The Book of Barra

ATLANTIC
OCEAN

South Uist
Daliburgh
Lochboisdale

Pollachar   Ludag

Sound of Eriskay

Lingay   Balla   Ben Scrien

Eriskay

Stack Is.

Fiaray
Scurrival Point

Eoligarry
CILLE BHARRA

Fuday

Barra

Orosay   Dìtir Mhor

Traigh Mhor

Grean Head   Cleat   Ben Cliad

Gighay

Hellisay

Bayherivagh

Floday

Borve Point   Fuiay

Borve
Hotel

Heaval
384m   Earsary

Bruernish Point

Ben Tangaval
333m

To Lochboisdale

Heishival Mor
191m

Castlebay
KISIMUL CASTLE

Vatersay

Vatersay

Muldoanich

To Oban

Floday   Sound of Sandray

Carn Galtar   Sandray

Lingay

Sound of Pabbay

Pabbay

Sound of Mingulay

Hecla   Mingulay

Berneray
Barra Head

Sea of the Hebrides

Outer Hebrides

Lewis   Stornoway

Skye

Barra

Rum

Coll

Tiree

Mull   Oban

0   5 miles
0   10 kilometres

The Book of Barra

BEING ACCOUNTS OF THE ISLAND OF BARRA IN THE
OUTER HEBRIDES WRITTEN BY VARIOUS AUTHORS AT
VARIOUS TIMES, TOGETHER WITH UNPUBLISHED
LETTERS AND OTHER MATTER RELATING TO THE ISLAND

Edited by
JOHN LORNE CAMPBELL

With Chapters on Catholic Barra by
COMPTON MACKENZIE
and on the Norse Place-names of Barra by
CARL Hj. BORGSTRÖM

Illustrated with photographs taken by
MARGARET FAY SHAW *and* J.L. CAMPBELL

acair
Acair

This book was first published by
George Routledge & Sons Ltd.,
Broadway house, Carter Lane, E.C.
in 1936 and printed by the Edinburgh Press,
Edinburgh and London.

Republished by Acair Ltd.,
7 James Street, Stornoway, Isle of Lewis,
in 1998 and republished again in 2006.

The publishers have in this edition kept as close as
possible to the style of the original book.

A CIP catalogue record for this title
is available from the British Library.

THIS EDITION:
Typescripted by Peigi MacLennan
Cover design by Mark Blackadder
Printed by ColourBooks Ltd., Dublin

Acair is grateful to
Dr. Margaret Fay Shaw Campbell, Canna,
for her permission to republish this book, and to
Hugh Cheape, Edinburgh, for his advice
and guidance throughout the publishing process.

info@acairbooks.com
www.acairbooks.com

ISBN 0 86152 104 8
EAN 9 780861 521043

Contents

*

Illustrations

*

Foreword

*

VERY REV ANGUS JOHN CANON MACQUEEN

John Lorne Campbell was a man of vision. It is easy to deduce this from the early direction of John's scholarly pursuits while still a young man, for he saw the urgency needed in order to collect and preserve everything of note about the people of the small island of Barra sixty years ago.

The nation was already distracted by the race to develop the modern means required to make quick progress and they saw no need to heed people in remote islands. John Lorne Campbell saw that the official attitude was endangering the language, culture and natural environment, the health of the land and ocean, the quality of bird plant and animal life.

As a little boy of ten on the neighbouring Isle of South Uist I was proud to wear the Badge of the Sea League founded in 1933 by John Lorne Campbell and Compton MacKenzie to ensure life and health for our fishing communities, and we were made aware of John Campbell's vision for our people by our enlightened headmaster who was a Barra man. During the next sixty years I would be frequently reminded of what one dedicated man could achieve.

To quote Compton MacKenzie in the Book of Barra — "When the stranger approaches me for bothering about 'politics' and 'economics' and 'better transport' and 'closing the Minch against trawlers', I long to set him down for a month of solitude upon one of the formerly inhabited Islands so that he may discover the IMPORTANCE OF HUMANITY to the NATURAL SCENE. The knowledge that there are still many who believe that it would serve the state to allow the islands to become a wilderness for sportsmen like so much of the Highlands, is always bitter with those of us who would rather see London a heap of ruins like Ur of the Chaldees than one more abomination of desolation like Rum." P. 30.

John was keenly aware of the importance of the Gaelic language but realised that its survival would only make sense against the backdrop of a healthy economic climate and he spent a whole long lifetime in preserving all that was good and worthwhile in the language while continually striving for the health of the land and the surrounding seas. With unbounded energy he travelled through the Southern Hebrides with cylinder, disc, wire, and later magnetic tape, to record and transcribe the music song and stories of an endangered people in a fragile economy.

John Lorne Campbell arrived in Barra in the summer of 1933 and this proved to be a happy event for himself and for posterity as his time in Barra was to have a lasting influence on the rest of his life. Compton Mackenzie was there enjoying the golden years of the Island's history, and John Campbell settled quickly under the patronage of John (Coddy) MacPherson, the uncrowned king of the Island. He soon discovered that here remained the true culture of traditional singing and storytelling and he felt that he had come home. The language and culture of the people had survived the boom years of the herring industry when Barra was the herring capital of the world. There was work at home for the women as well as for the men at the herring so that it was easier for them to preserve their traditional store of song during the winter months. John could now settle to give the world a picture of a small island community over the past four hundred years and his enthusiasm won over the talents of Compton Mackenzie and Carl Hj. Borgstrom. The final result was the finest researched book written about a small island community. John Campbell made no apology about not producing and editing the type of travel book about the Hebrides popular at the time. Though scholarly and thorough, the Book of Barra makes easy reading and we welcome the new edition.

While in Barra something else happened which was to influence and enrich his life beyond his wildest hopes and dreams. He met his future wife, the celebrated researcher and folklorist Margaret Fay Shaw who spent the years between 1929 and 1935 collecting songs and stories in the community of North Glendale in South Uist. An inspired researcher, she would encourage John in the work he had undertaken, she would listen to the recordings of the songs and compare the version given by the singers. They had a happy and fulfilling time in Barra and my window looks out on the spot where they made their happy home together among their friends in Northbay. We can safely say that Barra is the musical centre of the Gaelic world today because John and his wife convinced the old traditional singers that what they had was precious and must be passed on and preserved. Our own generation has produced world famous traditional singers like Flora MacNeil because John Campbell convinced her uncle Neil and others that the heritage was worth preserving. John Campbell and his wife worked hard to convince others that a national archive was much needed and they were happy to see the School of Scottish Studies at Edinburgh University established in 1951. He gave over three hundred recordings to the new centre.

In this work he made many friends among serious researchers and true friendship was of the greatest importance to him. He would work closely with scholars like Francis Collinson and they would collaborate to produce such works of great importance as the three volumes of *Hebridean Folksongs* between 1969 and 1981. Early research however made it very clear that they were already far too late, as many of the traditional singers and storytellers had passed on, and this sent John back to the end of the nineteenth century. He found what he wanted in the collections of the noted Father Allan MacDonald, priest of the Island of Eriskay until 1905. Father Allan had worked closely with Alexander Carmichael of *Carmina Gadelica* fame and John admired them both and used their work to help find alternative words and music so that the final product would be reliable. John soon discovered that Father Allan - who was so generous with his manuscripts to researchers - was frequently not acknowledged by those who published his work as their own. This would infuriate John Lorne Campbell and I remember him telephoning me late at night after discovering another unscrupulous writer publishing Allan's material without acknowledging the source.

Writing to Father Allan in July 1905 Alexander Carmichael lamented — "Everything Highland is becoming of interest. Let us try to meet this interest and show the world that our dearly beloved people were not the rude, barbarous, creedless, godless, ignorant, men and women that prejudiced writers have represented them. It is heartbreaking to me to see the spiteful manner in which Highlanders have been spoken of." (Èigse Volume V111 (1956-57), p. 262).

John Campbell welcomed the first two volumes of Carmina Gadelica while accepting that "Carmina does need an impartial critical examination in the light of modern scholarship." (Notes on Alexander Carmichael's *Carmina Gadelica* (1982), p. 13). John Campbell was deeply appreciative of the material collected by Carmichael and he encouraged Carmichael's grandson, James Carmichael Watson to prepare the remainder for publication. Sadly Watson lost his life in the Navy in 1941 after publishing volumes 3 and 4. Meantime John Lorne Campbell was busy with Father Allan's manuscripts and it turned out to be a life's work in itself.

With the publication of the Book of Barra John had shown how rich the Islands were in heritage and how urgent it was for the nation to help preserve and improve the fragile economy of the communities which kept the culture in being.

But now John would undertake his most important project. He would find an Island where he and Margaret would establish a Gaelic community which would survive off the land and the sea while preserving the culture. In 1938 he bought the Island of Canna where they would live happily for the best part of the next sixty years. Here they would continue their research, and those of his friends who were privileged to enjoy their hospitality in Canna House remember the studious atmosphere of their home and the serious conversations which were so enjoyable.

Here John would fulfil his greatest vision of a land where plant life and all little creatures like moths and butterflies would live sharing a well nurtured land of primrose and orchid and fern surrounded by a healthy sea teeming with lobster, crab and the finest of fish. Here he hoped for a happy community of Gaelic speaking islanders working the land and preserving the language and customs of their ancestors. He would have liked to see more young families in Canna, preferably from Eriskay, but that was not to be.

John presented the Isle of Canna to the National Trust for Scotland together with his unique library, archives and sound recordings in 1981; the final gesture of generous mind, the fruits of a lifetime of research, for the future use of the nation.

Now John Lorne Campbell (*Fear Chanaigh* as he liked to be known) has gone to his reward of lasting peace so richly deserved, while we look forward to the establishment of the University of the Highlands and Islands housed in Colleges throughout the Highlands and Islands. Could John's final vision be fulfilled? Canna would be the finest college of them all.

I have a dream of students from all over the world researching in the rarified atmosphere of Canna while delving into the finest archives of them all. The overdue reprint of the Book of Barra will afford scholars the study of one little Hebridean island over four hundred years against the music of ocean, laughter and song, while dance will while away the long winter nights for students of a worthwhile way of life, largely preserved by *Fear Chanaigh*. John Lorne Campbell and Compton MacKenzie would be well pleased.

Northbay, Isle of Barra. *Autumn*, 1997.

Preface

*

J.L. CAMPBELL

The editing of *The Book of Barra* has been for me a labour of love, undertaken as some small return for the hospitality and charm that is so readily afforded by the island of Barra, perhaps the most perfect of all the Outer Hebrides in its proportions and scenery, and certainly second to none in the richness of its associations and the drama of its social and religious history.

My intention in editing this book has been to give the reader some idea of the social and economic history of a small Hebridean island during the last four hundred years. If in doing so I have not found it advisable to observe the canons of contemporary tourist literature that is written about Scotland in general, and about the Hebrides in particular, I have no apology to offer. The recent social and economic history of the Highlands and Islands stands in urgent need of a thoroughly realistic examination from a nationalist point of view; and it would have hardly been worth the trouble of editing this book in order to add another volume to the large and ever-growing body of literature that is based upon an uncritical exploitation of the romantic aspects of Highland and Hebridean history. If such aspects have sometimes been a legitimate source of inspiration to our historians, they have also often been misinterpreted, and have served to obscure to many the less pleasant side of recent Highland history. For this reason, in editing *The Book of Barra*, I have tried to connect the past with the present in such a way as to present a picture of some continuity, in order that the reader may be able to form his own ideas of what the future of the Hebrides is likely to be, and what trends and tendencies from the past are likely to form that future.

The production of *The Book of Barra* in its present form has only been made possible by a most exceptionally fortunate combination of circumstances which has permitted the inclusion in the book of articles of unusual interest and authority upon various subjects intimately connected with Barra, without which *The Book of Barra* would have been of far less value. These articles have all been contributed freely and for nothing, as has the work of editing itself, and any royalties this book may earn are to be given to the Sea League (the local inshore fishermen's organisation) or else devoted to any other cause that is considered beneficial to the island of Barra.

I have to thank the Rev. Dr Donald Campbell for permission to print the hitherto unpublished letters of the last two MacNeills of Barra in the direct line to the Rev. Angus MacDonald, priest of Barra from 1805 to 1825; Mr Donald MacNeil, Castlebay, for the loan of a photograph of the portrait of General MacNeill, which is reproduced here as the frontispiece of this book; J.P. Day, B.A., B.S., D.Phil., and the London University Press for permission to quote the passages from Mr Day's *Public Administration in the Highlands and Islands*, which are reproduced on pages 220 and 270-4; the members of the Edinburgh University Biological Society's Expedition, who visited Barra in 1935, for the list of names of Barra fauna and flora that are printed at the end of this book; Miss Annie Johnston, Castlebay, and Mr Neil Sinclair, Northbay, for reading the book in proof, and many other natives of Barra for confirmatory information given to me upon various matters at different times. Mr Compton Mackenzie has also read the entire book, both in manuscript and in proof, and has made many suggestions regarding the editing besides adding a number of footnotes of his own.

The introduction to the various accounts and the footnotes, unless otherwise initialled, are by myself. The footnotes of the original writers are distinguished by being marked with asterisks. In editing the various accounts, I have, of course, made no attempt to standardize the spelling of personal and place-names, but in my own introductions I have used the spellings of the Ordnance Survey in the case of the latter. In the case of the personal name "MacNeill" (in local Gaelic pronounced MacNìll) which has a variety of forms, I have used this spelling in my introductions; it is one of the few Gaelic names which can preserve its correct literary spelling in English.

I regret that in editing this book I have not had time to read the Norse Sagas for references to Barra. The disappearance of the Gaelic manuscript called the *Barra Chronicle*, which is referred to on pages 26 and 282, is a disaster alike for Gaelic students and for historians. It is the more tantalizing, since the MS. is known to have been in existence quite recently. Canon MacNeil, Morar, tells me that the MS. was in the keeping of the MacNeills of Vatersay, who took it to Oban, where the last representative of this family died about fifty years ago. His father actually visited them for the purpose of getting the MS., which he did not succeed in obtaining. After the death of the last of this family, the effects were sent to a lawyer in the Lowlands, and the MS. could not be traced. A further search for it would be well worth making.

Northbay, Barra, *February* 1936.

CHAPTER 1

Catholic Barra

*

COMPTON MACKENZIE

This book is an attempt to collate all the available printed information about Barra; and although such a chronicle of a small Hebridean island is incomplete in many respects to a tantalizing degree, that is not the Editor's fault. At least the reader will be spared the burdensome task of trying to digest the ill-told tales of dubious truth and incontestable monotony with which the topographer of to-day is inclined to hide as with a flour-thickened gravy the stringy fare he offers.

My complaint as a reader, as a critic, and as an inhabitant against some of the numerous works published during the last decade about the Western Isles is not so much of their superficiality as of their effort to make the Islands and the Islanders conform to a sentimental preconception in the minds of their authors. The religious, political, and economic prejudices of the past which are apparent throughout *The Book of Barra* assist, if involuntarily, the triumph of the inexorable fact; but this nebulous twentieth-century impressionism will be of as much service to historians in the future as the posters of esurient railway companies. Therefore I hesitate to add a word to the straightforward descriptions of Barra which will be found in the various accounts collected, lest I should expose myself to the charge of indulging in that very impressionism condemned above. Yet it would be an excessive caution that ignored the peculiar magic, which to any experienced amateur of small islands declares Barra, immediately the voyager sets foot upon its soil, worthy to rank with the most renowned in travel, history and romance. We shall find the source of that magic by the light of our own dispositions. Some will discover it in the perfect proportions and variety of the natural scene, others in the humour, amiability, and engaging carelessness of a people who whatever its material suffering in the past has been spared the influence of the darker Calvinistic superstitions upon its spiritual health. "If we had travelled with more leisure, it had not been fit to have neglected the

Popish islands," wrote the perspicacious Dr Johnson in *A Journey to the Western Islands*. "Popery is favourable to ceremony; and among ignorant nations ceremony is the only preservative of tradition. Since Protestantism was extended to the savage parts of Scotland, it has perhaps been one of the chief labours of the Ministers to abolish stated observances, because they continued the remembrance of the former religion. We, therefore, who came to hear old traditions, and see antiquated manners, should probably have found them amongst the Papists."

It is indeed regrettable that Johnson and Boswell did not reach Barra in that autumn of 1773, especially as they might have done so toward the end of September when the festival of St Barr was still being observed, although by this time the venerated statue of the saint himself had probably disappeared. We may suspect, however, that Johnson would have derived a profounder imaginative comfort from a visit to Barra than the mere survival there of antiquated manners. His final reflection as he left behind him those 'illustrious ruins' of Iona was:

"Perhaps, in the revolutions of the world, Iona may be sometime again the instructress of the Western Regions."

In the event, Barra was represented to Johnson and Boswell as the Ultima Thule of desolation. We read in the latter's diary:

"We had a fine evening, and arrived in good time at Ostig, the residence of Mr Martin McPherson, minister of Slate. It is a pretty good house, built by his father, upon a farm near the church. We were received here with much kindness by Mr and Mrs McPherson, and his sister, Miss McPherson, who pleased Dr Johnson much, by singing Erse songs, and playing on the guittar. He afterwards sent her a present of his *Rasselas*. In his bedchamber was a press stored with books, Greek, Latin, French, and English, most of which had belonged to the father of our host, the learned Dr McPherson; who, though his *Dissertations* have been mentioned in a former page as unsatisfactory, was a man of distinguished talents. Dr Johnson looked at a Latin paraphrase of the song of Moses, written by him, and published in the *Scots Magazine* for 1747, and said, 'It does him honour; he has a great deal of Latin, and good Latin.'—Dr McPherson published also in the same magazine, June 1739, an original Latin ode, which he wrote from the isle of Barra, where he was minister for some years. It is very poetical, and exhibits a striking proof how much all things depend upon comparison: for Barra, it seems, appeared to him so much worse than Sky, his *natale solum*, that he languished for its 'blessed mountains,' and thought himself buried alive amongst barbarians where he was.—My readers will probably not be displeased to have a specimen of this ode:

> 'Hei mihi! quantos patior dolores,
> Dum procul specto juga ter beata;
> Dum ferae Barrae steriles arenas
> Solus oberro.

> 'Ingemo, indignor, crucior, quod inter
> Barbaros Thulen lateam colentes;
> Torpeo languens, morior sepultus,
> Carcere coeco.'

"After wishing for wings to fly over to his dear country, which was in his view, from what he calls *Thule*, as being the most western isle of Scotland, except St Kilda; after describing the pleasures of society, and the miseries of solitude, he at last, with becoming propriety, has recourse to the only sure relief of thinking men,— *Sursum corda*,—the hope of a better world, and disposes his mind to resignation:

> 'Interim fiat, tua, rex, voluntas:
> Erigor sursum quoties subit spes
> Certa migrandi Solymam supernam,
> Numinis aulam.'"

He concludes in a noble strain of orthodox piety:

> '"Vita tum demum vicitanda vita est,
> Tum licet gratos socios habere,
> Seraphim et sanctos TRIADEM verendam
> Concelebrantes.'

"Wednesday, 29th September."

The picture of poor Dr M'Pherson wandering solitary about 'the sterile sands of savage Barra' and contemplating across the Minch the outlined range of Skye like a great ship upon the horizon has for the lover of Barra an exquisite absurdity. However, none can regard with equal affection the Outer Isles and the Inner Isles, and no doubt the people of Skye among whom she lived and into whom she had married must have found it an inexplicable piece of eccentricity in Flora Macdonald to be availing herself of every excuse she could find to revisit her native South Uist. For all the fantastic beauty of Skye's airy battlements it would have seemed no more than an extension of the mainland to one who was desiring the sound of the Atlantic on the long line of the Uist sands. Perhaps Dr M'Pherson was reduced to such despair by his post on Barra less for lack of Skye's thrice blessed mountain-range than for lack of a congregation. It must have been unsettling to a scholarly Minister of the Established Church to find himself, at a time when Great Britain was enjoying the benefits of the Hanoverian Succession which had secured liberty to all except Catholics and property to all except the poor, exiled to a small and remote island, the inhabitants of which pitied his severance not from Skye, not from the continent of Scotland, but from the Faith they in their Catholic poverty had dared by the Grace of Almighty God to keep at whatever cost to their material welfare.

Those who will not look beyond this impressive fact for the magic of Barra, must remember that Barra has not been uniquely favoured in this regard. South Uist and Benbecula, Canna and Eigg, Knoydart and Moidart and blessed Morar, with many a glen in Banff and Aberdeen held fast to the Faith in a land more mercilessly ravaged by the Reformation than any in Europe. It will be wisest to call the peculiar magic of Barra a happy mixture of the natural scene, the character of the people, and the religious atmosphere combining to produce that effect of perpetual youth which expresses as well as anything our faint human apperception of Paradise.

The rigorous and almost incessant persecution of Catholics which followed the upheaval of the sixteenth century did not for many years affect the islands directly, except by spiritual starvation. The lack of apostolic zeal displayed by the Presbyterians bears a remarkable testimony to the predominance of the political aspect of the Protestant Reformation above any other. Years were to pass before the missionaries of the new religion attempted to minister without the help of political terrorization. Yet if we are astonished by the lack of Geneva fervour we are not less astonished by the supine attitude of Rome. In the Archives of Propaganda for 1669 we may read Cardinal Rospigliosi's representation of the state of affairs in the Hebrides:[1]

> "The natives of the islands adjacent to Scotland can, as a general rule, be properly called neither Catholics nor heretics. They abhor heresy by nature, but they listen to the preachers by necessity. They go wrong in matters of faith through ignorance, caused by the want of priests to instruct them in their religion. If a Catholic priest comes to their island, they call him by the name of the *tonsured one*, and show much greater veneration and affection for him than for the preachers. They sign their foreheads with the sign of the holy cross. They invoke the saints, recite litanies, and use holy water. They themselves baptize their own children when the ministers make any difficulty as to administering that sacrament, on the pretence that it is not essential for eternal salvation. *Rescriptum:* The Most Holy Father directs the appointment, as superior of that mission, of the present Archbishop of Armagh, who is to send labourers to these islands, and is hereby instructed to apply to the Holy Office for the extension of his faculties."

No excuse can be made for this neglect by the Congregation of Propaganda, and nearly a century later criticism of it was to be implied when the Rector of the Scots College in Paris, in writing to deplore the effect on the Jacobite cause of the Duke of York's becoming a Cardinal, consoled himself with the reflection that His Royal Eminence might be able to bring before Propaganda the paucity of Gaelic priests and the starvation of the Faith in the Highlands and Islands.

Bishop Hugh Macdonald, in a Report[2] to Propaganda of March 18, 1732, has to lament:

> "In the place of certain deceased priests, necessity has compelled the appointment of others from districts further south; and these, although of Highland family, want of practice has

1 Bellesheim's *History of the Catholic Church of Scotland,* translated by D. Oswald Hunter Blair, O.S.B., Vol. IV, p.85.
2 Bellesheim, *op. cit.,* IV, 390.

rendered almost useless at our mountain language, which they lost when studying at the colleges abroad. The faithful grievously deplore this scarcity of pastors; and while others enjoy in abundance every convenience for their spiritual welfare, they constantly complain that their souls are starving, by reason, not of the negligence, but of the fewness, of labourers in the vineyard. A great number of the heretics lament, in presence of the bishop or priest, with groans, tears, and words that might move stones, over their own unhappy errors and blindness;and having at length discovered the impiety, avarice, and carelessness of their ministers, and had their eyes opened to certain enormous errors, implore the help of Holy Mother Church, and ask with continual and unspeakable eagerness for Catholic pastors. Hence the greatest sorrow is enkindled in my heart, seeing as I do that the number of labourers amongst us who are versed in the Highland tongue is so scanty, that they are not only insufficient to assist Protestants of the kind I have described, but even the very Catholics themselves."

Although, as early as the decade from 1610 to 1620, the General of the Jesuits was writing repeatedly to the Superior of the Jesuit Mission in Ireland, urging him to send missionaries to the Scottish Gaels, it was left to Irish Franciscan missionaries to make the first real effort in the Highlands and Islands.

In a report from Father John Brady to Propaganda in 1627, 10,000 conversions, or more accurately 'reconciliations,' were claimed in the Montana Scotiae, the term used in Rome for the Highlands and Islands. This was the Father Brady that was attacked by fourteen ministers, thrown from his horse, and severely wounded. In 1633 Father Patrick Hegarty was reporting that in the Hebrides he had reconciled 2229 souls to the Church, baptized 1222, and solemnized 117 marriages. The following year Propaganda was decreeing the restoration of the See of the Western Isles; but the proposal fell through. In 1638 Father Cornelius Ward was writing in Latin[1] to the Bishop of Down and Connor:

"The labour of the mission in those remote and barbarous spots is almost indescribable, and beyond the belief of the Romans.

1 Bellesheim, *op. cit.*, IV, 71.

Sometimes the same missionary has been there in different years for six months together, without tasting any kind of drink except water and milk; *lacticinia* (butter, cheese, etc.) form their principal food, and in summer they can hardly procure bread. In the Hebrides and Highlands of Scotland there is no city, no town, no school, no civilization, no one can read except a few who have been educated at a great distance from home. At length when the aforesaid missionary found himself without wine or hosts for the holy sacrifice,he betook himself by long and circuitous routes, and not without great toil and hardship, to the city of Edinburgh. And when he at last made his way back to the mountains with the bread and wine, he fell into a very serious illness."

We may suspect that the abandonment of the Franciscan mission after Father Ward and Father Hegarty had both suffered imprisonment was due to the failure of the Propaganda to take energetic action and supply the necessary funds.

At last, in 1651, when Clanranald sent from South Uist to Ireland to beg for more priests, Propaganda asked St Vincent de Paul, the founder of the Lazarists, for missionary help. Father Francis White and Father Dermot Duggan, natives of Limerick and members of the congregation of the Mission, were sent at once. They set out, disguised as merchants, in the company of Young Glengarry, and they were in time to give the Last Sacraments to Old Glengarry who was drawing near to a hundred years. Father White stayed in the Western Highlands; Father Duggan was assigned to the Islands; and Father Lumsden, a Scottish Lazarist, laboured in Orkney, Ross and Caithness, the only three priests by now in Montana Scotiae. On October 28, 1652, Father Duggan was writing[1] to St Vincent de Paul:

"I set out for the Hebrides, where God in his Omnipotent Mercy has worked wonders even beyond my hopes. He has so softened hearts there that Clanranald, Laird of a great part of Uist, has become a convert, together with his wife, his son and their whole family. This lead has been followed by all the gentry, the tenants and their families.

1 Quoted by the Rev. Seán MacGuaire, C.SS.R., in *Ireland and the Catholic Hebrides*, from Abelly, *Vie de St Vincent de Paul*, Vol. V, p. 200.

"MacNeill, Laird of the island of Barra, having heard of me, sent a gentleman to beg me to do his island the same service as I had done for the Laird of Clanranald. . . . In these islands and in the whole of the Highlands of Scotland there are no priests except my companions and myself. We have accepted no recompense from the people for the services we have rendered. I have to employ two men; one helps me to row when I travel from island to island, and carries my Mass-box and my scanty luggage overland, for sometimes, before Mass, I have to travel four or five leagues on foot over wretched roads. The other man helps me to teach the *Pater, Ave* and *Credo* and serves my Mass, for I have nobody else capable of doing so.

"As a rule we take only one meal a day, consisting of barley bread or oaten bread with some cheese or salt butter. Sometimes we spend whole days without a meal because we cannot procure anything. This is the case especially when we have to cross the desert and uninhabited mountains. As for meat, we hardly ever eat it; in some places far from the sea, especially in the homes of the gentry, it is possible to procure it, but it is so unpalatable and so disagreeably served that one does not relish it. The people put the meat on the ground on a little straw which serves as table and chair, table-cloth and table-napkin. If we wished to buy some meat to cook and serve in French fashion, we could not get it in small quantities, for there is no butcher in the islands. We should have to purchase a cow or a sheep and this we cannot do, owing to our continual journeys to administer Baptism and the other Sacraments. There is fish in the sea which surrounds the islands, but the people, by temperament easy-going and unenergetic, make but little effort to catch any.

"It would indeed, be a great service to God to send to this country good apostolic workers acquainted with the language and prepared to bear with hunger and thirst and sleeping upon the ground. They should have an annual subsidy too; otherwise they would have nothing to live on."

Eighteen months later he was writing:[1]

"At the beginning of spring I landed upon another island,

1 Abelly, *op. cit.*, V, 202-205.

named Barra, where I found a people so devout and anxious to learn that I was astonished. It was enough to teach one child in each village the *Pater, Ave* and *Credo;* in two days the whole village knew them—children and adults. I have received all the leading inhabitants into the Church, including the young Laird with his brothers and sisters. There is hope of getting the old Laird on my next journey. Amongst the converts is a minister's son, whose devotion gives great edification throughout the whole district where he is known.

"As a rule I defer Communion for some time after the general Confession, so that the people may be better instructed and better prepared by a second Confession, and also that they may have a greater desire and appreciation of Holy Communion. Amongst the communicants were five whom God showed to be wanting in the proper dispositions, for when they put forth their tongue to receive the Sacred Host they could not draw it back. Three of them remained in this condition until the Sacred Host was removed. When, however, they had made their Confession with better dispositions, they received the Bread of Life without any difficulty. The two others have not yet returned to us. God has willed to allow these extraordinary happenings to give the other Christians of this country a greater reverence when they approach this Divine Sacrament.

"We have witnessed, too, many marvels resulting from the use of Holy Water. We baptized a great number of children and even adults of 30, 40, 60, 80 years and over, for we were sure that they had never been baptized. Amongst these were some troubled and annoyed by ghosts or evil spirits, who were completely delivered from them after Baptism and never saw them again."

It is clear from this letter that Father Duggan regarded Barra with particular affection. Father Hegarty or one of the Franciscan missionaries may have visited the island, but there is no record of it, and when we read of the baptism of octogenarians we have a right to presume that Barra had been deprived of the Sacraments for at least eighty years, and that when Protestant ministers like Mr Campbell of Harris visited them, though received with hospitality as Martin records, they found them too steadfast to be influenced. We must look to Jewry for a comparable display of fidelity and endurance.

The labours of Father Duggan to establish the Faith in the Outer Islands lasted for five years, by the end of which time the people from Benbecula to Barra Head were safe under God against the basest ingenuity of man. In Barra he is commemorated by a pass over the hills, Bealach a' Ghugain, a fit symbol of his devoted wanderings nearly three centuries ago. Throughout his apostolate Father Duggan was oppressed by the consciousness of the thousands of souls abandoned in the isles from North Uist to Lewis.

On May 5, 1657, he was writing:

"I am preparing to set out on the 10th of this month for Pabbay. I have not yet told you of this plan of mine fearing that the trouble and danger of it might make you anxious, for it really is a strange and weird place. Still, the hope we have of bringing back many stray sheep to the Lord's Fold, our trust in His goodness, and the grounds we have for hoping that the inhabitants of this island, not being infected with heresy, can, with God's grace, remain faithful to our religion if once instructed—these motives urge us to scorn the danger and even death and to set out with the Help of God to Whose Will I submit myself.

"This is why I am begging you not to defer your coming any longer. Take care not to tell the plan to anyone except M. Noeill, for we desire for many reasons to keep it secret."

This Pabbay must have been the larger island between Bernera and Harris, for the people of the Pabbay between Mingulay and Sandray would already have been reconciled, and in any case there would have been no necessity for secrecy, away from hostile lairds and Cromwell's lead and steel discipline. It may be presumed that other islands like Pabbay off the coasts of North Uist, Harris and Lewis held populations that only needed the advent of a priest to be reconciled immediately to the Faith.

I found on the island of Taransay a legend of a fight between Catholics and Protestants which might indicate some piece of profitable 'evangelization' with the dispossession of the Catholics. It is impossible to discover any information about Pabbay. About 1840 the people were driven off it for distilling and forcibly settled on Scalpay. The soil of Pabbay is among the richest of the islands, and for good land to be in the hands of the poor was a greater crime in 1840 than distilling. Pabbay is now under cattle, sheep, and deer. It would comfortably support a population of 300.

Father Duggan was not granted the fulfilment of his purpose. On May 10, 1657, he was in South Uist, preparing to set out upon that mission, more dangerous than ever now when the Cromwellian persecution had reached as far as Lewis. He fell sick, and a week later he was dead.

This was a grievous time for Scotland, and the bloody seventeenth century had still forty years to run. However, the persecution did not reach Uist and Barra. Dr Winster, the Prefect of the Scottish missions, was able to write in a Report to the Sacred Congregation in 1669:[1]

"The Catholics live in peace . . . in the islands of Uist and Barra . . . which are the most remote from the government residences. Such is the severity of the laws that the practice of the Catholic religion is not allowed; in the Highlands, however, and remote islands these laws are not carried into execution . . . The Highland families are, for the most part, Catholic or prepared to be so, if they had priests to instruct them; those, however, of the Lowlands are most fierce heretics and hate the Highlanders on account of their religion. The Highlanders are of excellent disposition, quick of intellect and taking a special delight in the pursuit of knowledge. They are desirous of novelties and have an unbounded passion for ingenious inventions. No greater favour can be conferred on them than to educate their children and render them suited to become priests or ecclesiastics.

"Their untiring constancy in all matters is truly surprising and is admitted and extolled even by their enemies, particularly in regard of religion, which they continue to profess as much as the severity of the persecution and the total want of priests permit.

"Their arms are two-edged swords, large shields, bows and arrows, which they continue to use, adding to them, however, fire-arms, which they manage with admirable dexterity . . . Almost all the families are Catholic or disposed to receive the Catholic Faith if for no other reason, at least to imitate their ancestors who were so zealous in the cause of religion.

"The remaining Scoto-Irish are heretics more through

1 Quoted in *Memorial of Dr Plunket*, p. 178.

ignorance than malice. They cease not, however, to cherish a great esteem for the Catholics, as appears in many things. If a priest visits them they show him more respect and honour him more than their own ministers. In fact the heretics amongst the Highlanders surpass in reverence for our priests the very Catholics of the Lowlands. They moreover retain many Catholic usages, such as making the sign of the Cross, the invocation of Saints and sprinkling themselves with Holy Water, which they anxiously ask from their Catholic neighbours. In sickness they make pilgrimages to the ruins of the old churches and chapels which yet remain, as of the most noble monastery of Iona, where St Columba was Abbot: also of the chapels of Ghierlock and Applecrosse and Glengarry which were once dedicated to the saints. They also visit the holy springs which yet retain the names of the saints to whom they were dedicated and it has often pleased the Most High to restore to their health those who visited these ruins or drank at these springs invoking the aid of these saints.

"The enmity of the Lowlanders has been a great source of injury to the Scoto-Irish, especially since heresy began to dominate in Scotland, for the inhabitants of the Lowlands being most furious heretics (with the exception of some few whom the Catholic missionaries restored to the bosom of the Church), and seeing the Highlanders most constant in the Faith and that there is no hope of alienating them from the Church they seek by all possible means to excite odium against them, designating them as barbarians, impious enemies of the reformed creed, etc., and they hesitate not to affirm of them everything that can be suggested by detraction and their own excessive hatred. They even deem it a glorious deed to show contempt for or cast ridicule on a Highlander."

We next hear of Barra in 1671, by which time the Hebridean mission had been placed under the direction of Blessed Oliver Plunket, the martyred Archbishop of Armagh. Notwithstanding the tremendous task he had before him of trying to repair the devastation of Cromwell in Ireland the Archbishop contemplated a visitation of the Hebrides. He was writing to the Marquis of Antrim on June 7, 1671:

"I need some assistance to enable me to visit the Scottish

Islands that is the Hebrides . . . it will be necessary for me to bring a priest and a servant with me and to dress after the manner of these people which is very different from that of every part of the globe."

There is something to beguile the fancy in the picture of the saintly Primate dressed in a belted plaid. "They still retain the language and costume of their earliest forefathers," a Scottish priest had written to Propaganda, "so that their dress is not very dissimilar from that of the ancient statues in Rome, loosely covered from the waist to the knee and they wear a bonnet on the head."

Father Francis MacDonnell, an Irish Franciscan from Louvain, wrote from South Uist to Blessed Oliver Plunket:

"The island of Barra is six miles long and three broad. The landlord is the laird of MacNeill, amongst whom is the laird himself. Father George Fanning, a Dominican, labours here with good results."

Father MacDonnell's Report to Propaganda is interesting:

"Father Francis MacDonnell   Armagh, 10th July 1671.
to Monsignor Baldeschi,
Secretary of Propaganda.

"When I heard that His Grace the Primate of all Ireland had received from the Sacred Congregation the care of the Scottish Islands, or Hebrides, I hastened hither to Armagh from the Isles, in order that I might suggest how the Faith might be propagated in those Islands. His Grace himself greatly desired this summer to return there with me, but I was of the contrary opinion, inasmuch as a report had spread of the arrival of the French whom the Scots are said to favour, so that if His Grace, the Primate, were to go there, everyone would think that he had come to prepare the way for the French. It is for this same reason that no missionaries are to be sent there this summer, as the news of their arrival would at once get abroad and they would be cast into prison.

"For it is proposed to effect the union of the two kingdoms of England and Scotland in one Parliament, to which union the

Islesmen are strongly opposed.

"Now, if the Primate were to visit them, it would at once be said that he came to foster the opposition to this union. The best and safest method of propagating the Catholic religion in the islands, and of strengthening it for the future, is to select some youths and to send them to Rome or to the seminaries on the Continent to be educated and promoted to the priesthood. Being natives, these may later do much good on the Isles and will be more gladly welcomed there. Meantime, His Grace the Primate should send thither some Irish priests or religious, since the people of these islands understand nothing but Gaelic, and they can hope for spiritual assistance from none but the Irish, since the Scots speak a corrupt form of English, and experience has long since proved that they afford no spiritual help to the Isles. From my receiving no answer to them I conclude that my various letters to the Congregation have been lost on the way, and hence in future I shall write through His Grace the Primate, and I shall hope for the reply also through him. It would greatly help our mission if a letter were sent to the Marquis of Antrim, who is of the family of MacDonnell, Chief of Clanranald, for though he externally professes to be a heretic, still he is very well disposed towards us and has a great number of Catholic dependents; lastly, it would be of great service to write to the illustrious Gillerane MacNeill of Barra, who is a Catholic."

To this report the Archbishop of Armagh added:

"The best method of propagating the Faith in these Islands is, first to send there missionaries knowing the Gaelic language, well grounded in virtue and inflamed with zeal for souls. The Procurator of the Mission, however, is of opinion that the Irish are scarcely fitted to minister there, inasmuch as there would be danger of the jealousy of the Royal Council, and if this were aroused the liberty now enjoyed would be lost. Hence it is necessary for many very important reasons to do everything as far as possible by means of priests of their own nation and to leave the jurisdiction over these people with those who are Scotch by nationality and that the Irish be there as their assistants."

This advice given by Blessed Oliver Plunket, with the substitution of other bodies for the Privy Council, is as pregnant to-day as when it was written. In an attempt to deal with the problem of nurturing a native clergy, a school was founded on Barra in 1675. The only other Catholic school in Scotland was in Glengarry. Propaganda tried to insist that Catholic children should be sent to these schools from all the rest of Scotland, and Winster had to protest to the Cardinals that Catholic parents in Scotland would as soon send their children to school in Jamaica as in Barra.

In 1679 Father Alexander Leslie made a visitation of the Scottish Vicariate. He reported to Propaganda that there were 12,000 Catholics in the Highlands and Islands with four priests, three of whom were Irish and the fourth, Father Robert Munro, the first native Gaelic speaker ordained since the Reformation, with whom he sailed to the Islands. They had intended to proceed from Canna to Barra, but a fog coming up the crew of their boat fell to fighting among themselves about the course, and in the end they went to Uist, moving thence to Eriskay where they stayed over a week. This looks as if Eriskay, had a bigger population then than when the Prince landed there in 1745. From Eriskay the priests reached Barra.

"Here we stayed thirteen days, treated right royally in various parts of the island, but particularly by the chief in his strong castle of Kismula. This is a huge building reared on a great rock and completely surrounded by the sea. Whatever member of the family is in possession of it, even though not the eldest, is regarded as chief of the whole island. I visited every district, and the Sacraments were administered and all the services held for the benefit of the Catholics, who gathered round us every day with equal joy to them and to us. When we were on the point of leaving the inhabitants showed themselves much displeased with Munro because he would not remain with them, and if I had not been with him I firmly believe that they would have kept him by force. Indeed they had some idea of keeping me, imagining that as I was an official of the Pope, if they detained me in their power they could make a treaty with His Holiness to obtain priests from him as a ransom for his delegate. I had as much as I could do, even backed by the laird, to escape from them, and then only by promising to go to Rome and throw myself at the feet of His Holiness and put before him their neglected condition and their spiritual needs. At length after much weeping and many laments they agreed that I should depart, and Munro with me, but they swore blood-curdling oaths that if they did not get a priest of their own, and Munro or any other came to the island he would not be allowed to leave except by swimming, as he would get no boat. They swore that they would sooner burn their boats than let another priest leave in one. Indeed, it would be quite in keeping with the character of these islanders that they would send an expedition to steal the priest of a neighbouring locality, and this would be the cause of deadly enmity between them."

That is an illuminating testimony to the Barra-man's strength of character. Father Munro was a devoted priest. Between 1671 and 1704 he was often imprisoned and twice banished from the country. In 1696 he was arrested in Flanders and charged with 'rebellion' against Dutch William. On his release he returned to Scotland, became acting Dean of the Isles, and in the winter of 1704 was arrested yet again and imprisoned in one of the dungeons of Glengarry Castle, without a wisp of straw for a bed or so much as a glass of water to cool the fever from which he was suffering. In two days he was dead. We may hope that his beatification will be granted.

In 1700 Father Munro was acting Dean of the Isles during the visitation of Bishop Thomas Nicolson, the first Vicar Apostolic for Scotland.

Bishop Nicolson was at this date fifty-five years of age. He had been brought up a Protestant and for fourteen years was a professor at Glasgow University. He had become a Catholic in 1682 and was ordained priest in 1685. He had been working on the Scottish Mission when the Revolution started in 1688. Escaping from Edinburgh he was imprisoned in Stirling, but after some months allowed to leave the country. In 1695 he was nominated Vicar-Apostolic and consecrated as Bishop of Peristachium. For a year he was kept in Holland, and when at last William gave him a licence to enter England on his way to his duties he was nevertheless arrested on landing and kept in prison for some months.

His first Report to Rome was sent from Aberdeen in September 1697. He gave a good account of the learning, zeal, and holiness of the scattered missionaries, but was much grieved by the harm done to Catholics by the growing infidelity and the general corruption of morals.

The persecution of Catholics on the mainland alike by Episcopalians and Presbyterians was intense during the intervals they could spare from persecuting one another, and it must have been a relief when the first Vicar-Apostolic reached the faithful islands. It was a black time.

"Men," wrote Chambers in his *Domestic Annals*,[1] "in trying to make each other Episcopalians and Presbyterians, had almost ceased to be Christians. The population was small and generally poor, and little had been done to advance the arts of life. Scotland had sent forth no voice in either literature or science; her universities could not train either the lawyer or the physician. No news-sheet, no stage-coaches, no system of police, existed in the realm. In certain intellectual and moral respects, the country was in no better state. The judge was understood to be accessible to private persuasions, and even direct bribes were suspected. The people believed as firmly in witchcraft as in the first principles of religion."

But Chambers was a bit of a Jacobite, and a quotation from Lecky,[2] the rationalist historian, will be less suspected of a bias in favour of Catholicism:

"There was one country in which the Puritan ministers succeeded in moulding alike the character and the habits of the nation, and in disseminating their harsh and gloomy tenets through every section of society. While England was breaking loose from her most ancient superstitions and advancing with gigantic strides along the paths of knowledge, Scotland still cowered in helpless subjection before her clergy. Never was a tyranny maintained with more inexorable barbarity. Supported by public opinion, the Scottish ministers succeeded in overawing all opposition, and prohibiting the faintest expression of adverse opinions."

The Bishop's account of his visitation of the Islands has been preserved.

1 Vol. II, p. 497.
2 Lecky, *History of Rationalism*, Vol. I, pp. 137-8.

After travelling by "rough and almost impassable paths, in order to avoid the soldiery, towards the west coast, which is inhabited by Catholics," he crossed to Eigg, "where he found all Catholics, 300 in number, very constant in the faith, and always loyal to their sovereigns." On Canna he found 130 Catholics, and passed from there to South Uist, where he found 1500 Catholics.

"About mid-day of June 23rd, which was Sunday, we landed at Loch Eynort in Uist, where Mass was said in a tent which we erected on the beach. Towards evening we went to the house of the laird at Ormaclate and were received with many marks of kindness by his lady in the absence of the chief of Clanranald, whom we had left on the mainland ... In South Uist all the people were Catholics, except about forty persons who attended the minister's chapel. At twelve stations such as presented themselves were confirmed, the numbers reaching over 800. We were greatly pleased with the kindness of the chief of Clanranald and of his lady.

"Our party arrived in Barra on the 10th July. The island is six miles long, productive of good crops of corn, with very rich grazing. The lord of the island, who is very zealous, received the Bishop with great respect. The people, who are excellent, really deserve a good priest, but we had only one of the Franciscans escaped from Ireland to place there until God should provide otherwise. In Barra there are the ruins of two or three churches and of a priory at Kilbar. There are six other inhabited islands, which belong to Barra, and there is a chapel in each. Of these Vatersay is the largest, with a circumference of five miles, while there are fourteen smaller islands that are only used for pasturage."

There is an interesting reference to the prevalence of the second sight in Barra:

"In this island many people are under the power of a kind of vision, called by the natives *second sight*, in virtue of which they foresee and predict unexpected and wonderful events. This power is quite beyond their own control, and the effects actually correspond to the predictions. The bishop proposes certain spiritual remedies with a view to delivering these poor people, but desires to refer the matter to the impartial judgment of your Eminences."

It is difficult in these days to persuade people afflicted with the second-sight to speak about it. If there has been on one side too much slick scepticism, there has been on the other a tawdry romanticism which has brought even greater discredit upon the subject. Therefore it was decided in editing *The Book of Barra* not to supply any more fairy-lamps for the Celtic twilight. Those who visit the Islands must discover their own road to the confidence of the people whom they will find equally contemptuous of the sceptic and the professional fairy-hunter.

If the Islands escaped the worst effects of the seventeenth century, the eighteenth century did not spare them. The Editor has collected as much as can be found about the echoes of the '45 in Barra. In the latter half of the century every laird in the Islands, for motives of material prudence, apostatized. The effect of that even on a Macneil will be evident in the letters printed on pp. 173-188.

It is melancholy to find Roderick, the great-grandson of Gillerane Macneil of Barra, sailing away to fight in Canada and leaving his son to be brought up by a Protestant relative. Of Gillerane, Bishop Nicolson had written that every Sunday he instructed them in the fear of God and the purity of the true faith, and that he had the merit of having thoroughly indoctrinated his people, and so kept them firm against the assaults of heresy.

Nevertheless, those who may be hurt and perplexed by the apostasy of lairds like Clanranald and MacNeil of Barra must remember in what their loyalty to the Faith might have involved them. Here is an extract from Lord Kame's *Statute Law Abridged* by a writer in the *Scots Magazine* of 1778:

"Heavy fines were imposed on noblemen or others sending their sons to be educated in foreign seminaries; and parents whose children became Catholics abroad had to find caution that they would send them no pecuniary assistance, except for the purpose of bringing them back to Scotland. Children under the care of Catholic parents or guardians were to be taken from them, and intrusted to some 'well-affected and religious friend,' the means for their support and education being provided out of the property of their parents . . . Catholics were incapable of acquiring real property, either by purchase or by deed of gift made in their favour, or in trust on their behalf, such deeds being by law absolutely null and void. They were also incapable, after the age of fifteen, of inheriting estates: if the heir, on attaining that age, refused to renounce his faith, his right of succession lapsed, passing to the nearest Protestant heir. If the latter declined to avail himself of it, it passed to the next Protestant after him, and so on until, as worded in the statute, the right was 'effectually established' in the Protestant line . . . A Protestant turning Catholic forfeited his whole heritable estate to his nearest Protestant heir . . . Catholics could be neither governors, schoolmasters, guardians, nor factors, a fine of a thousand merks being imposed on those who employed them in such capacities. They were forbidden to teach 'any art, science, or exercise of any sort,' under a penalty of five hundred merks. Protestants were prohibited from employing Catholic servants, under the same penalty; and the informer in such cases was entitled to the amount of the fine as his reward."

It is not surprising to find that at the general Assembly of 1779 Dr Robertson estimated that of the 20,000 Scottish Catholics not more than twenty owned land worth a hundred pounds a year, and that in the commercial world there was not a single Catholic of eminence.

When to their other disabilities is added the refusal of a commission in the Naval or Military forces to Catholics, and when it is remembered that at this date the chief livelihood of the Highlands and Islands was fighting for the aggrandizement of Great Britain, the weakness of the Catholic lairds is at least comprehensible. Some of them, however, with a load upon their consciences found the stead-fastness of the humble poor too sharp a reproach to be borne. Of such was the apostate Macdonald of Boisdale who in 1770 launched an odious persecution against the people of South Uist. He began with the children by driving them to Protestant schools where they were compelled to copy out scurrilous sentences and during Lent had flesh meat forced into their mouths. When the parents withdrew their children, Boisdale assembled his tenants and ordered them either to renounce Catholicism or lose their holdings. The poor people replied that they would rather beg from door to door than forsake their faith. Boisdale had already driven Father Wynne the priest from the island with threats of personal violence, and he now offered to leave the people in possession of their land if they would let the children be brought up as Protestants. To this the parents replied that the souls of the little ones were as dear to them as their own. Boisdale then proceeded to carry out his threat of wholesale eviction. Bishop Hay, the Vicar-Apostolic, published a memorial setting forth the case of the poor Uist people and raised subscriptions to meet the cost of transporting them to America in 1772.

The walls of Boisdale's garden are still to be seen, dry and grey as the ribs of a dead whale, but the great house he built himself has been pulled down to provide stone for byres. His line is extinct. On his death-bed he cried out in agony of mind for a priest, but the sons he had brought up as Protestants refused his last request, and he died with remorse and terror heavy upon his soul.

Barra escaped anything so violent as the laird of Boisdale's persecution; but readers of this book will have no difficulty in divining that the threat of eviction was always hanging over the heads of MacNeil's Catholic tenants. Reference may be made to letters 18, 21, 24, 25 of the MacNeil correspondence; and in fact Protestant tenants from North Uist were planted from time to time on the best holdings. It is noteworthy that the Protestants, all strangers, had increased form 60 in 1813 to 380 in 1840, the increase coinciding with a relative decrease in the whole population.

At the present day there are three Catholic churches in Barra— Our Lady, Star of the Sea at Castlebay, St Brendan's, Craigston, the first to be built, and St Barr's, Northbay. The raiding of the MacGillivray farm at Eoligarry after the Great War already shows a settlement prosperous enough to make a fourth church at the north end of the island a possibility in the future.

The present Macneil of Barra shows himself strangely confused about the religion of the island of his ancestors. Writing in *The Clan Macneil* he makes the statement that "with the Reformation some steps were taken toward looking after the spiritual welfare of the islesmen, and the Clansmen became nominally Protestant." Such a statement has no vestige of authority beyond the ignorant error of Martin Martin and Mr Macqueen, the author of the account of Barra in the *Old Statistical Account*, printed in full elsewhere. Macneil does a grave injustice to his forbears (who are expressly stated in Bishop Nicolson's Report of 1700 to have remained firm at the time of the Covenant) when he suggests that they were even Protestants before Roderick, son of the Roderick claimed as thirty-ninth chief, left his son behind in Vatersay to be brought up as a Protestant.

I have drawn particular attention to the Catholic history of Barra because the religious question is unfortunately still a dominant political issue in Scotland, and it is useful to remind some of my fellow countrymen both in the north and in the south that the Catholicism of the Highlands and Islands, which was the faith of Wallace and of Bruce, is as essentially Scottish as the Established Church. It is equally useful to remind some of my fellow Catholics in the south of Scotland of Blessed Oliver Plunket's recognition that Scottish Catholicism could *not* be treated as an Irish Mission.

This brings us to the question of St Barr, or Finbar, a Bishop of Cork, after whom Barra is alleged to have been named. The tradition may reasonably be accepted. Etymology provides no satisfactory Norse substitute, and that being the case it is easier, as well as being more grateful to the imagination, to accept Barra as the island of an early Celtic saint. The actual apostle of Christianity may have been a follower of St Barr, not necessarily the Bishop himself.

But what has happened to that statue of the saint which the people of Barra used to venerate? Martin writing in 1695 could have seen it if the inhabitants had not removed it from the altar in dread of Protestant ridicule. It may be that the Catholic missionary priests discouraged the public veneration of the saint's statue; but it is difficult to fancy that an object so profoundly cherished by the islanders was condemned to destruction. No tradition of its banishment can be discovered, but I have heard it darkly said that when it is found it will be found in the keeping of a certain family. It is unfortunate that we have no description of this statue which was evidently of considerable importance during the Middle Ages and which may have been much older. There was apparently no tradition of its having floated ashore, but the statues of patron saints in the small islands and coastal villages of the Mediterranean have often arrived in that way, and the legend related to Martin of the statue's invisible transportation to the site of the church in which it desired to abide is a familiar feature of popular hagiology.

Another regrettable disappearance is that of the *Barra Chronicle*. According to *The Clan Macneil* "several sheets either of the original or copies of the manuscript, were in the possession of the Reverend Angus Macneil of Vatersay" in whose guardianship was placed that young Roderick who succeeded his grandfather as reputed fortieth Chief of the Clan in 1763. Some say that the *Barra Chronicle*, which was a Gaelic chronicle of the Macneil clan, was carried overseas to

America: others say that one of the Macneil factors destroyed it. One may still hope that it is not irretrievably lost. No doubt by the eighteenth century it was no longer being faithfully kept; but the record of the two preceding centuries might have been of immense value to our knowledge of the life of the Islands, and the destruction may have been a deliberate attempt to obscure the history of the island to sectarian advantage, for it is clear that during the century between 1750 and 1850 the hope of forcing the people out of their obstinate Catholicism persisted.

The Editor had left little for me to say except on the religious question. His lucid introductions elsewhere to the various material he has collected are all that is required.

We are fortunate to be able to include an authoritative Fauna and Flora, thanks to the members of the Edinburgh University Biological Society's Expedition who visited Barra in the Summer of 1935, and have very kindly sent us a composite list embodying their own and other observations. Entomologists may be interested to hear that the Puss Moth *(Dicranura vinula)* is frequent, the larva feeding upon small poplars. The commonest of the more conspicuous moths is the Fox *(Macrothylacia rubi)*, the perfect insect being seen in May and the dark brown furred caterpillars being extremely numerous upon the moorland braes in Autumn. A Clouded Yellow butterfly *(Colias edusa)* was noticed by the Editor at Scurrival in September 1933, but the only species of butterflies always about are the Garden White *(Pieris brassicae)*, the Meadow Brown *(Epinephele jurtina)*, and the Common Blue *(Polyommatus icarus)*. However, the reader can gain an idea of the resident lepidoptera from the list printed on pages 317 and 318.

The charm of Barra is becoming more and more widely known. Every year brings a large number of visitors. On the whole we can congratulate ourselves upon their behaviour and pay a tribute to their good taste. Still, there have been signs of late that our immunity from unsympathetic guests is not secure. Let me remind such that there are other islands as remote as Barra where the manners they find suitable for Barra would not be tolerated. Freedom from Sabbatarian taboos does not mean that the people of Barra welcome the noise of a gramophone playing jazz when they are on their way to Mass. Liberty to make Sunday a day of recreation does not mean that the people of Barra view with equanimity the undress familiar to the Riviera. No doubt we are deplorably old-fashioned; but when there are so many up-to-date pleasure resorts attainable the least that our guests can do is exclude Barra from their patronage unless they are prepared to humour our prejudices. The privilege of enjoying the innocent freedom in which a Catholic community delights entails repayment of it with a sensitive respect for the customs and observances of such a community, however far they may seem to lag behind the spirit of the times. Barra will give to visitors much more than it can ever get from them, and it will only be through their awareness of this that newcomers can hope to move beyond the status of visitors and reach the enviable status of friends.

Then there is the visitor who longs to give the poor Barra people the benefit of organized uplift. I had a letter from a worthy gentleman recently, begging me to do what I could to start a public library, a recreation-room, a pipe-band, a choir, lectures, and I know not what besides. He had visited Barra in Summer, and his heart was heavy with compassion for the unhappy condition of the people in Winter. Now, if there is one place in Scotland which knows how to amuse itself that place is Barra, and if there is one place on which organized uplift would be completely wasted that place is Barra. And if I am willing to wager that the smallest number of wireless licences in proportion to the population is taken out in the Islands, I am equally willing to wager that the number of Islesmen who have voyaged round the world is relatively higher than among the population on the mainland. Whatever charges may be levelled against Barra the last to level will be mental stagnation. Conservatism in its non-political sense does not necessarily imply ignorance nor even self-complacency.

The Book of Barra has not been compiled with any notion of attracting the tourist or providing him with a guide during his visit. At the same time, the visitor who gets into his head the variety of information offered in it will be in a position to understand and appreciate something which the average guide-book does not attempt to explain—the spirit of a small people through nearly four hundred years of adversity, for an almost continuous denial of one right after another, spiritual and material, is an adversity far less endurable than the adversity which nature inflicts. Some of these wrongs have been redressed: others still demand redress. Those who buy *The Book of Barra* will have the satisfaction of knowing that whatever royalties it earns will be devoted to whatever Barra need requires help. At present the intention is to apply them to the funds of the Sea League, which was founded at Castlebay in the month of July, 1933, to fight for the rights of the inshore fishermen.

There is much work to be done in the future, work more valuable to the spirit of men than the organized uplift which too often acts as a soporific instead of a stimulant. There are islands in the West that need taking again for the people who have been driven from them in the past through the greed of proprietors, the supineness of governments, or the incompetency of permanent officials. There is the imperative need of taking practical measures, not merely for the preservation, but for the advancement of Gaelic. We do not intend to rest until every official communication in the Outer Isles is printed in Gaelic and in English. We are tired of being put to sleep by Gaelic lullabies to dream sentimental dreams. That is the risk which lovers of the island always run. It is so easy to fall into dreaming out there on the edge of the Eurasian continent, so easy in the glimmer of a Hebridean midnight to forget the practical needs of the people. When the stranger reproaches me for bothering about 'politics' and 'economics' and 'better transport' and 'closing the Minch against trawlers' I long to set him down for a month of solitude upon one of the formerly inhabited islands so that he may discover the importance of humanity to the natural scene. The knowledge that there are still many who believe that it would serve the state to allow the Islands to become a wilderness for sportsmen like so much of the Highlands is always bitter with those of us who would rather see London a heap of ruins like Ur of the Chaldees than one more abomination of desolation like Rum. We contemplate modern Europe, and observe the present rulers of Germany and Italy trying to stem the advance of Communism as if so many boy scouts should think to twist the tail of the Dragon of the Apocalypse, and we believe that in the revolutions of the world Iona in very fact will be sometime again the instructress of the Western Regions. In that belief we can afford to dream about the future, which would be an even greater waste of time than dreaming about the past unless it were accompanied by practical efforts to maintain the existing population of the Islands.

CHAPTER 2

Barra in 1549

*

DONALD MUNRO

Donald Munro was High Dean of the Islands before 1560, and in that capacity visited them in 1549, afterwards writing the account from which the following chapter is taken. Munro went over to the Reformed Church after 1560 and was employed to plant kirks in Ross and Caithness, in which he does not seem to have had much success. In 1570 a complaint was made to the General Assembly that he was not fluent in the Scottish, that is, the Gaelic tongue, which must have handicapped his labours considerably.[1]

Munro's account of the Islands is the oldest in existence. George Buchanan based his description of them in his History of Scotland (1582) *on Munro. Munro apparently had visited Barra, but it is clear that he writes of the smaller islands from hearsay alone. He confuses their positions and often wrongly describes their size. In some cases, his versions of their names are difficult to identify.*

*

LINGAY[2]
From the Ile of Sky towards the southwest be fourscoire myles of sea lyes ane Ile callit Lingay, guid for gressing and fishing, ane Ile of halfe myle lange. It hes a Falcon nest in it, perteins to the Bishop of the Iles.

GIGARUN[3]
Backwart to the north besydes the ile of Lingay lyes ane Iyl callit Gigarun, half myle lang, perteining to the Bishop of the Iyles.

1 H. B., p. 237.
2 S. H. S., LIII, pp. 285-289 (better), also H. B., pp. 258-261. These Islands are given in the wrong order by Munro.
3 Hume Brown identifies with Grianamul.

BERNERAY

Besydes the Ile of Gigarun toward the north lyes ane Iyle, Inhabit and manurit,[1] ane myle lange callit Berneray, verey fertill and guid for fishing, perteining to the Bishop of the Iyles.

MEGALY (MINGULAY)

Besydes the Ile of Berneray towards the north lyes ane Ile callit Megaly twa myle lang Inhabit and veill manuritt, guid for fishing and corne, perteining to the Bishop of the Iyles.

PABAY

Besydes the Isle of Megaly to the North northeist lyes ane Ile callit Pabay ane myle lange, manurit. In it is guid take of fisch, it perteines to the Bishope of the Isles.

FLADAY

Besides the Ile of Pabay lyes ane prettey litle Isle to the northwart callit Fladay, of ane myle lange, fruitfull in corne and als in fishing, perteining to the Bishope of the Isles.

SCARPNAMUT[2]

Neire the Ile of Fladay towards the North lyes ane Ile namit Scarpnamutt twa myle lange, with a hake[3] nest in it, full of pastures and verey guid for fishing, perteining to the Bishop of the Isles.

SANDERAY

Nixt to the forsaid Ile lyes ther ane uther callit Sanderay Inhabit and manurit, guid for corn and fishing, twa myle lange. It perteines to the Bishope of the Iles.

WATTERSAY

Besides this ile northwart lyes ane Ile callit Vattersay, twa myle in lenth and ane myle in breadthe, ane excellent Raid for shippes that comes ther to fische, ane faire maine land inhabit and manurit, abounding in corne and gersing with guid pastorage for sheepe. All thir nine Iles forsaid had a Chapell in every Ile. This Ile perteyns to the Bishope of the Iles.

1 Cultivated.
2 Now called Muldonich.
3 Hawk.

BARRAY

Not far from this Ile of Watersay towards the north be twa myle of the sea lyes the Ile of Barray, being seven myle in lenthe from the southwest to the northeist and be north, and foure in breadth from the southeist to the northwest; ane fertill and fruitfull (ile) in cornes, abounding in the fishing of Keilling,[1] Ling, and all uther quhyte fish, with ane paroche kirke namit Killbare. Within the southwest end of this Ile ther enters a salt watter Loche, verey narrow in the Entres, and round and braide within. Into the middis of the saide loche there is ane Casle, in ane ile upon ane strenthey Craige callit Kileuin perteining to Mckneill of Baray.[2]

In the north end of this Isle of Barray ther is ane round heigh know mayne grasse and greine round about it to the heid on the top of quilk ther is ane spring and fresh water well. This well truely springs up certaine litle round quhyte things less nor the quantity of ane confeit corne lykes to the shape and figour of ane litle Cokill, as it appearit to me.[3] Out of this well runs ther ane litle strype downwith to the sea, and quher it enters into the sea ther is ane myle braid of sands, quilk ebbs ane myle, callit the Trayrmore[4] of Killbaray that is the grate sands of Barray. This sand is all full of grate Cokills and alledgit be the ancient countrymen that the same cokills comes down out of the forsaid hill throughe (the) said strype in the first small forme that we have spoken off and after ther coming to the saidis sandis growis grate Cokills alwayes. Ther is na fairer and more profitable sands for cokills in all the world. This Isle perteins to Mckneill of Barray.

ORVANSAY (OROSAY)

Betwix Barray and Ywist ther lyes first Orvansay half myle lange with ane falcone nest, ane guid profitable Ile manurit, guid for sheepe, perteining to McNeill of Barray.

NACHARRACHE[5]

Besides this Ile Lyes Ellan Nacharrach by the Erische so callit and in English the Sheips Ile, ane litle Ile full of grassing and store, perteining to Mckneill of Barray.

1 Codfish.
2 Munro apparently confuses Bàgh Beag with Castlebay.
3 See p. 36.
4 Tràigh Mhór.
5 Not known now under these names.

NAHAKERSAIT[1]

Nairest this forsaid Ile lyes ane Ile callit Nahakersait half ane myle lange with ane heaven for heighland galleyis, perteynis to McNeill of Barray.

GARULANGA[2]

Besides this Ile lyes ane Ile callit Garulanga guid for fishing, and verey fruitfull, perteining to Makneill of Barray.

FLADAY

Besydes this lyes ane Ile callit Fladay halfe myle lange with ane Falcone nest in it, verey fertill and fruitfull, it pertaines to McNeill of Barray.

BWYABEG[3]

Besides Flada layes and Ile namit Bwyabeg halfe myle lange guid for gersing and fishing, perteining to Mckneill of Barray.

BWYA MOIR[3]

Narrest Bwya Beg lyes ane Ile namit Bwya Moir twa myle lange, manurit, full of gersing, and pasture with ane falcon nest in it, pertaining to Mak Neill of Barray.

HAY[4]

Not far from Bwya Moir lyes ane Ile callit Hay halfe a myle lange, fertill and fruitfull, and guid for fishing, perteining to McNeill of Barray.

HELLESAY

Besides Hay lyes ane Ile callit Hellesay ane myle lange, fertill and fruitful, weill manurit, and excellent for all sorte of quhyte fishe taking. It perteins to MakNeill of Barray.

GIGAY (GIGHAY)

Besides this Ile lyes ane Ile callit Gigay ane myle lange, fertil and fruitfull, guid for store and fishing, perteining to MakNeill of Barray.

LINGAY

Narrest to Gigay lyes ane Ile callit Lingay half myle lange ane verey

---

1 Not known now under these names.
2 Garbh-Lingay.
3 Not known now under these names.
4 Probably a misreading for Fuiay.

guide Ile for gressing pastures and for Sheiling, pertaining to MakNeill of Barray.

FERAY (FIARAY)

Besides this ile lyes ane Ile laiche, namit by the Erishe Feray haffe a myle lange, guid for corne and gersing and excellent for fishing, perteining to MackNeill of Barray.

FUDAY

Besides this Ile lyes ane maine sandey Ile callit Fuday, fertill for beare[1] and murenis, the quhilk Ile pay murenis[2] zierly[3] to MakNeill of Barray for part of mailles and dewties.

ERISKERAY

To the Eist of this Ile of Fuday be three myles of sea lyes ane Ile callit Eriskeray, twa myle lang, inhabit and manurit. In this Ile ther is daylie gotten aboundance of verey grate pintill fishe[4] at Ebb seas and als verey guid for uther fishing, perteining to Mackneill of Barray.

[According to Munro, the MacNeills then also owned the south-west end of South Uist, "callit Baghastill."]

1 Barley.
2 Eels.
3 Yearly.
4 Razor-fish?

CHAPTER 3

Customs of the Islanders (1582)

*

GEORGE BUCHANAN

George Buchanan, from whose History of Scotland *this interesting account of the sixteenth-century islanders is taken, was a famous scholar and historian. He was a tutor to James VI at one time, and had the reputation of being the best Latin poet of his day at a time when Latin was the international language of Europe. His* History of Scotland, *too, is a work of great importance. It was published in Latin in 1582, but not translated until 1821.*

Buchanan apparently knew Gaelic, at least well enough to interpret the meanings of the Gaelic place-names which occur in his History. *He was an enemy of Queen Mary, and the originator of some of the slanders which were used against her, and is criticized in the* Book of Clanranald[1] *for speaking ill of her and of Eòin Muideartach, which proves that the Mac Mhuirichs in South Uist must have known his* History.

*

CUSTOMS OF THE ISLANDERS[2]

It now remains that I say something concerning the islands, that part of the British history which is involved in the greatest confusion. Setting aside, therefore, the more ancient writers, from whom it is impossible to extract any information, I shall follow the writers of our own time, upon whose accuracy and veracity more reliance may be placed. The islands, which, as it where, surround Scotland, form three distinct classes, the Western, the Orcades, and the Zetland isles. Those are called the Western Isles which are spread over the Deucaledonian Sea, on the west side of Scotland, from Ireland almost to the Orcades. The British historians, of the last and the present age, commonly style them the Hebrides, certainly a new name, of whose origin no trace can

1 R. C., Vol. II, p. 170.
2 H. B., pp. 232-235.

be found among ancient writers. In that part of the ocean some place the Aebudae, or Aemodae; but they are at so much variance among themselves, that they scarcely ever agree in situation, number, or name. Strabo, to begin with the oldest, may perhaps be excused for having followed uncertain report, that part of the world not having been sufficiently explored. Mela enumerates seven Hemodae, Martianus Capella as many Acmodae, Ptolemy and Solinus five Aebudae, and Pliny seven Acmodae, and thirty Aebudae. I shall retain the name most frequently used by the ancients, and designate the whole of the Western Islands Aebudae. Their site, relative condition, and produce, I shall describe from more recent and more certain authority; following chiefly Donald Monro, a pious and diligent man, who went over the whole of them himself, and minutely inspected them in person. They lie scattered in the Deucaledonian Sea, upwards of three hundred in number, and from time immemorial belonged to the kings of the Scots, until the time of Donald, the brother of Malcolm the Third, who ceded them to the king of Norway, in order to obtain his assistance in his unjust usurpation of the Scottish crown. The Danes and Norwegians retained them for about one hundred and sixty years, until, being vanquished in a decisive battle[1] by Alexander the Third, of Scotland, they restored them. Sometimes, however, trusting to their strength, and enticed into seditions, the islanders have asserted their liberty, and erected kings of their own. Among others, John, of the family of Donald[2], lately usurped the royal title.

In their food, clothing, and in the whole of their domestic economy, they adhere to ancient simplicity. Hunting and fishing supply them with food. They boil the flesh with water poured into the paunch or the skin of the animal they kill, and in hunting sometimes they eat the flesh raw, merely squeezing out the blood. They drink the juice of the boiled flesh. At their feasts they sometimes use whey, after it has been kept for several years, and even drink it greedily; that species of liquor they call bland[3], but the greater part quench their thirst with water. They make a kind of bread, not unpleasant to the taste, of oats and barley, the only grain cultivated in these regions, and, from long practice, they have attained considerable skill in moulding

1 Largs, in 1263. The Norwegian occupation of the Isles was of course much longer than 160 years.

2 John, last King of the Isles, who submitted to James III in 1476 and surrendered his lordship to James IV in 1494.

3 From Old Norse *blanda*, a mixture of fluids. The same term was used in the Orkneys and Shetlands. (O.E. Dict.)

the cakes. Of this they eat a little in the morning, and then contentedly go out a-hunting, or engage in some other occupation, frequently remaining without any other food till the evening.

They delight in variegated garments, especially striped, and their favourite colours are purple and blue. Their ancestors wore plaids of many different colours, and numbers still retain this custom, but the majority now, in their dress, prefer a dark brown, imitating nearly the leaves of the heather, that when lying upon the heath in the day, they may not be discovered by the appearance of their clothes; in these, wrapped rather than covered, they brave the severest storms in the open air, and sometimes lay themselves down to sleep even in the midst of snow. In their houses, also, they lie upon the ground; strewing fern, or heath on the floor, with the roots downward and the leaves turned up. In this manner they form a bed so pleasant, that it may vie in softness with the finest down, while in salubrity it far exceeds it; for heath, naturally possessing the power of absorption, drinks up the superfluous moisture, and restores strength to the fatigued muscles, so that those who lie down languid and weary in the evening, arise in the morning vigorous and sprightly. They have all, not only the greatest contempt for pillows, or blankets, but, in general, an affectation of uncultivated roughness and hardihood, so that when choice or necessity induces them to travel in other countries, they throw aside the pillows and blankets of their hosts, and wrapping themselves round with their own plaids, thus go to sleep, afraid lest these barbarian luxuries, as they term them, should contaminate their native simple hardiness. Their defensive armour consists of an iron headpiece, and a coat of mail, formed of small rings, and frequently reaching to the heels. Their weapons are, for the most part, a bow, and arrows barbed with iron, which cannot be extracted without widely enlarging the orifice of the wound; but a few carry swords of Lochaber axes. Instead of a trumpet, they use a bagpipe. They are exceedingly fond of music, and employ harps of a peculiar kind, some of which are strung with brass, and some with catgut. In playing they strike the wire either with a quill, or with the nails, suffered to grow long for the purpose; but their great ambition is to adorn their harps with great quantities of silver and gems, those who are too poor to afford jewels substituting crystals in their stead. Their songs are not inelegant, and in general celebrate the praises of brave men; their bards seldom choosing any other subject. They speak the ancient Gaelic language a little altered.

CHAPTER 4

Barra in 1620

*

The following account of Barra is taken form "Ane Description of Certaine Parts of the Highlands of Scotland" in the second volume of Walter MacFarlane's Geographical Collections Relating to Scotland.[1]

Walter Macfarlane (c. 1690-1767) was a chief of the MacFarlanes, and a famous antiquarian; his work upon the genealogies of various Scottish families is still considered authoritative. The famous Gaelic poet Alexander MacDonald dedicated his volume of poems (published in 1751*) to him. As this dedication has not been printed since* 1802, *and is the only piece of Gaelic prose of MacDonald's that is now known, it is worth reproducing:*[2]

Do an Uasal Onarach, Bhaltair Mac-Pharlain, Triath Chlann-Pharlain.

Uasail Oirdheirc,
Is e ar stuiddeara mor doi'-chíosaicht', agus ar n eolus neamhchum-manta, anns gach ni a bhuineas do dh'fhaolum agus do sheanchas; go sonraicht', ar gaol gun choi'-meas do na nithe sin a bhuineas do ar duthaich agus do ar canoin mhathaireil féin, a bhrostaich me chum an obair so chuir fo ar dídionn. Uimesin tha me dochusach go fuiling sibh fo ar tearmann i, chum gur luaithite ghabhar speis agus tlachd dh'i, ann measg gach dream a thuigeas a chanoin so. Oir, feadaidh me radh gun bhrosgul, nach b'urrainn i bhi ni ba shábhailte fo thearmann neach air bioth eile.

Tha ar cliu mor agus ar n alladh chomh-lan-shoilleir cheana, as nach ruig mise leas ann so toiseachadh ri mheadachadh; a bhar gur fior chinnteach me, nach bheil ni air bioth is graineile, agus is fuathaiche libhs', na ni sin a bhiothas cosoil ri brosgul no miodul. Agus ann lan dóchus, go faidh an obair mheanbh so, ar dion agus ar comaradh,

Tha me le mor spéis agus urram,
ar seirbheiseach fior umhuil,
Alastair Mac-Dhonuill.

1 S. H. S., LII, p. 177-180.
2 The spelling of the original is retained. *Ar* stands for both *ar* and *bhur*.

To the distinguished nobleman
Walter MacFarlane, Chief of Clan Parlan.

Illustrious Noble,
It is your great and indefatigable researches, and your uncommon knowledge in everything which pertains to learning and to history, especially your incomparable love for the things that pertain to our country and to our own mother-tongue, that encouraged me to place this work under your protection. Therefore I hope that you will suffer it to be under your patronage, in order that it may be the sooner appreciated by everyone who understands this language. For I may say without adulation, that it could not be safer under the patronage of any other person.

Your great fame and reputation are so clearly evident already, that I need not begin to elaborate them here; besides, I am truly certain that nothing is more abhorrent to you, than anything resembling fawning or flattery. And in the full hope, that this little work will obtain your protection and your help,

I am, with great affection and respect,
your most humble servant
Alexander MacDonald

This dedication did not prevent the book being burnt as seditious literature in 1752.

The name of the author of this description of Barra is unknown, and the description itself is undated. It is possible, however, to fix its date with some degree of certainty. The "Rorie McNeill" described is obviously Rory the Tartar, who succeeded in 1598, and died about 1622. The date of his birth is apparently not known, though it is doubtful if he actually attained the age of "sex or sevin score of years" which, according to this account, he attributed to himself. Some of Rory's exploits are related on page 75. He married first, a sister of MacLean of Duart, and secondly, a sister of MacDonald of Clanranald. There was considerable strife between the half-brothers by these marriages, especially from 1610 to 1613.[1] Rory the Tartar was no longer alive in 1622; therefore this account was most probably written between 1613 and 1622.

*

1 See C. M., pp. 62-74.

BARRA IN 1620[1]

Barray is one Illand being in the Maine seas farr from the Mainelands. It is of fyve myles of Length with certane glenns verie profitable for goods to feed therintill. And this Illand is verie fertill of corne and milk and abundance of fish is slaine in the sea of Barray. There is certane Illands on the North-end of Barray pertaining to the Superior which are named Erisgae, Fuda, Linga, Fara, with certaine other litle Illands.

On the South-end or southwest there are severall litle Illands which are profitable and fertill both of corne and abundance of milk.

And none can goe with scutts or boatts to those Sowthwest Illands but in those tymes of the yeare such as Aprill and Summer and in the beginning of August.

The Master or Superior of these Illands hath in due payment from the Inhabitants and tennants of the saids Illands for his dewtie, the half of ther cornes, butter, cheese and all other comodities, which does Incres or grow to them in the yeare.

And hath ane officer or serjeant in everie Illand to uptake the samen.

The names of those Illands is called Watersa, Sandira, Pappa, Mewla,[2] and Bearnera.

These Illands are farr off from all countries. There is one church in Barray on the North or Northeast end of it which is called Kilbarray, and in this toune there is one springand fresh water Well. And the Inhabitants and ancient men and woemen both of men and woemen in this toune and of the Countrie especiallie one ancient man being of five or sexscoir zeares old doeth say that when appearance of Warrs wer to be in the Countrey of Barray That certaine drops of blood hath oftymes bein sein in this springand fresh Water Well.

The Laird and Superior of this Countrey was called Rorie McNeill being ane verie ancient man of sexscore yeares old or therby did report this to be true.

And also did report this to be true lykewayes. Whensoever appearance of peace would be in the Countrie That certain litle bitts of Peitts wold be sein.

There is one litle springand fresh water running out of ane grein hill above the Church, which doeth flow into the sea, and there is

---

1 Walter MacFarlane's *Geographical Collections*, S. H. S., LII, pp. 177-180. The punctuation has been corrected but the spelling is left unchanged.
2 Mingulay, Gaelic Miùlaidh.

springand there certane litill Cockles shells which they alleadge that
the samen doth flow into the sea out of the Well and doeth grow in
another place next the Church not the tenth part of ane myll from the
church of Barray called Killbarray.[1]

And there is abundance of choice litle cockle shells found.

The wholl countreymen and tennants doe conveen togidder to
this place when the sea doeth ebb and bring with them certaine
number of horses and gather in this place abundance of Cockles.

The length of this sandie place is ane myll and ane half or therby,
and no less broad.

Certaine of these Inhabitants will come fyve mylls with ther horses,
and bring home as much with them as their horses will beare of these
cockles.

And if ten thousand cold come, they should have als many as there
horses were able to carrie everie day gotten and gathered in this place.

And it is gotten below the sand, and when you doe come and stand
on that sand with your horses you will think the place verie dry, but
when you doe put zour hands below into the sand you shall see
abundance of the saids cockle comeing above the sand, and als much
of the sea Water as will wash them from the sand.

Next to this place there is ane plaine ground of faire green earth
on the Westsyde of this sandie place, and this is called Mealloch.[2]

In this Mealloch there is ane litle Chappell called Kilmoir[3] and it
lyeth on a verie pleasant grein. And one litle hill of green ground is
betwixt this chappell and the principall Church of the Countrie, for
this Church of Kilmoire is on the northsyde of the litle hill, and the
Chappell of Kilmoire on the Southsyde.

In this Chappell as the Inhabitants say that there is cretaine earth
within this Chappell which if anie man wold carrie the samen with him
to the sea, and if the wind or stormie strong weather were cruell and
vehement, if he wold caste a litle of this earth into the sea it wold
pacifie the wind and the sea wold grow calme immediatlie efter the
casting of the earth into the sea.

The Main seas and the seas next to Scotland are on every syde of
this Chappell. The Main seas doth come from the West and the other
seas from the east, and almost the saids two seas doth forgadder and

1 See p. 28.
2 Gaelic *mealbhach*, from Norse *mel-bakki*, a name applied to places where bent grass
grows in sandy soil.
3 Now apparently known as Caibeall Mhichil.

meet with other.

And they have cutt and broke the lands in divyding the Illand of Barray into two parts almost next to the litle Chappell of Kilmore.

The Inhabitants of this Illand are called Clan Neill Barray.

There is one castle in this Illand on the South end in one litle Illand of Craig or rock builded verie strong.

And there is ane fresh water Logh betwixt Kilbarr and this Castle of Kilsimull. And there is a little toure of stone and lyme builded in ane litle Illand in the midst of this Logh,[1] and the toune wherein this litle toure is builded is called Arnistill.

There is no great rivers of fresh water in Barray but one litle Water in a toune called Quir[2], and there is a litle mill in that water and no more mills in all the Illand.

Bot everie husbandman in the countrey hes ane Instrument in their houses called one Kewrne[3] and the two stones doth lye on the house floore, and that place is made cleane.

The most corne which doeth grow in this countrie is good barley and one verie fertill countrie of that kinde of Corne and there are manie Wyld birds or fowls in this Countrey.

The inhabitants thereoff are verie antient Inhabitants and the Superior or Laird of Barray is called Rorie McNeill. He is sex or sevin score of years as himself did say.

This ancient man in tyme of youth being a valiant and stout man of warr and hearing from skippers that oftymes were wont to travell to ane Illand which the Inhabitants of the Illand alledged this McNeill and his predecessors should be their Superiors, which Illand is sein oftymes from the tope of the mountains of Barray. This Rorie hearing oftymes the same newes reported to him and to his predecessors, he fraughted a shipe but nowayes could find the Illand, at last was driven to Ireland on the west syd thereoff, and took up a Spreath,[4] and returned home therefter.

This McNeill[5] had severall Noblemens daughters and had sundrie bairnes, and at last everie one of them thinking and esteeming himself to be worthie of the Countrie after the father's deceass, being on lyff

1 Loch St Clair.
2 Cuier.
3 Quern, or hand-mill.
4 A booty of cattle.
5 He seems to be Ruairi an Tartair, who had families by a sister of MacLean of Duart, and by a sister of MacDonald of Clanranald. There was strife between the half-brothers, but this account is exaggerated. See C. M., p. 67; and *The Celtic Review*, Vol. III, p. 218.

as yet, the saids sones haveing sundrie mothers, at last everie one of them did kill others except one that is alyff and another drowned in the sea.

CHAPTER 5

Barra in 1695
*
MARTIN MARTIN

*Martin Martin (c. 1660-1719) was the third son of Donald Martin of
Bealach, near Duntulm in Skye. The exact date of his birth is not known, but
he graduated M.A. at Edinburgh in* 1681. *From some subsequent date until*
1686 *he was governor to Donald MacDonald younger of Sleat, and from* 1686
to 1692 *to young MacLeod of Dunvegan. From* 1692 *until* 1697 *he travelled
the islands at the suggestion of Sir Robert Sibbald, the antiquary, and in* 1697
he contributed a short paper on this subject to the Royal Society's Philosophical
Proceedings, xix, 727. *This was expanded and published, with a map, in*
London *in* 1703 *under the title of* A Description of the Western Islands of
Scotland. *He made a visit to St Kilda in* 1697, *of which he published an
account in* 1698. *He entered Leyden University in* 1710 *and graduated M.D.
there. He died in London in* 1719.[1]

*Owing to the excessive scarcity of early accounts of life in the Islands,
Martin's* Description *is of great value. It is the only description of the isles
written by a Hebridean, and the author's sympathy with, and understanding
of his subject are strongly in evidence, compared with the superficiality and lack
of sympathetic insight which is often apparent in the writings of strangers like
Burt and MacCulloch and others. If occasionally we meet a story in Martin
which is not too easily believed, it must be remembered that such tales are
repeated from hearsay and do not themselves impugn the accuracy of the
author's own observations. Martin's book accompanied Dr Johnson and
Boswell on their famous tour. Johnson, who found Martin in error over some
stone crosses on Raasay, doubted his accuracy, disliked his style, and thought
that he had missed a unique opportunity to describe a vanished social organization. MacCulloch plagiarized Johnson's criticism, and like Burt[2] derided
Martin's accounts of second sight. Second sight is a subject on which we are
entitled to hold our own opinions while respecting those of others. As for the
social organization about which Dr Johnson and MacCulloch were so anxious*

---

1 This account is based on the biographies in *The Dictionary of National Biography* and in Dr D. J.
MacLeod's edition of Martin's book (1934).
2 Author of *Letters from the North of Scotland* (1726).

for information, the truth is that Martin describes very adequately what remained of it in his own time. It had been in decay since the Reformation (1560) and the Union of the Crowns (1603), and when Martin wrote, many of its most characteristic customs had been abandoned for at least a generation. In spite of Dr Johnson's irritation and the sneers of Burt and MacCulloch, most modern readers will prefer Martin to the two latter writers. But for him we should depend almost entirely upon references in the Gaelic poets for our knowledge of seventeenth-century life in the islands.

Like Dean Munro, Martin clearly had not visited the smaller islands round Barra, but had got his information about them at second hand. On his map, the positions of Mingulay and Pabbay are reversed. Much of Martin's account of Barra and its islands refers to Mingulay and not to the mainland of Barra, a fact which has apparently eluded both the author of The Clan Macneil *and Miss Goodrich Freer in her* Outer Isles.

*

The island of Barray[1] lies about two leagues and a half to the south-west of the island South-Uist; it is five miles in length and three in breadth, being in all respects like the islands lying directly north from it. The east side is rocky, and the west arable ground, and yields a good produce of the same grain that both Uists do; they use likewise the same way for enriching their land with sea ware. There is plenty of cod and ling got on the east and south sides of this island. Several small ships from Orkney come hither in summer, and afterward return laden with cod and ling.

There is a safe harbour on the north-east side of Barray, where there is great plenty of fish.[2]

The rivers on the east side afford salmon, some of which are speckled like these mentioned in North Uist, but they are more successful here in catching them. The natives go with three several herring nets, and lay them cross-ways in the river where the salmon are most numerous, and betwixt them and the sea. These salmon at the sight or shadow of the people make towards the sea, and feeling the net from the surface to the ground, jump over the first, then the second, but being weakened, cannot get over the third net, and so are caught. They delight to leap above water and swim on the surface. One

1 Taken from *A Description of the Western Isles of Scotland* published in 1703, reprinted in 1884. Pp. 89-100.
2 Northbay.

of the natives told me that he killed a salmon with a gun, as jumping above water.

They informed me also that many barrels of them might be taken in the river above mentioned, if there was any encouragement for curing and transporting them. There are several old forts to be seen here, in form like those in the other islands. In the south end of this island there is an orchard which produces trees, but few of them bear fruit, in regard of their nearness to the sea. All sorts of roots and plants grow plentifully in it. Some years ago tobacco did grow here, being of all plants that most grateful to the natives, for the islanders love it mightily.

The little island Kismul lies about a quarter of a mile from the south of this isle. It is the seat of Macneil of Barray; there is a stone wall round it two stories high, reaching the sea, and within the wall there is an old tower and a hall, with other houses about it. There is a little magazine in the tower, to which no stranger has access. I saw the officer called the Cockman,[1] and an old cock he is; when I bid him ferry me over the water to the island, he told me that he was but an inferior officer, his business being to attend in the tower; but if (says he) the constable, who then stood on the wall, will give you access, I'll ferry you over. I desired him to procure me the constable's permission, and I would reward him; but having waited some hours for the constable's answer, and not receiving any, I was obliged to return without seeing this famous fort. Macneil and his lady being absent was the cause of this difficulty, and of my not seeing the place. I was told some weeks after that the constable was very apprehensive of some design I might have in viewing the fort, and thereby to expose it to the conquest of a foreign power, of which I supposed there was no great cause of fear. The natives told me there is a well in the village Tangstill,[2] the water of which being boiled grows thick like puddle. There is another well not far from Tangstill, which the inhabitants say in a fertile year throws up many grains of barley in July and August. And they say that the Well of Kilbar throws up embryoes of cockles, but I could not discern any in the rivulet, the air being at that time foggy.[3] The church in this island is called Kilbarr, i.e., St Barr's Church. There is a little chapel by it, in which Macneil and those descended of his family are usually interred. The natives have St Barr's wooden image[4]

1 Gocman, or Usher.
2 Tangusdale.
3 See pp. 28 and 36.
4 See p. 22.

standing on the altar, covered with linen in form of a shirt; all their greatest asseverations are by this saint. I came very early in the morning with an intention to see this image, but was disappointed; for the natives prevented me by carrying it away, lest I might take occasion to ridicule their superstition, as some Protestants have done formerly; and when I was gone it was again exposed on the altar. They have several traditions concerning this great saint. There is a chapel (about half a mile on the south side of the hill near St Barr's Church)[1] where I had occasion to get an account of a tradition concerning this saint, which was thus: "The inhabitants having begun to build the church, which they dedicated to him, they laid this wooden image within it, but it was invisibly transported (as they say) to the place where the church now stands, and found there every morning." This miraculous conveyance is the reason they give for desisting to work where they first began.[2] I told my informer that this extraordinary motive was sufficient to determine the case, if true, but asked his pardon to dissent from him, for I had not faith enough to believe this miracle, at which he was surprised, telling me in the meantime that this tradition hath been faithfully conveyed by the priests and natives successively to this day. The southern islands are: (1) Muldonish, about a mile in circumference; it is high in the middle, covered over with heath and grass, and is the only forest here for maintaining the deer, being commonly about seventy or eighty in number. (2) The island Vattersay[3] lies southerly of Barray, from which it is separated by a narrow channel, and is three miles in circumference, having a mountain in the middle. It is designed for pasturage and cultivation. On the south side there is a harbour convenient for small vessels, that come yearly here to fish for cod and ling, which abound on the coast of this island. (3) The island Sandreray, two miles in circumference, is fruitful in corn and grass, and separated by a narrow channel from Vattersay. (4) To the south of these lies the island Bernera, about two miles in circumference.[4] It excels other islands of the same extent for cultivation and fishing. The natives never go a-fishing while Macneil or

1 Kilmoire, see p. 37.
2 It is a possible explanation of this tradition that this statue came to land in Barra after some shipwreck, and its possession was for some time an object of dispute between the inhabitants of Kilbar and those of Vaslan.
3 Sandreray in original, erroneously.
4 Throughout the following passage Martin confuses Bernera with Mingulay, while other editors have taken it to refer to Barra itself. In reality the next three pages refer to Mingulay and Bernera, mostly to Mingulay.

his steward is in the island, lest seeing their plenty of fish, perhaps they might take occasion to raise their rents. There is an old fort in this island, having a vacuity round the walls, divided in little apartments.[1] The natives endure a great fatigue in manuring their ground with sea-ware, which they carry in ropes upon their backs over high rocks. They likewise fasten a cow to a stake, and spread a quantity of sand on the ground, upon which the cow's dung falls, and this they mingle together, and lay it on the arable land. They take great numbers of sea-fowls from the adjacent rocks, and salt them with the ashes of burnt sea-ware in cows' hides, which preserves them from putrefaction.

There is a sort of stone in this island, with which the natives frequently rub their breasts by way of prevention, and say it is a good preservative for health. This is all the medicine they use. Providence is very favourable to them, in granting them a good state of health, since they have no physician among them.

The inhabitants are very hospitable, and have a custom, that when any strangers from the Northern Islands[2] resort thither, the natives, immediately after their landing, oblige them to eat, even though they should have liberally eaten and drank but an hour before their landing there. And this meal they call Bieyta'v;[3] i.e., ocean meat; for they presume that the sharp air of the ocean, which indeed surrounds them, must needs give them a good appetite. And whatever number of strangers come there, or of whatsoever quality or sex, they are regularly lodged according to ancient custom, that is, one only in a family; by which custom a man cannot lodge with his own wife, while in this island. Mr John Campbell, the present minister of Harris, told me, that his father being then parson of Harris, and minister of Barray (for the natives at that time were Protestants)[4] carried his wife along with him, and resided in this island for some time, and they disposed of him, his wife and servants in manner above mentioned; and suppose Macneil of Barray and his lady should go thither, he would be obliged to comply with this ancient custom.

There is a large root grows among the rocks of this island lately discovered, the natives call it Curran-Petris,[5] of a whitish colour, and upwards of two feet in length, where the ground is deep, and in shape

1 Dùn Briste in Bernera.
2 The other islands of Barra.
3 Biadh an t-saimh.
4 This is not correct. See p. 8 *et seq.*
5 Parsnip.

and size like a large carrot; where the ground is not so deep it grows much thicker, but shorter: the top of it is like that of a carrot.

The rock Linmull,[1] about half a mile in circumference, is indifferently high, and almost inaccessible, except in one place, and that is by climbing, which is very difficult. This rock abounds with sea-fowls that build and hatch here in summer; such as the guillemot, coulterneb, puffin, etc. The chief climber is commonly called Gingich,[2] and this name imports a big man having strength and courage proportionable. When they approach the rock with the boat, Mr Gingich jumps out first upon a stone on the rock-side, and then, by the assistance of a rope of horse-hair, he draws his fellows out of the boat upon this high rock, and draws the rest up after him with the rope, till they all arrive at the top, where they purchase a considerable quantity of fowls and eggs. Upon their return to the boat, this Gingich runs a great hazard by jumping first into the boat again, where the violent sea continually rages; having but a few fowls more than his fellows, besides a greater esteem to compensate his courage. When a tenant's wife in this or the adjacent islands dies, he then addresses himself to Macneil of Barray representing his loss, and at the same time desires that he would be pleased to recommend a wife to him, without which he cannot manage his affairs, nor beget followers to Macneil, which would prove a public loss to him. Upon this representation, Macneil finds out a suitable match for him; and the woman's name being told him, immediately he goes to her, carrying with him a bottle of strong waters for their entertainment at marriage, which is then consummated.

When a tenant dies, the widow addresseth herself to Macneil in the same manner, who likewise provides her with a husband, and they are married without any further courtship. There is in this island an altar dedicated to St Christopher, at which the natives perform their devotion. There is a stone set up hereabout seven feet high, and when the inhabitants come near it they take a religious turn[3] round it.

If a tenant chance to lose his milk-cows by the severity of the season, or any other misfortune; in this case Macneil of Barray supplies him with the like number that he lost.

When any of these tenants are so far advanced in years that they are incapable to till the ground, Macneil takes such old men into his

1 Lianamul, off the west of Mingulay.
2 Not in the dictionaries; there is *gingein*, a thick-set person.
3 Sunwise.

own family, and maintains them all their life after. The natives observe, that if six sheep are put a-grazing in the little island of Pabbay, five of them still appear fat, but the sixth a poor skeleton, but any number in this island not exceeding five are always very fat. There is a little island not far from this called Micklay,[1] of the same extent as Pabbay, and hath the same way of feeding of sheep. These little islands afford excellent hawks.

The isles above mentioned, lying near to the south of Barray, are commonly called the Bishop's Isles, because they are held of the Bishop. Some isles lie on the east and north of Barray, as Fiaray, Hellisay,[2] Buya Major and Minor, Lingay, Fuda; they afford pasturage, and are commodious for fishing; and the latter being about two miles in circumference is fertile in corn and grass. There is a good anchoring place next to the isle on the north-east side.

The steward of the Lesser and Southern Islands is reckoned a great man here, in regard of the perquisites due to him; such as a particular share of all the lands, corn, butter, cheese, fish, etc., which these islands produce: the measure of barley paid him by each family yearly is an omer, as they call it, containing about two pecks.

There is an inferior officer, who also hath a right to a share of all the same products. Next to these come in course those of the lowest posts, such as the cockman and porter, each of whom hath his respective due, which is punctually paid.

Macneil of Barray and all his followers are Roman Catholics, one only excepted, viz., Murdock Macneil; and it may perhaps be thought no small virtue in him to adhere to the Protestant communion, considering the disadvantages he labours under by the want of his Chief's favour, which is much lessened, for being a heretic, as they call him. All the inhabitants observe the anniversary of St Barr, being the 27th of September; it is performed riding on horseback, and the solemnity is concluded by three turns round St Barr's church.[3] This brings into my mind a story which was told me concerning a foreign priest and the entertainment he met with after his arrival there some years ago, as follows:—This priest happened to land here upon the very day, and at the particular hour of this solemnity, which was the more acceptable to the inhabitants, who then desired him to preach a

---

1 Martin mixes the southern islands up. All the proceeding passage refers to Mingulay, not to Barra itself, as has been supposed, and is obviously written from hearsay.
2 Mellisay in original.
3 See p. 54.

commemoration sermon to the honour of their patron St Barr, according to the ancient custom of the place. At this the priest was surprised, he never having heard of St Barr before that day; and therefore knowing nothing of his virtues, could say nothing concerning him: but told them, that if a sermon to the honour of St Paul or St Peter could please them, they might have it instantly. This answer of his was so disagreeable to them, that they plainly told him he could be no true priest, if he had not heard of St Barr, for the Pope himself had heard of him; but this would not persuade the priest, so that they parted much dissatisfied with one another.[1] They have likewise a general cavalcade on St Michael's Day,[2] in Kilbar village, and do then also take a turn round their church. Every family, as soon as the solemnity is ended, is accustomed to bake St Michael's cake, as above described; and all strangers, together with those of the family, must eat the bread that night.

This island, and the adjacent lesser islands, belong in property to Macneil, being the thirty-fourth of that name by lineal descent that has possessed this island, if the present genealogers may be credited. He holds his lands in vassalage of Sir Donald Macdonald of Slate, to whom he pays £40[3] per annum and a hawk, if required, and is obliged to furnish him a certain number of men upon extraordinary occasions.

1 St Barr's name is not to be found on the Calendar.
2 Similar cavalcades at Michaelmas are stated by Martin to have taken place in Lewis, Harris, North Uist, Skye, Coll and Tyree, so that the custom was once widespread in the Hebrides.
3 £3, 6s. 8d. in English money.

CHAPTER 6

Barra in the Forty-five [1]

*

J. L. CAMPBELL

Though the MacNeills were not 'out' in the Rising of 1745, the island of Barra did not come through these troubled times unscathed, especially during the time that the hunt was being made after Prince Charles by land and sea, while he and his small band of followers were hiding in South Uist and Benbecula from 11th May to 28th June 1746.

Barra Head was the first piece of Scottish territory upon which the Prince and his followers, the 'seven men of Moydart,' set eyes as they approached the Highlands in their ship the *Du Teillay*. It was sighted on 22nd July 1745.[2] On board the *Du Teillay* was Duncan Cameron, who had been brought up in Barra, and who had fought at Fontenoy in Lord John Drummond's regiment. Duncan Cameron had come at the instruction of Aeneas MacDonald (Kinlochmoidart's brother) to guide the *Du Teillay* in approaching the Long Island, and his account of the Prince's landing and the march to Edinburgh was taken down by Robert Forbes, compiler of *The Lyon in Mourning*, in the course of several conversations.

Barra Head was sighted on 22nd July 1745. On the same or the next day Cameron put off on Barra to find a pilot to take the ship to Eriskay. His own description of this incident is as follows:[3]

"When they were near the shore of the Long Isle, Duncan Cameron was set out in the long boat to fetch them a proper pilot. When he landed he accidentally met with (Macneill of) Barra's piper, who was his old acquaintance, and brought him on board. The piper piloted them safely into Erisca (about July

---

1 Most of this chapter is based on information contained in *The Lyon in Mourning*, Scottish History Society, Vols. XX-XXII. But *The Lyon in Mourning* is so badly indexed that it is possible that some details may have escaped notice. Unindexed references to Barra occur in Vol. XXI, pp. 177, 204, 328; and Vol. XXII, p. 29.
2 S. H. S., Vol. XXIII, p. 1.
3 S. H. S., Vol. XX, pp. 204-205.

21st),[1] a small island lying between Barra and South Uist. 'At this time,' said Duncan Cameron, 'there was *a devil of a minister*[2] that happened to be in the island of Barra, who did us a' the mischief that lay in his power. For when he had got any inkling about us, he dispatched away expresses with informations against us. But as the good luck was, he was not well believed, or else we would have been a' tane by the neck.'

"When Duncan spoke these words, *'a devil of a minister,'* he bowed low, and said to me, 'Sir, I ask you ten thousand pardons for saying so in your presence.[3] But, good faith, I can assure you, sir (asking your pardon), he was nothing else but the *devil of a minister.'*

"When they landed in Eriska, they could not find a grain of meal or one inch of bread. But they catched some flounders,[4] which they roasted upon the bare coals in a mean low hut they had gone into near the shore, and Duncan Cameron stood cook. The Prince sat at the cheek of the little ingle, upon a fail sunk,[5] and he laughed heartily at Duncan's cookery, for he himself owned he played his part awkwardly enough."

According to Aeneas MacDonald,[6] who accompanied the Prince on the *Du Teillay,* "From Eriska some of the company sent to Roger MacNeil, Esquire of Barra, as relations, being come thither, and who would be glad to see him: but he happened to be from home."[7] MacNeill's absence on this occasion was probably due to diplomatic reasons. In Scotland many a good cause has been ruined by its potential supporters waiting to see which way the cat would jump. MacNeill was one of the chiefs who played for safety in 1745 in this manner, but his caution neither helped his countrymen, nor prevented his own arrest and imprisonment a year later, as remains to be seen.

From Eriskay the Prince and his friends sailed to Loch nan Uamh, where they landed; and nothing more is heard of Barra until April in

---

1 Actually July 23rd. The dates are old style.
2 This was the Rev. John MacAulay, grandfather of Lord Macaulay, the famous Whig historian.
But see The Dictionary of National Biography, where this relationship is denied.
3 Robert Forbes was an Episcopalian Clergyman.
4 Flounders are still plentiful in Barra Sound.
5 A turf seat.
6 S. H. S., Vol. XX, p. 289.
7 S. H. S., Vol. XX, p. 289.

1746. But there must have been comings and goings, and it is clear that enough must have gone on to implicate MacNeill sufficiently to justify his subsequent arrest and confinement. According to one account,[1] arms had been landed in Barra for the Jacobites by a Colonel Kendela or Ultan Kindelan, in the Spanish service, which were later found by the Hanovarians. In April 1746, shortly before Culloden, Donald MacLeod, who later piloted the Prince from Borrodale to Benbecula, and Aeneas MacDonald, the brother of Kinlochmoidart, visited Barra to bring back a sum of about £380 that had been left there.[2] As the Minch was "swarming with sloops of war, boats and yawls full of militia, viz., the Campbells, the MacLeods, and the MacDonalds of Skye," they had the greatest difficulty in getting to Barra, and were nearly captured by Captain Ferguson of the *Furnace* in South Uist on their way back. They managed to return in safety by Canna and Eigg to Kinlochmoidart's house on the mainland.

After Culloden (16th April 1746), there was a lull of about two weeks before the hunt for the Prince was taken up. As is well known, the Prince decided to go to the Outer Islands with the hope of getting a boat to take him to France or to Orkney; his original intention was to go to Sir Alexander MacDonald of Skye or MacLeod of MacLeod, but this he was persuaded to abandon. The Prince sailed from Borrodale to Benbecula, thence to Scalpay in Harris with the hope of getting a vessel at Stornoway; when he failed, he returned to Benbecula and South Uist where he was 'on the run' from 11th May until 28th June, sheltered and helped by the MacDonalds of Clanranald, his staunchest supporters. In the meantime his enemies endeavoured to hem him in, landing in Barra and North Uist, and even going to St Kilda.

According to the account[3] of Alexander MacDonald, the famous Gaelic poet:

"About the latter end of June Captain Ferguson landed at Barra with some hundreds of red-coats. Three hundred of the MacLeods of Skye likewise at the same time arrived in Benbecula, all in quest of his royal highness. General Campbell with a squadron had gone about to St Gilda, the remotest of all the western Isles, the Laird of MacLeod proprietor, and from thence

1 S. H. S., Vol. XXI, p. 286.
2 S. H. S., Vol. XX, pp. 159-160.
3 S. H. S., Vol. XX, p. 328.

was come to Uist. Besides all this the channel between Uist, Skie, and Canna was all full of ships and scooners, so that at once his royal highness and his few adherents were to be attacked from all quarters environed by sea and land."

The Prince escaped from Benbecula on 28th June disguised as 'Betty Burke,' maid to Flora Macdonald. On 5th July Donald MacLeod was captured in Benbecula and taken to Barra to appear before General Campbell, whom, however, he did not see there.[1] Meanwhile, MacNeill of Barra had been arrested by Captain Ferguson, and Rev. James Grant, priest of Barra, had been taken by the notorious Captain Caroline Scott in Mingulay.[2] According to John Cameron, Presbyterian Chaplain at Fort William, Scott also landed in Barra to search for arms and hanged a man whom he heard had been in arms,[3] though the man protested he could find fifty witnesses to prove he had "never been out of the country or under arms in it." "What made this the more surprizing," Cameron goes on to say, "is that tho' in the islands belonging to (Macneill of) Barra there will be about 4 or 500 souls, there is but one gentleman and 7 or 8 common people that are Protestants, of whom this poor unfortunate man was one."

MacNeill of Barra was arrested in June 1746 by Captain Ferguson, and suffered with the other Jacobite prisoners the most disgraceful ill-treatment. The Rev. James Taylor, Episcopalian Clergyman in Caithness, who was one of these prisoners, later wrote a vivid account of their hardships for Robert Forbes:

"Simon, Lord Lovat, MacNeil of Barra, John Gordon, younger, of Glenbucket, were by this time (June) apprehended, as were great numbers of inferior persons, severals of whom were treated most cruelly by some of the officers, specially by Captain Ferguson, a fellow of very low extract, born in the county of Aberdeen, who, being naturally of a furious, savage disposition, thought he could never enough harass, misrepresent and maltreat every one whom he knew, or suppos'd to be an enemy for the goodly cause he himself was embarked in."[4]

1 S. H. S., Vol. XX, p.178.
2 O. I., p. 400.
3 S. H. S., Vol. XX, p. 94.
4 S. H. S., Vol. XXII, p. 29.

Ferguson's brutalities are well known to every student of the Forty-Five.[1] Ferguson was representative of a type of Scotsman that has too often disgraced his country. Vindictive, ungenerous, cruel, self-seeking, bigoted, without a shred of chivalry or honour, he personified the very worst qualities of Scottish Whiggery. MacNeil was taken to Inverness, and from Inverness on the prison-ship *Pamela* to Woolwich. The *Pamela* was ordered to anchor off Tilbury on 27th August,

"where[2] some other transports were lying with prisoners, which was no convenient station for people so confined, for the country on each side the river is very wet and marshy, which occasions frequent unwholesome fogs, and all the grand necessaries of life sell there at a much higher rate than in many places in England.

"At length by the indulgence of the Court every prisoner was allow'd half a pound weight of bread a day, and an quarter of an pound weight of cheese or butter for breakfast, but no ale or beer. But by the avarice and villainy of the victualler, one Bonny, a broken taylor, they seldom or never received above three fourths of the said weights, and sometimes not so much. Besides, it was the opinion of many that the fleshes were none of the wholesomest kind, as being purchased from butchers who were suspected to deal in diseased cattle. But they were oblig'd to use such victuals or starve. And even such of the prisoners as had money were greatly straitned to obtain healthy provisions by the boundless avarice of the soldiers and backwardness of the sailors to bring them honestly from Gravesend."

The escape of one of the prisoners in September resulted in the more rigorous confinement of the others. But in October the ship's officer, Laurence, was relieved by one Barker, "a rank atheist of a most scandalous life and lost character" who "oblig'd honest Mr MacNeil of Barra and Mr Gordon, younger, of Glenbucket, who was almost blind, to sleep in the hold, and put all the hardships he was capable of inventing upon them and all the captives there."

MacNeill was not kept long in these unsavoury quarters, however.

1 Donald MacLeod, the Prince's pilot, describes the sufferings of the prisoners under Ferguson's care, and at Tilbury. S. H. S., Vol. XX, pp. 180-181. The treatment seems to have been designed deliberately to destroy slowly men for whose summary execution there was not sufficient pretext.
2 S. H. S., Vol. XXII, p. 31.

"On the first day of November (1746), Barra and Mr Gordon, in company with the Laird of Clanranold, Bysedale, etc., were carried by Mr Dick, a messenger, to his house in London, where they were confin'd till Summer 1747." The order for MacNeill's discharge was made on 28th May 1747;[1] in the list of "Prisoners of the '45"[2] it is stated that he turned King's Evidence, but no details are given. His caution had not prevented his undergoing a humiliating and unpleasant imprisonment. The last echo of the Fort-Five occurred in 1750, when Lochgarry reported to the Prince[3] that amongst others, "MacNeill of Barra would bring 150 men to aid a new Rising in the Highlands." The whole of this scheme was betrayed to the Hanovarian Government by Young Glengarry (Pickle the Spy), one of the blackest of the traitors who have disgraced Scotland's history, so that nothing came of it.

1 *Scots Magazine*, Vol. IX, p 244.

2 *Scottish History Society*, Vol. XV of third Series, p. 175.

3 See Andrew Lang's *Pickle the Spy*, pp. 214-218.

CHAPTER 7

Barra in 1794

PARISH OF BARRAY

(COUNTY OF INVERNESS, SYNOD OF GLENELG, PRESBYTERY OF UIST)[1]

*

THE REV. MR EDWARD MACQUEEN[2]

Name, Situation, Extent, Etc.

The ancient name of this parish is not known. Its present name seems to be derived from St Barr, the tutelar saint of the island, and to whose memory the 25th of September is dedicated as a holiday. On this day the Priest says mass, and all those of the Romish religion used punctually to attend. After mass the people amused themselves with horse-races, and spent the evening in mirth and conviviality. Of late years this custom has been much on the decline. Formerly there was an image of the saint in the churchyard of Kilbar (the principal place of worship, and probably the burial-place of the saint), which was clothed with a linen shirt every year upon his own anniversary. Some of the priests who resided here informed me that it was not enjoined as a necessary part of their duty to pay so much veneration to Saint Barr, as he never had the honour of being ranked with the Saints of Rome, nor was his name at any time inrolled in the Roman kalendar. From this it appears that the churches in these parts, which were subject to Icolumkill, never recognized the authority of the church of Rome.[3] It appears from Bede, who wrote in the beginning of the eighth century, that the monastery of Icolmkill was not subject to Rome at that time. Later writers have shown the same in their times; besides, if at any subsequent period it had submitted to Papal jurisdiction, it is more than probable that some Pope or other would have dignified with canonization, a person who had sanctity enough to render him worthy of being appointed the patron or protector of any

1 O. S. A., Vol XIII, pp. 326-342.

2 Church of Scotland minister in Barra from 1774 to 1813. He wrote this description of Barra for the *Old Statistical Account of Scotland*, to which all parish ministers contributed, under the editorship of Sir John Sinclair.

3 This conclusion is quite unjustified.

district of ecclesiastical territory. On the N. this parish is divided from Uist by a channel of 8 miles; the island of Tyree, in the county of Argyle, and the property of the Duke of Argyle, is the nearest land to it on the S. and lies at the distance of about 40 miles; Canna and Rum, in the parish of the small isles, lying at the distance of 24 miles; on the W. it is exposed to the Atlantic Ocean. The parish of Barray consists of the main island of Barray, particularly so called, and a number of other islands, distinguished by their respective names, the largest of which are inhabited, such as Watersay, Sanderay, Pabay, Mengalay, and Bernaray, to the S.; Flodday, Heillesay, and Gigay, on the E.; besides a number of small islands not inhabited. The main island of Barray is 8 computed miles in length, and from 2 to 4 in breadth, being intersected in different places by arms of the sea. The compilers of the *Encyclopaedia Britannica* will do well to correct their error in calling Barray a rock half a mile in circumference, inhabited only by solan geese and other wild fowls.[1] The island of Watersay, separated from the main island by a channel of one mile, is about 3 miles in length, in some places a mile and a half broad, and is divided into two distinct farms; the one, possessed by Mr McNeil of Watersay; the other is now in the hands of the proprietor, called the farm of Kilis.[2] The next is Sanderay, distant 5 miles from Barray; it is 2 miles in length, 2 in breadth, and contains 9 families. Pabay, lying at the distance of 8 miles from Barray, $1^{1}/_{2}$ in length, and 1 in breadth, contains 3 families. Mengalay, at the distance of 12 miles, 2 miles in length, and 2 miles in breadth, contains 8 families. The last is Berneray, which, from its being called the Bishop's Isle,[3] seems to have once belonged to the Bishop of the Isles[3]; it is 16 miles distant from Barray, 1 mile in length; $^{3}/_{4}$ in breadth, and contains 3 families. These islands are fertile in corn and grass, but liable to be blasted by the S.W. winds, which frequently blow here. They are very difficult of access, on account of the strong currents running between them, and landing is sometimes not only difficult, but hazardous. Close by the island of Mingalay is a high rock,[4] with very luxuriant grass growing on the top of it. The inhabitants of this island climb to the top at the risk of their lives, and by means of a rope carry up their wedders to fatten. This must be the *Scarpa Vervecum* mentioned by Buchanan. To this, and to the island of Bernera, great

1 Suliskeir, sometimes called Barra, was intended.
2 Caolas, see p. 140.
3 All the isles south of Barra were held of the Bishop of the Isles. See pp. 26-28, and p. 46.
4 Lianamul. See p. 45.

numbers of sea-fowls resort every year in the month of May, the same with those in St Kilda, though not in such variety; they come in the latter end of April or the beginning of May to clean their nests from the rubbish of last year, then set off, and after some days return to lay their eggs and hatch, and so soon as the young are able to take the wing, they disappear, and are not to be seen till the same season next year. The inhabitants of these two islands catch some of them in the rocks, which they think very good eating, and from which they get very fine feathers; these feathers they sell at 6d. the lb. in the country, as they never have them in such quantities as to send them to a public market. The main island of Barray has a barren appearance, from the great quantity of rock to be seen everywhere, excepting the north end, which, for its fertility, if the climate were equally good, might be compared to any of the same extent in any part of Scotland. In the middle and south end are very high hills, and some flat; the hills are a mixture of green, rock, and heath; and seem to be better calculated for a sheep-walk, than for rearing black cattle, but lie at too great a distance from market.

Agriculture, Soil, Etc.
Agriculture has been almost invariably the same here (as in most of the western isles) for time immemorial, till within these last five years, when Mr Macneil, the proprietor, returned from visiting foreign countries, has begun to introduce the method used in the low country, as far as he thinks the soil and climate can admit of. The soil in general is thin and rocky (excepting the north end, which is a mixed soil, and almost free of rock); there is also a great deal of sand, which is blown one way or other with every gale of wind, so that a great part of the best cornland has been thus blown away, or covered with sand. There is some meadow ground between the hills. The ground here requires that the manure be thick laid, in order to procure a tolerable crop; there are some meadows that yield three successive crops with one coat of manure, viz., one of potatoes, and two of oats.[1] The people here use the plough for the most part; but in their rocky ground they dig or turn up the ground with a kind of lever, which they called the crooked spade, and which Dr Johnson has described in his tour through the Hebrides. They lay their potatoes for the most part in lazy beds, in the following manner:—1st, They mark out a ridge of about

1 A common rotation in the Highlands at this time. The potato was introduced into Barra in 1752.

four feet wide, then lay on the manure, and with a spade cover it with earth taken out of the furrow; in this state it remains till the beginning of April, when they begin to plant the potatoes by means of a dibble, or pointed stick, with which they penetrate the earth thus laid on (making a hole to receive the seed), then break the earth with a hand-rake, which serves the purpose of harrowing; this is a more tedious operation than laying the plant upon the manure before it is covered with earth, but is the only method that can be used on these meadows, which are deep and wet, and the season must be very bad when they do not make good returns. They have of late begun to plant potatoes in light sandy soil, which answers very well; and Mr Macneil,[1] the proprietor, plants almost all his with the plough, which gives ample satisfaction, and everyone begins to follow the example. The principal crop here is barley and potatoes; there is some small black oats, and little rye. The returns in barley are from 10 to 15; in potatoes from 15 to 20. Seaweed is the principal manure here; as that is sometimes precarious, the crop must be so also, for when a sufficient quantity of seaweed is not cast upon the shore, a plentiful harvest is not to be expected. Formerly the seaweed that grows upon the shore was used for manure; but since kelp has become so valuable, the proprietors everywhere have restricted the people from cutting it for that purpose, which is certainly prejudicial to agriculture. The people also make some compost. In good seasons they raise as much crop as will be sufficient for their subsistence, otherwise there is a scarcity; but the proprietor supplies the country with low-country meal at the market price. It is to be hoped that a scarcity may not happen so frequently henceforth, if the people in general could adopt the improvements lately introduced in raising crops and rearing cattle. The cattle here are generally small. Mr Macneil, who has an extensive farm in his own hands, having bought from the best folds in different parts of the Highlands, can now produce a fold of his own rearing equal to any of them. The lands here, as in many other places in the Highlands, are distinguished into single and double lands, and the division of them is into pennies, halfpennies, and farthings.[2] No tenant here possesses more than halfpenny, for which he pays from £3 to £4 for single lands, and £6 for the halfpenny of double lands. The souming of the halfpenny, that is, the number of full-grown cattle, is 8, young stock

1 Colonel Roderick MacNeill, proprietor from 1763 to 1822. See p. 116.
2 The origin of these divisions is unknown, and no trace now remains of them except in place-names.

and sheep included; 2 three-year old queys, or 3 two-year olds, are equal to a soum, and 8 sheep. So that the stock of the possessor of a halfpenny of single lands, consists of 3 horses, 4 cows, and 8 or 10 sheep. The tenants pay their rents by manufacturing kelp and sale of their cattle. The proprietor employs a number of them in making kelp upon his farm, for which he pays from £1, 10s. to £2, 2s., and for the kelp made upon their own shores, which he also has at his own disposal, £2, 12s. 6d. the ton, which is the highest manufacturing price given in the Highlands, so far as I know. So that, from the sale of their cattle, and making of kelp, the people live very easy, excepting in bad years, when there is a scarcity of bread, they are under the necessity of buying low-country meal. There are 5 farms which were let for 19 years at stipulated rents; the leases are nearly expired. The distance of this place from market, and its insular situation, has prevented the price of cattle from advancing in the same proportion as it has done in places more accessible, and more conveniently situated. Notwithstanding this disadvantage, the price has advanced to a third more at least within these 18 years; for a cow that sold then at £1, 10s. would sell now at £2, 5s. or £2, 10s.; and parcels that sold then at £2, sell now at £3; milch-cows sell at from £3, 10s. to £4; whereas, at the period above mentioned, they sold for £2 and £2, 10s. according to their quality. They are bought by drovers who come hither from different places at stated times. The expense in carrying them from this to the nearest part of the continent, which lies at the distance of 20 leagues, is 2s. 6d. the head, besides the buyer's expense and trouble in coming for them, and the risk of losing some by the way, as they sometimes make a tedious passage.

Population
According to Dr Webster's report, the number of souls in 1755 was 1150. There has been no exact list taken of the number of inhabitants here since it was erected into a parish; at least I could find none. But it is evident that population must have increased considerably within these last 20 years, from this circumstance, that then there were some lands unoccupied, and many of the tenants possessed a whole penny; whereas, lately, the proprietor was obliged to divide the lands into smaller portions, in order to accommodate the inhabitants. At this time, no tenant occupies more than 1/2 penny, and many have but 1/4 and 1/8 of a penny. In the last case, it is to be observed, the land is what is called double; at present the number of souls in this parish is 760

males, and 864 females, in all 1604, of which only 80 are Protestants. Besides this number, upwards of 200 left this country within the last 2 years; some emigrated to the island of St John's, and Nova Scotia, in North America, being inveigled thither by a Mr F . . .[1] upon promises of the undisturbed profession of their religion (being all Roman Catholics), and of free property for themselves, and their offspring for ever; but how soon they were landed, he left them to their shifts, and returned back to his native country. These poor people were left in the most deplorable situation. If the inhabitants of the different places in which they landed, had not exerted themselves for their relief, many of them must have perished, for want of the common necessaries of life. They became sensible of their folly when it was too late; others went to Glasgow, being invited thither by Mr David Dale, to work in his cotton manufactory; but Mr Dale's terms not coming up to their expectations, some of them returned home; and many of them, from a change of diet and occupation, contracted distempers, of which they died; many more prepared themselves for emigration, but repented time enough to avoid the snare into which their friends have been inconsiderably led, by going to America; they also sold their effects, and spent the money arising from the conversion, so that they would have been destitute in their native country; but Mr Macneil, the proprietor, not only gave them, and such as returned from Glasgow, lands, but likewise money enough to purchase a new stock of cattle, and all the other necessary implements of husbandry. The spirit for emigration is now happily and totally suppressed.

Superiority
Barray held originally of the Kings of Scotland[2] till the reign of James VI when an English ship was seized upon the coast by Roderick Macneil, then Laird of Barray, surnamed Ruary 'n' tarter, or Rory the turbulent,[3] probably so called, from the frequent depredations he committed in different places, which were not uncommon in those days. Queen Elizabeth complained to the Court of Scotland of this act of piracy committed upon her subjects; upon which, the Laird of Barray was summoned to appear at Edinburgh, to answer for his unjustifiable behaviour; but he either refused or despised the summons. Several attempts were made afterward to apprehend him, which

1 Possibly the person referred to on pp. 122-3.
2 Barra was held of the Kings of the Isles until 1494.
3 Chief from about 1600-1622.

proved unsuccessful. Mr Mackenzie, commonly called the tutor of
Kintail, predecessor to the late Lord Macleod, undertook to effect by
stratagem, what others could not do by more direct means. Having
come, under cover of a friendly visit, to the Castle of Kisimul, where
the laird then resided, he invited him and all his retainers on board,
who not suspecting any hostile design, suffered themselves to be
overpowered with excess of liquor, so that all his friends were easily
persuaded to go on shore, and trust their chief in the hands of one
who had so hospitably entertained them. Kintail improved the
advantage put into his hands, hoisted sail under night, and the wind
proving fair, he was soon out of reach of his pursuers. He at length
arrived with his prisoner at Edinburgh, where he was tried for his life.
Being interrogated why he treated Queen Elizabeth's subjects with
such barbarity, he replied, that he thought himself bound, by his
loyalty, to retaliate, as much as lay in his power, the unpardonable
injury done by the Queen of England to his own Sovereign, and his
Majesty's mother. By this answer, he obtained his Majesty's pardon, but
forfeited his estate, which was given to Kintail, who restored it back to
the Laird of Barray, on condition of holding of him, and paying him
60 merks Scots[1] as a yearly feu-duty. Some time after, Sir James
Macdonald of Slate, great-great-grandfather of the present Lord
Macdonald, married a daughter of Kintail's who made over the
superiority to Sir James, either as a present or as a part of his
daughter's dowry. The superiority continues in the family of
Macdonald to this day.

Antiquities and Curiosities
There are several duns in this parish, most of which were built by the
Danes, others of greater antiquity, built by the natives, to defend
themselves against the encroachments of the neighbouring clans, as
also of the Danes, when they invaded those islands. The Danish duns
are 11 in number, 5 on the island of Barray, 2 in Watersay, 1 in
Sanderay, 1 in Pabay, 1 in Mengalay, and 1 in Berneray, the last of
which is taken notice of by the learned Dr Macpherson of Slate, in his
antiquities, and is more entire than any of the rest. Each of these duns
is in sight of some other, that, in case of an invasion, the alarm might
be the more speedily communicated to the whole. That upon the
island of Berneray, being the farthest south, it may be supposed,
served for a pharos or watch tower, as well as a place of defence, as did

1 £3, 6s. 8d. in English money.

another in the island of Eriskay (the property of Colin Macdonald, Esq. of Boisdale, but at that time the property of the Laird of Barray), on the east. While the Danes were in possession of these islands, they confined the natives to their own duns, which are all built on fresh-water lochs, or small creeks formed by the sea; whereas those of the Danes are built upon eminences. At one time, the Danish governor made alliance with Macneil of Barray, by marrying his daughter.[1] But after the battle of Largs,[2] the power of the Danes began everywhere to decline; and such of them as remained here, after the Ebudae were restored to the King of Scotland, were expelled or massacred by the natives. In one of the adjacent islands, there is a collection of human bones, where it is said the last of the Danes were murdered. In Kilbar are two churches, built by the monks, belonging to Icolmkill; another at Borve, dedicated to St Michael. In Castle-bay, is a fort, built upon a rock, which must have formerly been almost covered with the sea. This fort is of a hexagonal form; the wall is near 30 feet high; in one of its angles is a high square tower, on the top of which, at the corner immediately above the gate, is a perforated stone, through which the gockman or watchman, who sat there all night, let a stone fall upon any person who attempted to surprise the gate by night. Within the wall are several houses, and a well dug through the middle of the rock. The tradition here is, that this fort was built upwards of 500 years ago. Buchanan calls it an old castle in his time.[3] It has always been the residence of the Lairds of Barray, till the beginning of the present century. Here are also several Druidical temples, none of them remarkable for extent or structure; near one of these is a well, which must have been once famous for its medicinal quality, as also for curing or preventing the effects of fascination.[4] It is called *tobbar nam buadh*, or the well of virtues. There are a few mineral springs.

Fishery

There are quantities of cod and ling catched upon the E. coast of this island. The fishing banks extend from the mouth of Loch Boisdale to Barray-head; from 20 to 30 boats are generally employed in this business from the latter end of March, or the beginning of April, to the end of June, and five hands in every boat; at an average they kill

1 According to *The Clan Macneil* this was Niall, twenty-first Chief.
2 In 1263.
3 1582.
4 Witchcraft.

from 1000 to 1500 ling to each boat. Mr Macneil of Watersay, who took an exact account of the number of ling sent to Glasgow in the year 1787, found it to amount to 30,000 besides a great number sold in the country. They have not been equally successful at all times; but one year with another the quantity may be computed at 30,000 ling, besides cod. They carry their fish to Glasgow in the very boats they use at the fishing, where the ling sell from £5 to £6 the hundred. Herring has often been got here in great abundance; but the want of salt has sometimes prevented the inhabitants from deriving any considerable advantage from it. It is to be regretted, that the severity of the salt-laws[1] hinders the poor people here from using any other than what is got from the custom-house, which lies at the distance of 20 leagues; if the Legislature thought proper to remove this grievance, fishing of various kinds might become a source of affluence to the people in general, of wealth to individuals, and the public markets would be more plentifully supplied. They have been at times so successful in the caraban[2] fishing as to be entitled to some of the premiums granted by the Board of Trustees; they also make some dog-fish and cuddy oil, some of which they burn in their lamps, the overplus they sell at 7d. or 8d. the Scotch pint. Some have even been known to pay their rents with the oil extracted from the small fish called cuddy. Shell-fish abound here, such as limpets, muscles, wilks, clams, spout fish, or razor-fish, lobsters, crabs, &c., &c., but what is singularly beneficial to the inhabitants, is the shell-fish called cockle. It is found upon the great sand on the N. end of Barray, in such quantities, that in times of great scarcity all the families upon the island (about 200) resort to it for their daily subsistence. It has been computed, that the last two summers, which were peculiarly distressing on account of the great scarcity, no less than from 100 to 200 horse-loads of cockles were taken off the sands at low-water every day of the spring-tides during the months of May, June, July, and August. If the people made use of the cockles in plentiful years, they might save as much bread as would prevent a scarcity in the worst of times. Buchanan is undoubtedly mistaken, when he asserts,[3] that the cockle originated from small animalculi coming down along with the water of a spring in the top of a green hill above the sand. It is true, there is such a hill, with a spring

---

1 The duty on salt was repealed in 1817. It helped to protect the kelp industry, so it was not completely harmful to the Islands as might be supposed.

2 Sail-fish. Not now caught, though still often plentiful.

3 Copying Donald Munro. See p. 28.

on the summit of it; but any water running from it does not come to the sea, being absorbed by the intervening ground, which is sandy; besides, that it is allowed by all naturalists, that every animal procreates its own species. But this vulgar notion prevails among the inhabitants to this day. The shell of the cockle makes the whitest, if not the strongest lime; they lie in great banks on the sea-side, where a small vessel may be loaded in a tide.

Harbours

The first towards the N. is Ottirvore, which is more properly a road than a harbour; the entrance to it is from the E. between the islands of Eriskay and Gigay. The next further S. is Flodday Sound, surrounded by a number of islands, and opens to the S.E.; here the largest ships may ride with safety all the seasons of the year. Tirivah, or the inland bay, so called from its cutting far into the middle of the country; here vessels may ride out the hardest gales; it opens also to the S.E. On the S. end of Barray is Kisimul-bay, so called by the natives, and by mariners Castle-bay, from the old castle formerly mentioned; it opens to the S. In the island of Watersay is a very commodious harbour for ships of any burden; it is accessible from the S.E. between the islands of Sanderay and Muldonich, or the Deer Island. Ottirvore and Flodday are much frequented by ships to and from the Baltic. The convenience of these harbours, and the great quantity of fish killed upon the coast, should make Barray a more eligible situation for a village than any that the joint-stock company[1] have yet pitched upon. These harbours have good outlets from the S. and N. and are near the fishing-banks; they also abound in small cod and flounders. There are some fresh-water lochs with plenty of trout.

Religion, Stipend, School, Places of Worship, Poor, Etc.

The Protestant religion universally prevailed here till after the Restoration;[2] when the Church of England was established in Ireland, some Irish priests took banishment from that kingdom to those islands; at that time Harris and Barray made one parish, the minister

1 The British Fisheries Society, founded in 1786.
2 There is no record of even a formal conversion of the people of Barra to Protestantism having ever taken place. After the Reformation (1560), no priest was able to come to the Island for a considerable time, and there must have been a complete cessation in the holding of religious services for many years. The first priest to come to Barra after the Reformation was the Rev. Dermit Dugan who visited the Island in 1651, and was welcomed in a way which makes it clear that the people had not become Protestants. See the First Chapter.

always resided in the former, and was at too great a distance from the latter; so that the inhabitants were exposed to the artifices of the priests, who taking advantage of the absence of the minister, and the ignorance of the times, perverted the people. The stipend of this parish is 2 chalders meal, and 900 merks Scots, of which 300 are paid out of the unaffected tiends of South Uist, together with 50 for communion-elements. There is no manse. A short time after the present incumbent was settled in the parish, Mr Macneil, the heritor, went to America at the commencement of the last war.[1] The minister agreed with his man of business at Edinburgh to accept of £10 a-year for his manse, and melioration for any house he should build to accommodate himself, till the heritor should return. The matters stands so still. The glebe is a small farm given by the heritor, when this place was erected into a parish, to the Presbytery, on condition that every incumbent should pay 46 merks Scots yearly rent; the whole may be valued at £12. The number of Protestants has been always so small, that it was thought unnecessary to put the heritor to the expense of building a church. There is no school here but one granted by the Society for Propagating Christian Knowledge, which is now upon a more respectable footing than formerly, as the Society, since the last visitation by the Rev. Mr Kemp, their secretary, have augmented the salary from £12 to £15; the heritor has built a good schoolhouse, as also a house for the master, and has furnished the schoolmaster with all the conveniences required by the Society. At the last visitation upwards of 40 scholars attended; it might be of benefit if it was equally well attended throughout the year; but in the busy seasons, such as seed-time and harvest, the parents are obliged to withdraw their children. There are three places of worship, viz, Kilbar, Borve, and Watersay. The minister preaches two Sundays at Borve, which is only a mile and a half from his own house; the third Sunday at Kilbar, at the distance of 3 miles; and the fourth at Watersay, which, including a ferry of 1 mile, is at the distance of 5 miles. The inhabitants of the South isles are all Roman Catholics; the priest goes there only twice a-year, unless by a particular call to visit the sick, and to administer extreme unction. What renders this parish singularly troublesome, is its distance from the seats of Presbytery and Synod; the first is in North Uist, at the distance of 40 miles, besides a ferry of 8 miles, where he attends two stated Presbyteries in the year, the one in the beginning of December, and the other the middle of March; besides occasional

1 The war of the American Revolution.

meetings, and attendance upon sacraments in North Uist and Harris, the last of which is at the distance of near 60 miles, besides the ferry already mentioned, and that between North Uist and Harris, 12 miles in length; this distance the minister is sometimes under the necessity of walking on foot, though at other times, when horses are in good order, he is obliged to the generosity of the principal gentlemen on the way for the use of their horses, which he takes this occasion to acknowledge. The seat of the Synod, which is Glenelg, on the continent of Scotland, is at the distance of 30 leagues by sea, when he must be at the expense of boat and crew; and if he goes from hence to North Uist, to take passage by the packet-boat to Dunveggan,[1] and then through Sky, the distance is much greater, and the expenses more considerable.—The number of poor is generally from 40 to 50; there are £400 Sterling of a fund for them, £200 of which is a mortification by Archibald Macneil, late tacksman of Sanderay, and £100 by Roderick Shaw, tacksman of Alasdale, now living; they never go anywhere else to collect their subsistence.

Servants, Wages, etc.

The number of servants depends upon the extent of land a man possesses; a farm of any considerable extent, according to the present mode of farming, employs 5 or 6 men, 4 or 5 maid servants, and 2 or 3 boys; the wages of a labouring man servant, for the whole year, are from £1, 10s. to £2; the boys have from 15s. to £1, 5s.; women from 15s. to £1. Besides the above wages, the men and boys get a seventh part of the crop to divide among them, the grieve has double wages. Giving them a share of the crop, makes them more industrious, and binds them faster to the master's interest, as it is for the time inseparably connected with their own. Such a number of servants must be very burdensome to a farmer, and must run away with a great share of the produce of his farm; but the difficulty of winning their peats, which is the only fuel used here, renders it necessary to keep so many servants, and double the number of horses that would be sufficient for their ploughing; for a farmer that must keep such a number of servants, must also keep 16 or 18 horses, both which are almost wholly employed drying and carrying home their peats, from the beginning of June, when the sowing is at an end, till the latter end of August, when the reaping comes on. If the Legislature thought proper to take the duty off coal, it might, in a great measure, alleviate this grievance;

1 In 1883 the postal service still followed this route.

and if farmers could use coal, instead of peats, they might employ their servants for very useful purposes, such as, making kelp, building walls, making inclosures, composts, etc., etc.

Miscellaneous Observations

The Gaelic is the only language commonly spoken here, and I believe the purest dialect of it to be met with in any country; though by their frequent excursions to Glasgow, the people have introduced a number of English words. Numbers of the inhabitants, who attended the school, speak English tolerably well. —There are 200 tons kelp sent annually to the markets of Liverpool and Leith, and fetch the best price that is given for any that is sent from any part of the Highlands; fish and oil are sent to Glasgow; price as formerly mentioned. There are also from 200 to 250 head of cattle sold to drovers, at an average, about £2, 5s. a-head, great and small, besides about 100 hides of beef sent to Glasgow, or sold on the nearest part of the continent. The number of horses here is 557; cows, 1170; the number of soums in sheep, 277, which, at the rate of 8 sheep to the soum, is 2216. —The weather is rather inconstant. The W. and S.W. winds blow more frequently here, and prove very destructive to corn. This last winter was very wet and stormy, much the same with that of 1790,[1] both which have been the most distressing to the people here, in the memory of any man living. We have had very little snow this winter or spring, and none at all the two preceding. The sea seems to have made some encroachments here. The tradition here is, that 3 or 4 generations back, the cattle used to feed in places where kelp is made at this day; but now it can hardly go any farther, as the shore along the west coast (where the sea could have made any progress formerly), is almost all rocky, and may serve as a sufficient barrier against any future encroachments. It is to be observed, that notwithstanding the great quantities of fish killed upon this coast, the proprietor never claimed any emoluments from that lucrative business,[2] but allowed the people to make the best of it for themselves, and he always gives premiums to the first people that discover the arrival of the herrings upon the coast; nor does any proprietor in the neighbouring parish derive any advantage from the fishing there.—The island of Barray, with all the surrounding islands, is the property of Roderick Macneil, Esq. of Barray, whose predecessors are said to have been in possession of those

1 Both very bad winters all over the Highlands.
2 See p. 116.

islands before the Danes, and were the first of that name who came from Ireland, whence they derive their pedigree; so that they have always been acknowledged the chief of the Macneils in Scotland.

CHAPTER 8

The Gaelic Schools, 1818-1825

*

J. L. CAMPBELL

In 1811 the Gaelic Schools Society supported by charity was founded in Edinburgh with the object of sending itinerant teachers around the Highlands and Islands to teach the Highlanders to read the Scriptures in their own language. In 1803 it had been estimated that "out of 335,000 persons in the Highlands it was computed that 300,000 understood no other language than Gaelic, so far, at least, as not to comprehend a book written, or a continued discourse spoken in any other."[1] As Gaelic was then excluded from the curricula of the parochial schools, which in any case were totally insufficient in numbers, many islands having no schools whatever, it is not surprising that the Highlanders had remained for the most part in a state of complete illiteracy.

The Gaelic Schools Society adopted the excellent policy, not of establishing permanent schools, which would have been financially impossible, but of opening schools for from eighteen months to two years in different places, and then removing the teachers to fresh localities. The idea was to stimulate an interest in reading, and to found a tradition of literacy which might continue under the impetus originally received. By deciding that the reading of the Bible and Psalms should be taught without comment, the Society surmounted what would otherwise have been serious denominational differences, and Highlanders of all creeds were in consequence able to avail themselves of the school's teaching. Moreover, the Society, in spite of some ill-conceived opposition, stuck nobly to its intention of teaching the reading of Gaelic and of Gaelic only, as the spiritual and not the material needs of the Highlanders were in view; indeed, under this policy the Society dismissed several teachers who disobeyed the orders of the Society by teaching English. The point of view of the Society is well expressed in its Report for 1822.[2]

1 First Report, p. 10.
2 P. 10.

"It is well known that it was long a favourite political maxim, that, to subjugate the Highlands, it was necessary to obliterate their language; and it seems to have been under the influence of this opinion, that in all the Schools established by the Venerable Society for propagating Christian Knowledge, the English was the language primarily taught. The light of the pure Gospel, however, which has broken forth within these few years from amidst the mists of prejudice, has persuaded the religious public, that it is not fit, that even for the attainment of a political improvement, if success could be ensured, multitudes of immortal souls should be left without remedy to perish everlastingly. The political relations, too, in which the Highlands now stand, in connection with the rest of the empire[1], have, under the benign providence of God, co-operated to abate the hostile wish, and to put an end to the vain efforts directed against a language, venerable from its antiquity, rich in its structure and variety, and dear to the people from every association which can attach the mind. It is therefore now a matter of universal consent, that the Gaelic must remain the language of the Highlands, till it is vanquished by the sapping influence of commercial intercourse; and this being the case, your Committee refer, as conclusive evidence in favour of your plan of teaching, not the English, but the Gaelic, to the change in their mode of procedure, which the Venerable Society for propagating Christian Knowledge thought it their duty to recommend in all those stations, where, as in yours, the vernacular language of the people is the Gaelic. When the report of their experience of the result of that
recommendation shall come before the Public, your Committee doubt not that it will evidence its wisdom, and consequently afford an additional confirmation in favour of your plan.

"But, although your Committee believe the Gaelic, as the only language fully understood by the sequestered Highlanders, to be the only language which can promote their eternal interest, they are not blind to the advantages which must be conferred on them in regard to their temporal interests, by giving them the opportunity of acquiring the English. It does indeed appear to your Committee, that the Gaelic language is the best and easiest channel for the acquisition of the English; and they have some

1 This must be one of the earliest examples of the use of the word 'empire' in this connotation.

hopes of soon seeing introduced into use, elementary books for teaching the English through the Gaelic, which they consider a great desideratum[1] in the system of Highland education. It would, however, tend materially to paralyze your operations, were your Teachers permitted to teach both languages in your Schools; for the temptation to which the people would be thereby exposed, of preferring what they would deem their worldly to what is really their eternal interest, would be so strong, that the main object you have in view would certainly be left unaccomplished. Your Committee have felt it their painful duty, under a strong conviction of this truth, and the vital importance of maintaining the simplicity of your principles, to suspend some of your Teachers, who, notwithstanding repeated admonitions, have persevered in teaching English in your Schools."

These Gaelic schools were at once welcomed in the Highlands, and abundant testimony was at once forthcoming to their good effect. They did in fact fulfil a most pressing need, for the scandalous neglect of the Gaelic language in both the parochial and S.P.C.K. Schools—a neglect which was really animated by the Westminster Government's determination to stamp out the language—made it impossible for the Highlanders either to acquire any knowledge through the best—in many cases the only—medium of conversation known to them, while at the same time preventing the Gaelic language from undergoing the cultivation that could have made it a first-rate medium for the exchange of ideas. As it happened, the taste for Gaelic reading, insofar as it was introduced into the Highlands by these Schools, never really became much more than a taste for purely religious literature. However, the Schools did the most excellent work, and produced proof of the obvious fact that a foreign language is best acquired after and not before the native tongue has been mastered.[2] From all quarters came testimony to the fact that by being taught to read Gaelic the Highlanders were stimulated to learn to read English, and that by first having been taught their own language they acquired the other with much greater facility and understanding than did those unfortunates who were condemned to learn English, usually by rote and without understanding what they recited, before they had ever been

---

1 This still remains a great desideratum.
2 This has been strenuously denied by persons interested in the obliteration of the Gaelic language, but it is nevertheless the opinion of leading modern educationists.

taught to read even a word of their native Gaelic language.

Although the Society was founded in 1811, it was only able to progress slowly at first, and a School was not opened in Barra until 1818. In the Eighth Report[1] an interesting account of this is given:

"As it has been the invariable desire of your Committee to reach, if possible, the most destitute and distant parts of the Country, an opportunity of opening a School in the Island of Barra was gladly embraced. Though the number in attendance has not been great, your Committee hope to succeed better in securing attendance than they have hitherto done; and, in the meanwhile, they avail themselves of the present occasion to lay before you the Report of the Rev. Angus M'Donald,[2] Roman Catholic Minister of Barra, dated the 2d. of April last.

"'I use the liberty', says he, 'though not personally acquainted with you, to express my satisfaction, as the Pastor of the Roman Catholics in this Parish, for the choice you have made of a Gaelic Teacher for this Island. The happy result of his assiduity and attention in the discharge of his professional duty, endears him to every body in that part of this parish wherein he taught, and especially to me, who am in duty bound to take interest in their spiritual welfare. I have made it my duty, since the commencement of this first Session to the end, to visit the School from time to time; but Mr Cameron's method of teaching, his assiduity and attention all along, gave me pleasure. I can venture to assure you, that, in my humble opinion, the Pupils under his tuition made as much progress in reading and spelling their mother tongue, as could be expected in one Session, especially the first. The Schoolmaster's exertions and endeavours in checking vice and immorality deserve no less credit—the happy consequence of which is, that cursing and swearing are almost banished from that part of the country. The Institution is charitable, and merits the thanks and applause of all true Highlanders, who should take pleasure and extreme satisfaction in seeing their mother tongue, a language in itself so expressive and energetic, so much encouraged. We only wish for such a School among us, and earnestly desire the Teacher's return.'"

1 P. 15.
2 See p. 115.

This School was taught at Kilbar by Alexander Cameron, who had sixty pupils.

In the Ninth (1819) Report[1] another interesting paragraph is given to Barra:

"In the Report of last year, your Committee intimated the opening of a School in the Island of Barra, one of the most destitute and distant Islands of the Hebrides; and the very favourable opinion of the Rev. Angus Macdonald, the Roman Catholic Minister, of the progress of the Scholars, and the assiduity of your Teacher; your Committee have now the pleasure of laying before you a report of the examination of the School by the Rev. Alexander Nicolson, the Parish Minister, on 4th June last. 'The Gaelic School at Kilbar was examined by me two days ago, in presence of Major Macdonald, the factor of the country, and most of the parents of the children who attended the School, and I have peculiar pleasure in stating to you, for the information of the Society by whom the School is supported, that the children in general acquitted themselves in a very satisfactory manner, and have made such progress in reading the Scriptures, as could scarce be expected in a much longer period of time than they have attended. Many of them, though very young, read the Bible and New Testament in a most clear and distinct manner, and several of them were able to repeat by heart some of the longest Psalms.

"'Before I conclude, it may not perhaps be improper to give a short statement of this Parish, to which your Society have extended their charitable views. The Parish of Barra consists of eight inhabited Islands, separated from one another by wide channels, some many miles broad, strong currents, and boisterous seas. The main Island, properly called Barra, is about 12 miles long, and from 4 to 6 miles broad; the population of the whole Parish amounts to about 900 Catholics, and 120 Protestants. Of this immense population no more than 30 are capable of receiving religious instruction in English, a few understand English imperfectly, but hardly any were able to read the Gaelic language, until your Circulating School was established among them. The total ignorance of the greatest number of the inhabitants of every kind of religious knowledge,

1 P. 17.

is melancholy indeed. Their peculiar situation precludes them from many advantages which their more fortunate brethren enjoy; secluded as they are, in a great measure from the rest of mankind, in one of the remotest of the Western Islands, they have few opportunities of cultivating their minds by moral or religious instruction. Their means of acquiring knowledge were indeed very scanty; for there has not been a Parochial School established here for a long time back, although there is now a prospect of having one soon, the only School in the Parish being one on the establishment of the Society in Scotland for propagating Christian Knowledge. You may now judge of the peculiar usefulness of Circulating Schools in such Parishes as this, by which, in a certain time, every individual, however remote his situation, or however low his means, may have an opportunity of acquiring the most useful of all knowledge—the knowledge of the way that leads to salvation.'"

In 1819 Alexander Cameron was still teaching in Kilbar, with thirty-four pupils, all between the ages of six and fourteen years; six were reading elementary books, eleven the Bible, and seventeen the New Testament. At the beginning of 1820 he was removed from Kilbar to Greian, where he had twenty-nine pupils, between the ages of five and twenty-six; seven were reading elementary books and the others the Bible and New Testament.

In October 1821 the Right Reverend Ranald MacDonald, Catholic Bishop of the Isles, wrote as follows:[1]

"Rev. Dear Sir,
"I was from home when your letter was received here, otherwise it would have been answered much sooner. I can never forget the attention you were kind enough to pay to my former application. I have written to Mr Angus Macdonald in Barra, who, I am confident, will do all he can to make the School answer the end proposed by the zealous promoters of that laudable Institution. I have likewise written to Mr Norman Macdonald about the School in Ardnamurchan; but as he lives in Moydart at a distance, and has few of his hearers in Ardnamurchan, he can be of little service to that School. I hope you will be able through time to extend the benefit of these Schools to some new Districts that are

1 Appendix to Eleventh Report, p. 43.

equally needful. I have the pleasure to be, Rev. Dear Sir, yours truly,

"Rand. Macdonald"

At the end of 1821 Cameron was removed from Greian to Bruernish; and in June 1822 the Rev. Angus Macdonald, priest of Barra, and the Rev. Alexander Nicolson, minister of Barra, wrote of the school:[1]

(Rev. Angus MacDonald)
"I have this day attended the examination of the Gaelic School of this parish, along with the Rev. Alexander Nicolson, and Messrs. Campbell and Cameron, Gaelic Teachers in the parish of South Uist. The number of scholars examined was not great, merely owing to local circumstances. This season of the year requires attendance at home in domestic concerns; it was not so till of late, during winter and spring the School was attended by a considerable number. The number that attended this day, consisted of boys and girls; 12 read the Bible, 9 the New Testament and Psalms, and 1 the Guide. Several parents were present, who felt the most gratifying sensation on hearing the Divine Word read in their own language by their children. We had every reason to be satisfied (considering the short time of attendance) with the progress these youths have made during the course of this year. They read with ease, and distinctly, and spelt to admiration; their memories were exercised in like-manner; they repeated whole Psalms *verbatim*, with great ease. In confirmation of the Teacher's attention to his charge, I understand he keeps Sunday Schools for such as choose to attend, to prevent any violation of the Sabbath, and check immorality. As a pastor of souls, I have cause to be satisfied with his conduct and assiduity in promoting the good of his pupils, and hope the Society may be pleased to continue him, if it be his own desire. As a Catholic clergyman, I return thanks to the Society for their liberality of sentiment, set forth in their instructions to their Teachers, in confining these instructions to teaching alone, abstracting from controversial points, and giving trouble to such as are of a different persuasion, at same time affording equal advantage of education. As a true Highlander, my gratification is still

1 Appendix to Twelfth Report, p. 40.

increased, from a consideration of the encouragement given, to the revival of a primitive language which has scarcely a rival. It is rare to find, if at all, a language which expresses the most sublime sentiments and ideas, still intelligible to the lowest peasant, its charms and beauties are only known and admired by those who possess it. Deeply impressed with these sentiments, I have the honour to be, etc."

(Rev. Alexander Nicolson)
"The Gaelic School established at Bruinish in this parish, taught by Mr John Macleod, was examined yesterday by me, along with the Rev. Angus M'Donald, the Catholic Clergyman in this place, when several of the parents of the children attended. The number of scholars present on the occasion, did not exceed 22, owing to the severe fever which raged in the neighbourhood, by which some of them were confined, and others from apprehension of the infection afraid of attending. Such, however, as were present, exhibited sufficient proofs of the attention of the Teacher to the trust committed to his charge. The Teacher produced his former lists of the scholars who attended during the session, by which it appeared, that for the first two months he had 61. On the fourth month he had 41. The School was examined March last, by a committee of Presbytery, when 41 scholars were present, who, considering the short period of their attendance at that time, gave very great satisfaction. Upon this occasion, such as were present exhibited sufficient specimen of the progress they had made; 12 read the Bible with great accuracy; 9 the New Testament and Psalm-book, and 1 the Guide. I cannot in sufficient terms express the pleasure it gave me, to behold these little children read the word of Life with such accuracy, who, without the fostering hand of your humane and benevolent Society, might ever pass their life in ignorance and darkness. The Teacher appeared to have paid particular attention to the spelling of the scholars, as the youngest among them could spell the longest and the most difficult word with the same ease as the shortest. Several of them repeated some of the longest Psalms, with very great correctness, and even large portions of the Scriptures themselves. At the first Examination in March, I was delighted to see a few heads of families exhibit along with their children, and read verse along with them, with

tolerable ease and correctness, out of the New Testament. The parents who attended this Examination, seemed highly gratified with the progress of their children, and deeply sensible of the great blessing conferred upon them by your Society; and they requested me to apply for a continuation of the School at the same place, for another Session, to which I hope the Society will agree, as there is now a sufficient house provided for the accommodation of the School-master.

"I have likewise to request the attention of the Society to the destitute situation of the Island of Sandra * in this parish. The Island is about 8 miles distant from the Main-island of Barra. It is inhabited by several families, who have never as yet had an opportunity of acquiring the least degree of knowledge. They are all Roman Catholics, and as far as I know, have not a single Bible among them. I have spoken to the people since my return from Edinburgh, about the prospect they had of a School from your Society, and they seemed highly delighted at the idea of their children soon being able to read. They promised to have a comfortable house provided for the Teacher's reception, and that the number of scholars would amount to from 25 to 30.— One man said he would send eight of his own family to school. As the Directors were kind enough to promise me, when in Edinburgh, a Teacher for this needful place, I have every confidence that they will have one in readiness against the beginning of next Session. I have pledged myself to the people, that your Society would attend to their application and wishes. I shall be glad to hear from you as soon as convenient on this subject."

At the end of 1822 the teacher's name is given as John MacLeod; there were forty-one pupils in the Bruernish school, between the ages of five and forty years, nine reading elementary books, and the others the Bible.

There are no further reports of the schools in Barra. In 1823 the teacher was removed from the Bruernish school, having that year taught twenty-six pupils; there was also a school at Languinish, taught by Fergus Ferguson, who had there twenty pupils. At the beginning of 1824 the only school in Barra was at Kentangaval, taught by John Swan;

* A Gaelic Teacher has been appointed to Sandra; the School was opened in November last, and was then attended by 22 males, and 10 females.

but he was removed before November 1826, and there is no record of his pupils given.

So ended the Gaelic schools in Barra, through which a considerable number of people became literate in their mother tongue, which otherwise they would never have learned to read. There is no record of the schools having continued without official teachers from the Society. The Society itself ended in 1843 from lack of funds; great destitution had prevailed in the Highlands and Islands in 1836 and 1837, owing to bad harvests, the failure in the herring fishing, and the reduced price for kelp, and charity found more necessitous objects. There were signs too that in certain areas the efforts of the Society were degenerating into sectarianism and the hysteria of revivalism. Meanwhile the parochial schools—such as they were—continued, until the Education Act of 1872[1] revolutionized education in Scotland by introducing the principle of State intervention, and dealt the Gaelic language what was probably its death-blow by refusing to recognize it either as a medium for instruction or a special subject, a refusal which has since been only partially mitigated, and that in the second case alone.

1 Whatever benefits may have followed this Act in the way of enabling the Gaelic-speaking inhabitants of the Islands and Highlands to compete economically with the English-speaking inhabitants of the industrial areas and the Dominions, it is still an undeniable fact that Gaelic culture and Gaelic tradition are still best preserved to-day amongst the generation that had passed their childhood before the Act came into effective operation.

CHAPTER 9

Barra in 1816 [1]

*

JOHN MACCULLOCH (1773-1835)

John MacCulloch, the well-known geologist, was born in Guernsey. His father, James MacCulloch, was descended from the MacCullochs of Nether Ardwell in erst-while Gaelic Galloway, and his mother was a daughter of a jurat of Jersey. He was educated in Cornwall and at Edinburgh University where he graduated M.D. in 1793. He remained at the University and formed friendships with Walter Scott, to whom he wrote in a series of letters the descriptions of the Western Isles from which the account of Barra on page 102 is taken, and with the Earl of Selkirk, who was a promoter of emigration schemes. He became surgeon to the royal regiment of artillery, and in 1803 was appointed chemist to the Board of Ordnance. In 1807 he commenced a private practice at Blackheath. In 1811 he was sent by the Board of Ordnance to Scotland to determine what kinds of rock could most safely be used in powder-mills. From 1811 until 1821 he travelled extensively every summer in the Western Isles, visiting nearly all of them including St Kilda and North Rona, and accumulating a vast amount of geological information which he published in 1819 under the title of A Description of the Western Islands of Scotland, including the Isle of Man; *his letters to Scott, published in 1824, contain material collected on these journeys. He was president of the Geological Society of London in 1816-17, and was appointed physician to Prince Leopold of Saxe Coburg in 1820. In 1826 he was commissioned to make a geological map of Scotland and he travelled every summer there from then until 1832 for this purpose. He died in Cornwall in 1835 as the result of an accident. He was the author of a number of books and articles on geology and natural history, and as a geologist, his reputation was high. His energy in overcoming the difficulties of transport in the Western Isles is a testimony to his keenness, and the geological descriptions of the islands themselves are reliable and often extremely well written.[2]*

Less happy are his all too frequent excursions into the realm of political economy. MacCulloch was the kind of man who could not see a community of

---

1 Approximate date.
2 This account is based upon that in the *Dictionary of National Biography*.

peasant cultivators without thinking how much more profit could be got out of the land if their holdings were thrown together and given over to a single farmer.

It was a common way of thinking in his time, but the manner in which he puts it forward proves him to have been an insufferable intellectualist utilitarian doctrinaire. There is not space enough here to deal with his theories in detail; it is enough to say that any one who may wonder why Lowlanders have often been unpopular in the Highlands, or who may think that the majority of Highlanders supported Jacobitism out of a merely sentimental personal attachment, will find in MacCulloch's pages ample reasons for the detestation of Whigs and Whiggery that prevailed in Gaelic Scotland. Those who, like MacCulloch, may be disposed to take the Highlanders' antipathy to industrialization as evidence of their laziness and inertia, will do well to remember that the economic theories in which he believed are now nearly entirely discredited. The division of labour and enlargement of farms which MacCulloch and other Whigs advocated have led in the end to a far more widespread unemployment and misery than existed before the failure of the '45 finally left it in the power of men of his type to wreck their country under the pretext of improving it. Let any one who shares MacCulloch's views to-day go to the unemployed in the towns and tell them that they are idle and redundant, as MacCulloch termed the Highlanders; such an action is itself unthinkable. It is impossible to calculate the cost in human misery and degradation that has been involved through the application of the philosophy which MacCulloch here states with such ineffable coldness, suavity and aplomb. Its inevitable concomitants have been the evictions (such for instance as that described on page 221 of this book), rural depopulation, the exploitation of child labour, the growth of the slums and the destruction of almost every amenity that does not conform to utilitarian and commercialized standards. Nowhere, alas, have the excesses of the utilitarians cost so much as in Scotland, which, bound hand and foot by the Treaty of Union of 1707, has thus been deprived of any effective control over them, and has in this way provided a peculiarly fertile field for the cultivation of the damnable fallacies of laissez-faire, with the result that in Scotland to-day excessive emigration and uncontrolled industrialization have produced on the one hand an almost deserted countryside and on the other some of the worst and most overcrowded slums in Europe.

It is fortunate to be able to publish this account, since it shows clearly the economic ideas that actuated men like General MacNeill,[1] and Colonel Gordon.[2] In other chapters MacCulloch expresses them most succinctly. Of the

1 See p. 136-7.
2 See p. 170-1.

Highland home manufactures he says:

"Their want of employment for a great portion of the year necessarily leads them to construct for themselves those things for which a richer and more fully employed population has recourse to the industry of the towns."[1]

And of farming:

"There is no doubt that the population of any country like this will be greater under such a system (i.e., the old system) than under one which shall convert many small pastoral farms into a large one, or which, by uniting in a similar manner the small arable farms, shall dispense with the numerous incumbents who under such an improved (sic) system would find no employment on the soil. But in these cases the same quantity of the given manufacture, cattle or corn, is produced by fewer hands, or the agricultural machine is more perfect. And as the perfection of agriculture, as of manufactures, is that state in which the greatest produce is obtained at the least expense, it would be difficult to admit the principle that this perfection in the first of all arts was advantageous in a general view, while in the details it was injurious."[2]

The destruction of the home manufactures so slightingly referred to here, has made the country still more dependent on the towns, and has consequently led to further urbanization, though it has of course, increased the profits of the middleman. The enlargement of farms as here recommended involved the degradation of small tenants to the rank of agricultural labourers, and, in practice, the eviction and enforced emigration of the consequently 'redundant' population; such economic theories were carried out over most of the Highlands to the great misery of the people. They are now discredited, but it is far more difficult to undo the harm than it was to do it. It is to be hoped that when a free Scotland undertakes as a national task the restoration of rural life in the Highlands, the Islands will be first called upon to fill the gap, for they can provide the men who are familiar with the way of living that best answers in this country.

In conclusion, it cannot be stated too often that the real reasons for such abuses as inefficient farming, bad housing, and inertia at which MacCulloch girded were (1) the depression and hopelessness caused after the '45 by the fact that the Highlanders felt themselves deprived of their freedom, (2) lack of

1 *Description of the Western Islands*, Vol. 1, p. 538.
2 *Ibid.*, Vol. I, p. 113.

security of tenure, and (3) lack of compensation for improvements made by the tenant. In a country where the small tenants were continually in the danger of being removed to make room for what MacCulloch describes as improved methods of farming, it is not surprising that they failed to put heart or energy into their cultivation, or housed themselves poorly; the more so when any improvement they might effect not only became automatically the landlord's property, but was sometimes even made a pretext for the raising of their rents.

*

BARRA AND VATERSA[1]

If you are wearied of rocks and lochs and islands and waves, you must lay all the blame on the steam engine, not on your correspondent. I do not mean that this writing, replete will all manner of sapience and adventure, was written by a steam engine; though if mathematics and algebra can now be ground in a mill, and equations and logarithms bolted out like bran, I do not see why novels and travels, and much more, should not also be manufactured by a forty horse power: Swift's machine was not quite visionary. What I do mean is this; that as the essence of forty horses, or of a whole regiment of cavalry, can, in these days, be comprised in a kettle and distilled, a man may now drive his ship and forty from Cantyre to St Kilda, with the same facility as he formerly drove his gig and one to Loch Lomond; and that too, without paying for those ruinous Scottish turnpikes. Bishop Wilkins foresaw a day coming when a man was to call for his wings instead of his boots; but the Bishop did not foresee that, instead of ordering his wings to be put on, or his horses to be put to, the traveller will now shortly order the cook to boil his kettle. Such is the efficient and real cause of at least two of these very volumes: otherwise, I might as well have directed travellers to the mountains of the moon as to the mountains of Sky, and have described the islands and bays in the Mare Hyperboreum Lunare. But I see the day coming when, instead of Loch Cateran and Aberfoyle, it shall become the fashion to chase happiness to North Rona and Barra Head; when the greasy thumbs that have just been contesting for cold fowl and Yorkshire ham, shall be leaving their marks on these pages, and when mates and cabin boys, weavers and tobacconists, shall be trying to spell those little grey Greek words, and wishing that Sir Walter Scott's letters were in gude broad Scotch. In time, the fire-teaser, or some other learned Sawney, shall condense us

1 *Highlands and Western Isles of Scotland*, Vol. III, p. 1.

into a neat little pocket abridgement for the ladies and gentlemen who have taken their places on board the *St Kilda*, Alister Mac Kettle, master, bound on a tour of pleasure to the Western Islands. Why should not all these events happen? Greenock can now circumnavigate Loch Lomond after breakfasting on its own herrings, and return at night to its own lime-punch. Ten years ago, it might as well have attempted to go to Gibraltar to breakfast. Our friend Staffa has even been obliged to put a lock and key on his island, lest it should be stolen; and its very existence was not known fifty years ago.[1] I do not despair of seeing an Opera and a Royal Institution in Sky before long, and a Gaelic newspaper at Stornoway. Such is the apology for two volumes of sea and islands; and if indeed *non omnis moriar*, if all the copies are not worn out before this prophecy is fulfilled, our joint fame shall be beginning to bud when I am food for fishes, and you for worms. It is the fate of him who goes first, to bear all: first through the ford. All the risk is his; the risk of not being cared for, the risk of not being read, the risk of not being understood, the risk of being abused. But he who braves must bear. The path of a book, like the way to Staffa, is smooth enough when it has been well trodden: and if the Serjeant who leads the forlorn hope comes off with his head, why then he is three chevrons less and an epaulette more. To cut matters short, imagine a gale of wind, a head sea, two reefs in the mainsail, Barra on the lee bow, and last and best of all, Ottervore road.

On Eriska, there is a tower[2] which has been a stronghold of the Mac Niels: though small, it is striking, from the scarcity of objects of art in this doleful country. We entered into conversation with some old people, who attempted to amuse us with tales, probably more interesting to them than to us. The ship that brought Prince Charles from France, first anchored in this harbour; and it was remembered with some feelings of hereditary pride, that he had landed on Eriska, where he found some women roasting shell-fish on a fire in the open air, and that he had partaken of their fare; thus commencing the career of that popularity which, as it continued to the end, must have been as much the result of good-nature as of policy. The opinion of a few old women in this wild place could have been of as little value to him as that of the people in general after his project was overthrown and he had become a proscribed fugitive. Political feelings and opinions have however much changed on this subject, even within my

1 The first stranger to visit Staffa was Sir Joseph Banks, who went there in 1772.
2 Caisteal a' Bhreabadair; possibly in a better state of preservation then than now.

memory. The few also who felt or inherited an attachment founded on family connexions, on ancient habits, or on imaginary national affections, have nearly vanished from the stage. If we yet meet a few persons in the remote Highlands who talk the talk of 'sixty years since,' it is but the repetition of what they have heard and read; sentiments which they have scarcely examined, and to which they attach no definite ideas. But enough of Eriska and ancient politics. Of the numerous other islands of this bay I need take no notice: and I may now make a general apology for the future omission of hundreds which, though I have examined them, afford remarks for none but a geologist.

Toland[1] has given an absurd etymology for the name of Barra. It is evidently named after St Bar,[2] to whom the principal church is dedicated, and St Bar was a bishop of Caithness; but it is imagined by the people, that some of the ecclesiastical buildings which remain here, if not all, were dedicated to St Columba. It is impossible for me to decide a question of this nature between rival saints; but if you are anxious on the subject you may read the fifty-five folios of the Bollandists; where you will not find it. It is difficult to comprehend the nature of this establishment; as there are four[3] independent buildings, collected, or rather huddled together, within one enclosure bearing the traces of a ditch outside; all of which appear to have been chapels. None of them are large; and one is not much bigger than a good sized chest; being only six feet by ten. They are utterly deficient in style or ornament; and therefore, in an architectural view, quite uninteresting; unless it may be thought otherwise, that the windows have inclined straight stones above, instead of the Gothic arch. It is probable that some of them have been votive buildings; as this was not an uncommon practice in the Islands, in the Roman Catholic ages. The burying ground contained some ancient tombs and a heap of unburied skulls; proving that the superstitions of the elder times are not fashionable in Barra.

This place, Kilbar, and its village, are built on a part of the island which is separated from the principal portion by a low southern isthmus, over which the eastern and western seas nearly meet at high water. The larger southern division contains one rocky mountain of

1 Toland (1670-1722) was a Gaelic-speaking Irishman, a deist and a Whig pamphleteer, and no doubt congenial enough to MacCulloch. I have not been able to trace this reference.
2 See, however, p. 226.
3 This is wrong; there are only three.

about 2000 feet high; which descends somewhat abruptly into Chisamil Bay, and declines to the north and east by a succession of lower hills terminating on the shores in various rocky points that separate the small valleys in which the population is found. The land is sandy and of little value, even where it is susceptible of cultivation; while the rougher tracts are appropriated to the pasturage of black cattle. As to the commercial department of agriculture here, since the proprietor of the land buys the cattle of his tenants for exportation, there can be no competition of offers. It is easy to imagine why this ought not to be a very good plan for the sellers.

It is often a misfortune to the Highlanders, and particularly in these remote situations, that the communication by posts is frequently tedious and uncertain. With respect to this island, its letters are brought from Loch Maddy in North Uist, through Sky; so that two or three weeks may be occupied in the transit. On the west side of Sutherland, a great sheep-farming country, the post office is, or was, Tain, on the east side of the island, distant nearly eighty miles; and that, by roads which make the inconvenience three times as great. Thus speculators in kelp, wool, or cattle, have opportunities of profiting by the ignorance of the producers, who may thus remain uninformed of the fluctuations in the prices of their commodities. Where agriculture has remote commercial relations, as is here the case, the frequency of communications cannot be too great. Much has indeed been done for the improvement of the Highlands, in the matter of roads, ferries and ports; and, in general, it has been well and liberally done; while it is equally certain that it has produced effects which have repaid the advances, though the details of the benefits may not be always perceptible to those who look no further than to the immediate balance of expenditure and profit. That much might yet be done, and with further good consequences, is most obvious; and it surely cannot be doubted that it is a just principle in government to do for the general welfare, that which proprietors and inhabitants are unable, for want of means, to effect. In the same manner, it has itself an interest, in the shape of contingent advantages, in such improve-ments. It has been said, even in recent writings, very idly, that it is unjust to 'tax the inhabitants of Middlesex' for the purposes of building bridges or making roads for the Highlanders. As well might it be argued that the salary of an English judge should be paid exclusively out of English revenue, or that a grant of money to the harbour of Ramsgate is a fraud on the Highlanders who pay taxes. But it is useless to dwell on an argument so utterly inconsiderate; the philosophy of those who see not beyond the length of their noses.

That agriculture in general is in no very flourishing state in this island, might be imagined from the use of the ristle plough; an ancient instrument carrying the coulter alone, and preceding that which contains the share. One circumstance relating to it, is, however, remarkable; namely, the superior cultivation of the farms in the possession of the Roman Catholic population. It is not the only instance, where the Priests of that persuasion in Scotland, laudably interest themselves in the temporal prosperity of their flocks.[1] This island affords one miserable instance, out of too many, of the evils arising from excessive population. The number of houses at Kilbar seems to be about twenty, and the population should therefore be nearly a hundred; while this village was the refuge of those who had been unable to procure any land, after the island had been allotted. It is difficult to conceive how people do contrive to live without land in this country; nor, in fact, is it possible for them to do more than exist miserably. The men caught fish, and the women and children were all employed at low water in digging cockles; but all the vegetable food they could have had to eke out this diet was to be procured from an acre of land which the proprietor had given them from his own farm.

If I have represented the Highlanders as deficient in industry, I have also admitted that this fault is neither universal nor irremediable. It is not only just, but useful, to point out instances of activity; as it may lead those who despair of rousing this people to exertion, or who culpably neglect that duty, to make the attempt, instead of abandoning the pursuit as hopeless. If a Highland proprietor imagines that his tenant will not exert himself in draining or improving his farm, in cultivating his fishery or in working his quarries, it is certain that by importing Lowland, or foreign, tenants, fishermen, or labourers, he cuts off all hope from his people, and is not entitled to pronounce that an incorrigible state which is in a great measure fostered by his own impatience or want of exertion. I wish they would all recollect what has been said by one who has concealed much sound philosophy under the cap of folly: "Comme enfant nouvellement nay, les fault allaiter, bercer, esjouir,—espargner, restaurer, appuyer, asseurer." They are children; and kindness and care might do much for them. To say that the Highlanders are incapable of being roused to industry, is as injurious in its effects as it is untrue: it is often difficult; but time,

1 See p. 127.

patience, and method, will effect a great deal. It is those with whom this power lies, who are deserving of censure; not the critical traveller, who excites their anger, chiefly because he pricks their consciences; who merely tells useful truths, and who points out faults, only in the hope that they may be corrected.

The Barra men are among the most active and industrious fishermen in Scotland. They carry on an extensive ling fishery solely by their own exertions and on their own accounts; disposing, themselves, of the produce, at the Greenock market, to which they go in their fishing-boats through the Crinan Canal. They are thus comparatively wealthy; although, going quietly on in their old habits, their houses are no better than those of their neighbours. Their fishing-boats alone indicate their superior wealth; being large and well found, compared with all those which are seen in the Western Islands. This is not exactly the best system which could be adopted, as the labour, which might be much better bestowed on the fishery, is expended on a tedious navigation, and as want of capital both cramps them in laying up sufficient stores of salt and leaves them at the mercy of the purchasers. How this system originated among these people in particular, or why it continues, I could not discover; but it is no less remarkable that in South Uist and Benbecula, lying almost at their very doors, and possessing the same advantages, the people are noted for poverty, indolence, and neglect of the fisheries.

The construction of the Barra boats is very peculiar; and, like many others of the insular Highlanders, the boatmen are their own builders, purchasing the timber from the northern traders. They are of considerable size, so as easily to carry ten or twelve men, and extremely sharp, both fore and aft. They have no floor, but rise with an almost flat straight side, so that a transverse section somewhat resembles a wedge. Yet they are swift and safe; offering another example, in addition to the numerous ones already known, to prove in how many and in what apparently contrary ways, the objects of a shipbuilder may be attained. A seaman accustomed to a wall-sided boat is naturally surprised at their form; forgetting that in proportion as they heel to the breeze, their bearings are increased; while, from their lightness, they are almost as buoyant in a bad sea as a Norway skiff.[1]

It is a draw-back on the merits of the Barra men, that they are addicted to the use of whisky; a propensity fostered by their great gains

1 Which from this description they appear to resemble.

as much as by their mode of life. The ancient prowess of the Highlanders in this respect, is well known; and like their ancestors, the Scythians, they were notorious for quarrelling over their cups. It was almost the inevitable consequence of a Highland compotation, to terminate in bloodshed. The reputation has descended, where the merit, such as it was, is lost. Some years are now past since a meeting of Highlanders would sit down to their whisky bottle, just as, in these degenerate days, we do to our port wine; and the quantity of this strong spirit which they could drink without apparent inconvenience is incredible. The excuse for it still continues, when the means are gone. A damp climate is considered, not only a justification for the morning dram, but as the disease for which, whisky, whenever it can be got, is the only remedy. To say, however, that the Highlanders are addicted to drinking, it to make the mistake that has often been done, of forming a judgment of their present manners from books long since written. I have no doubt that, like the common people elsewhere, they would drink whisky could they get it; nor do I know why they should not seek the consolation which poets and philosophers have joined in praising. But in the present state of things they are nearly as much cut off from the use of whisky as from that of Tokay. Greater vigilance on the part of the Excise has raised the price of illicit spirits nearly to that of the licensed, and it is no longer in their power to procure it. They are in fact a sober people; whether from necessity, I will not pretend to say; but I really believe that, as happens in the case of many other habits abandoned from compulsion, they would be far soberer than their English neighbours, even if they had the power of being otherwise. This is a natural consequence of their laudable economy and foresight; of the care they take of their families, and of the provision they are attentive to make for their rents, as for futurity. Exceptions there must be; but it is high praise to a Highlander that he does not, like his profligate neighbour of England, consume in riot and personal gratification that which is necessary for those who are dependent on him. These are among the real and solid merits which are overlooked by those who are fierce in the defence of idle and visionary ones. It is the fate of poor Donald to find least justice from his pretended friends; as is not uncommon. There is more ardent spirit drank in London alone than in all the Highlands collectively; and indeed a traveller like myself will often have occasion to lament, when wet and weary, that he cannot procure it, even at their inns. 'Withers, Prynn, and Vicars,' never drank 'viler liquors' than is this common whisky, I must admit, as far as my own taste at least goes; but we do not wait to taste in on these occasions.

I was here amused with the distress of the people from the want of tobacco; the American War having raised its price beyond the means of purchase. The Highlanders are reputed to be very much addicted to its use; but this is just as true of tobacco as of whisky. They are doubtless very glad to get it, as are most idle people; but it is not often in their power to purchase it. It is indeed as snuff that their sole consumption, at any time, lies; nor do I recollect to have once seen a pipe in the country. Here they had tried all manner of experiments, by roasting various plants, and thus manufacturing a sort of Barra blackguard. The root of the daisy was said to have produced the best substitute.

This Long Island is a strange country. There is land, it is true, and water, for nature has but these two geographical elements, and therefore you might suppose that you could walk or ride over the one and swim or sail over the other. It would be impossible to make a greater mistake; for, hence at least to Harris, it is seldom either sea or good dry land. You may tread the crude consistence; but it must be, like Satan, half on foot, half flying. It is a country only fit for wild ducks; who "o'er bog, o'er steep, through strait, rough dense or rare, with head, hands, wings, and feet pursuing their way," may perhaps contrive to see it all. You may perhaps ride a few yards, but in ten minutes you will have to flounder through a bog, or scramble over rocks, or you will find a firth or a loch to cross; it is too wide to swim, and there is no boat. If there should be one, there is a second sea, and a third, and a fourth; you land on an island instead of the main, or lose yourself in the labyrinth of inextricable chaos. The Gaelic proverb says well when it says, "It is not every day that Mac Niel mounts his horse." It could not be of less use in Venice.

On the southern part of Barra, there is a small town on an islet in a fresh-water lake, an ancient seat of the Mac Niels. After much toiling through sand and rocks, I arrived on the shores of Chisamil Bay, at a village ornamented with dried skate, having "a most ancient and fish-like smell," as this animal is preserved without salt, and is, in consequence, very delectable. Every one knows how a Highland house is built; but every one does not know the architecture of a Barra house. In these, the roof springs from the inner edge of the wall, instead of the outer; in order that all the rain may be caught by it and make its way among the stones; thus preventing the inconvenience of "minute drops from off the eaves." All other points correspond; as is proper in architecture. We may say of them what Ovid does of the palace of Night and Erebus: "Janua quae verso stridorem cardine reddat, Nulla domo tota":[1] the only door is a bundle of heath. As to the rest of the comparison, I fear it does not very well hold. The 'solliciti canes' and the 'sagacior anser' do their duty admirably here; as the one barks at you before you are in sight, and continues to yelp long after you are out of smell, while the 'anser' answers them, hissing like Megaera's snakes; the 'vigil ales,' the 'ferae,' the 'pecudes,' and the rest of the clanjamfray, loining in a concert with the 'humanae convicia linguae' enough to rouse Nox and Erebus both. But I must not forget a principal part of the description; for here indeed the resemblance is perfect: "Nebulae caligine mixtae Exhaluntur humo, dubiaeque crepuscula lucis."[2] It is probable that Ovid lived in a sort of Barra house during that philosophical retirement of which he so bitterly complains. If there is no chimney, and if a Highland hut is varnished with black pitch, that pitch is bistre, and the artist who has lost his colour box may use it for drawing. If it smokes at every crevice like a melon bed in heat, there is no want of chimney sweepers; or of a society for their suppression, which is still better. Thus the wise man extracts good from every thing. Besides, you can truly and mathematically draw round a Highland fire: round our own, we do it only by a figure of speech. And as a circle is the double of its half, like most things, one Highland fire is as good as two. It is a hospitable fire also; because there is room for the pigs and the chickens and the three black collies: and it is further a genial fire because it conduces to the laying of eggs: as all good housewives know. Even the Cockneys need not affect to despise the Highlanders for their want of chimneys: the fashion is not very ancient in England. "Old men," says Hollinshed, who is a very good chronicler of the times if not a very brief one, "noticed the multitude of chimneys lately erected," "whereas, in their young days, there were not above two or three, if so many, in most uplandish towns of the realm." The progress can be traced now in this country, just as it crept on in England; at least where things are left to take their natural course. The fire in the middle of the house is first transferred to the gable; a canopy with a chimney is next placed over it; those who formerly sat near the fire, then sit within the fire-place; in progress of time, this is contracted so as to exclude them; and, lastly,

---

1 "Throughout the house there is no door to creak on its hinge in answer."
2 "Clouds mixed with darkness are exhaled from the ground, and the twilight of doubtful light."

this eventful history ends in Carron grates and Bath stoves and registers, in bright brass and brighter steel, the pride of housewives, the dread of chilly guests, and the torment of housemaids.

To compensate the artist, however, for the bistre within, though the roofs and the walls generally bear a plentiful crop of grass, corn, and weeds, which sounds picturesque enough, they offer no consolation for his drawings. No human art can possibly represent a Highland cottage so as to render it a picturesque object. If alone, it is a shapeless pile of stones and turf; if congregated into a town, that looks like a heap of dunghills or peat-stacks. Were it not for the occasional wreath of blue smoke, a southern traveller would never suspect their presence at a small distance. Hence the unfortunate artist in Highland landscape is deprived of the aid which is elsewhere afforded him by the infinite varieties of rural architecture; of the life and interest which human habitations bestow on a picture; and of that source of contrast and scale of measurement which are afforded by a mixture of the petty works of man with the bold and wild features of Nature.

Chisamil Castle is a fine object, compared to most of the Highland ancient residences; as it is of considerable extent and occupies a striking position on its insulated rock, which, to the great surprise of the people, contains a spring of fresh water, though surrounded by the sea: being the only spring, I believe, in the Long Island.[1] This very valuable possession to such a strong hold, is secured by masonry and covered by an arch. This castle lies about half a mile from the shore, and is still tolerably entire; its extent being such as probably to accommodate not less than five hundred men; a considerable army in those days.[2] The family of Mac Niel was one of the powerful Clans of the time, yet the size of this garrison is remarkable; as it was not usual to keep an army on foot when it could be levied in a few hours by sending round the acknowledged signal for gathering, the burnt and bloody stick, or fiery cross. Martin describes his difficulty in getting access to it, upwards of a century ago, owing to the ill nature of the Constable, or Cockman (Gokman), as he calls him;[3] so that all the discipline of a fortress seems to have been preserved in these castles, even down to the late period at which he wrote.

---

1 This is absolutely wrong.
2 An excessive estimate; in any case, it is doubtful if the MacNeills could have raised so many armed men at any time. Lochgarry's estimate (see p. 65) in 1750 was a hundred and fifty men.
3 See p. 42.

Though Mac Niel is said to have been a tributary to the Lords of the Isles at one time, this Clan professes to be of Irish origin, which is probable, considering the absolute community which seems in former times to have existed between that country and the West Highlands; though that Irish origin is still Norwegian. He is the Nialson of the Sagas. It appears to have kept up a degree of state absolutely ridiculous, if we may trust to two tales, one of which at least is true. In Carstares's state papers, there is a letter from the Earl of Argyll, laughing at the formality and state with which an ambassador from that chief had presented to him a letter offering aid, "as if he had belonged to another kingdom." The other story relates to the wreck of a Spanish vessel which the gentlemen of the Clan had proposed to appropriate; and respecting which, when it was questioned what the King of Spain would say, the answer was that Mac Niel and His Majesty must settle that between themselves. If he was the thirty-sixth chief of his race in Queen Anne's[1] time, as Achmar says, he had indeed something to boast of.

Chisamil Castle consists of an irregular four-sided area within a high wall, containing many distinct buildings ranged along its sides which appear to have been the barracks. One of the angles is filled by a high and strong square tower, which must have been the keep; having no entrance from the ground, and only accessible at one door about half way up, the ascent to which is by a narrow outside staircase. In the opposite angle is a small tower which seems to have been the prison; as the situation of this castle rendered it impossible to have a dungeon under ground. The walls are embattled on one side, and provided with a covered way and loop-holes, so as to render the defence in that quarter very complete. It is altogether a work of more art than most of the Highland Castles, and constructed on better principles The keep is also flanked by a small circular defence; but the protection of the rest has been trusted to the strength of the masonry. The entrance to this castle is near one of the angles; and, near it, are the remains of a round enclosure, or basin, which was probably a place of security for the boats. There is no date on the building, nor could I discover when it was erected; but it cannot be very ancient.[2]

It was with some difficulty we reached Vatersa, which is separated from Barra by a channel that is very narrow on the west side, and only

1 Thirty-ninth, according to the official genealogy.
2 This is correct. The Castle probably was built in the fifteenth century. It is not mentioned in Fordun's list of the Hebridean castles.

deep enough for small boats. This island consists of two green hills, united by a low sandy bar where the opposite seas nearly meet. Indeed if the water did not perpetually supply fresh sand to replace what the wind carries off, it would very soon form two islands; nor would the tenant have much cause for surprise, if on getting up some morning, he should find that he required a boat to milk his cows. The whole island is in a state of perpetual revolution, from the alternate accumulation and dispersion of sand-hills; which at least affords the pleasure of variety, in a territory where there is none else but what depends on the winds and weather. I had here an opportunity of imagining how life is passed in a remote island, without society or neighbours, and where people are born and die without ever troubling themselves to enquire whether the world contains any other countries than Vatersa and Barra.[1] The amusement of the evening consisted in catching scallops for supper, milking the cows, and chasing rabbits; and this, I presume, is pretty near the usual round of occupation. The whole group of the southern islands is here seen from the southern part of the island, forming a maritime landscape which is sufficiently picturesque. They are all high, and some of them are single hills rising abruptly out of the water. They are inhabited by small tenants and fishermen; and, except a small quantity of grain cultivated by the people for their own use, are appropriated to the pasture of black cattle. Sheep, here as elsewhere in the remote islands, cannot be adopted, owing to the impossibility of transporting them far by sea. The highest of these islands seemed to range from 800 to 1000 feet; and Sandera, named rather more properly than Vatersa which contains no water, is covered on the west side with sand, to such a height as to look like a hill of snow. The other principal islands are Pabba, Muldonich, Mingala, and Bernera, which latter is the southernmost and is generally known by the name of Barra Head. These islands present a curious mixture of Scandinavian and Gaelic denominations; the four just mentioned being of Gaelic origin, while Sandera and Vatersa, with Fladda and Linga, have northern designations.[2] Muldonich is named after St Duncan, who has probably been a personage of considerable importance, as Sunday is, in the Highlands,

1 This is a piece of unwarrantable affected imagination, and a most unjustifiable slight upon a community whose fishermen went regularly in small open boats to Greenock and Glasgow, and who already at the time this account was written had many relations in America.
2 These names are in fact probably all of Norse origin; but the derivations of Sandray and Vatersay are not so simple as MacCulloch supposed. See pp. 227, 228.

frequently known by the name of Di Donich, or Duncan's Day.[1] We were promised a boat in the morning to visit all these islands, and I therefore went to bed full of hope. I had forgotten that I was in a Highland land.

Morning came, and six; but breakfast did not come till ten. Then came the cows to be milked and the calves to be admired; for in these countries of blatant cattle, a calf is a much more important object than a child, and its nursing an affair of the purest affection. At length we arrived at the beach, and then the Laird recollected that, a few days before, his boat had been carried away by the tide and dashed in pieces; as he had forgotten to anchor or fasten her. But there was another boat on the island;[2] we should probably find it; which we accordingly did. With unusual foresight, he had borrowed some oars the preceding evening; but they had been left on the beach within high water mark, and had floated off in search of the original boat. There was now a boat without oars; but what are these difficulties in a land so full of expedients? There were oars to be borrowed somewhere: they would be ready at twelve, or one, or two o'clock: we should not be many hours too late, and could only be benighted. I knew we should be benighted though we were to stay there a month; and the oars were sent for. We then however discovered that there were no men; our kind host having sent all his people to Barra. But there was an expedient ready for this also; and another messenger was despatched to borrow four of the islanders. The borrowed oars of one fisherman were at length fitted to the borrowed boat of another: but when the second messenger returned, all the islanders were absent making kelp. It remained to find another expedient; and that was, to return to Barra. Need you wonder how happily people can live in the Highlands, how easily they can find employment, even in such solitudes as this, and how little time can hang heavy on those hands that have found so many expedients for occupying it? In fact, Time does not enter into the list of their categories. It is never present, but always past or to come: what a delicious illustration for Harris's Hermes. It is always too soon to do any thing, until it is too late: and thus vanishes that period of weariness and labour, and anxiety, and expectation, and disappointment which lies between the cradle and the grave.

1 Muldonich, formerly called Scarp, which was probably its original Norse name, is in Gaelic *Maol Domhnaich*, "the island of the tonsured one of the Lord"; Sunday in Gaelic is *Di-domhnaich*, from Latin Dies Dominica (MacBain). Neither has anything to do with St Duncan.

2 Vatersay, as the narrative shows. The laird is presumably Colonel Roderick MacNeill, who died in 1822.

I could not have lost much in point of pleasure or information; except the pleasure of boasting hereafter that I had visited the southernmost as well as the northernmost point of the Long Island. Many heroic acts, indeed, are undertaken, and performed too, from as worthy motives every day. Moralists, since it is their trade to moralise, laugh at mankind for despising what is in their reach. But mankind here, is more in the right than the moralists: the main object is, to overcome: and that which is attainable becomes therefore as important as if it were attained.

But I must end the history of this barren expedition, with an account of the fashions of these islands in the articles of marriage: not under the New Act however, be it marked. The Fathers say that the intention of marriage is to propagate the Church. But the MacNiels maintained that it was to propagate the Clan. When a tenant's wife died, he applied to the Chief for a new one, on the ground that he had become useless, and that the deficiency was a public loss. Mac Niel then sent him a wife, and they were married over a bottle of whisky. This would have satisfied Marshall Saxe;[1] who, viewing men, probably, much as Mac Niel did, seems to have been alarmed in his latter days lest he should not have enough to kill; if we may judge from his Essay on Population, where the old soldier seems not a little out of his element.

BARRA[2]

This island is of a very irregular and indented shape, containing but a small surface compared with its extreme dimensions, which are ten miles in length, by seven in breadth. If indeed the hill above Kilbar be considered only as an appendage, its length will be reduced to seven miles. This appendage of Barra consists of a single hill, connected with the remainder of the island by a flat sand, over which the western and eastern seas almost meet at high water. They have probably been at one time separate islands, subsequently united by the sandy isthmus which the action of the waters has thrown up; nor is it impossible that in some of the revolutions to which these shores seem exposed they may again be separated. Toward the southern and western side of the isle arise one high hill scarcely attaining the height of 2000 feet, descending to Chisamil Bay and declining to the north and east in a succession of lower hills which terminate in various rocky points on

1 Or Hitler or Mussolini at the present time.
2 *Description of the Western Islands*, Vol. I, p. 70.

the shores. The intervals of these rocky promontories are occupied by sandy bays communicating with small vallies in which the population is accumulated. These valleys present a soil composed of a mixture of peat and sand, and near the shores, of sand only; while the hills offer nothing to the eye but a motley mixture of peat and rocks, affording but scanty pasture to the black cattle which form the chief agricultural wealth of the island.

Fisheries

The rocky shores abound with fish, principally ling; in the pursuit of which the inhabitants are very industrious. When cured they are carried by the fishermen themselves to Greenock, and in this way much time is unprofitably occupied; an evil, which the greater extension of the fishery and a proper commercial arrangement would easily remedy. But society here is not yet advanced to the state that admits of those arrangements; and to this want is in part owing the very inadequate manner in which fishing is conducted along many parts of this productive shore. The impediments arising from the want of commercial arrangements, and the deficiency of capital, are not, however, universal in the maritime Highlands; as establishments under the direction of capitalists exist in various parts of the western coast, and are followed by the results that might naturally be anticipated.[1]

To the preceding causes must be added the difficulty of reconciling the often incompatible pursuits of farming and fishing; the most active season of the fishery being frequently that where the attention of the fisherman is also required at home, to conduct the operations of agriculture, on which he must depend for the chief part of his subsistence. It is obvious that the state of the country is not such as to admit of a ready or constant market for immediate consumption, which is therefore limited to the families of the fishermen themselves. Under these circumstances, there can be no effectual or extensive fishery, nor any endeavours to take more than is required for domestic use; unless where the small fishermen are enabled to salt and retain their several stocks, till they accumulate so as to render them sufficient for a distant market. To the natural impediments arising from a want of capital, by which this is checked, must be added the difficulties arising from the nature of the salt laws. To favour the fisherman and

1 This probably refers to the British Fisheries Society, which was incorporated in 1786 and had harbours at Lochbay in Skye, Tobermory, Ullapool, and Wick. It was hampered by the Salt Duty and various Government restrictions, and had sold all its West Coast properties by 1842.

promote the commerce in the salted commodity, and at the same time to check the frauds that might follow the misapplication of the salt allowed for that purpose, have been found matters of considerable difficulty. Complaints, as may naturally be expected, abound on this subject, and, to remedy the real inconveniences, many regulations have at different times been adopted, with more or less success. It would here be out of place to attempt a description of these several regulations; as the subject is not only trite, but the changes have been so numerous, that to notice them would lead to a considerable length of discussion.[1] To render the Highland fisheries effective, has been an object of much anxiety, and if the expedients have sometimes failed, they have at least been intended to reconcile the more local interests of the country with the general advantages of the empire.

Similar attempts have been made to temper those regulations which, in the case of these remote islands would, if rigidly enforced, produce inconveniences without any adequate advantages to the revenue. The restrictions on the private manufacture of candles are of this nature. Such restrictions can be attended with no inconveniences in a commercial country, but they would here be oppressive as well as useless; as there is no market for the sale of the raw, or the purchase of the wrought material, and the former would of course be unconvertible. A discretionary power is therefore judiciously entrusted to the officers in this department of the revenue, by which this manufacture is permitted for domestic use, under certain regulations capable of checking abuse without producing inconvenience.

As grievances, real or imaginary, must exist everywhere, it will not be a subject of wonder if many other complaints are found among these remote islanders; although a patient submission to inconveniences and privations, forms no small feature in their character. It is pleasing however to observe, that they are never directed towards the government; an attachment to which is one of the most striking traits of the Highlander's character, to him who has been accustomed to the political ill-humour of the lower orders in England. These grievances are generally however the consequence of circumstances so essentially interwoven in the system of the country, as to be irremediable; often proceeding more or less directly from a crowded population, from poverty, and from the remoteness of the situation. In a few instances,

1 The Salt Duties, which protected alike the English salt manufacturers and the Highland kelp industry, were incredibly complicated and for a long time nearly stifled the fishing industry in Scotland. They were repealed in 1817.

they appear rather to be traditional than real; the gradual influence of a number of concuring circumstances, having long since removed most causes of complaint. If we consider the general poverty of the people, the distance of the seats of justice, the great competition for land, and the dependance on the landlord thence generated, together with the accumulated influence which the situation of proprietor and magistrate combined, gives to the great landholders or their agents, it is gratifying to reflect that so little just cause of complaint exists. The instances of oppression which are occasionally related to strangers, will be found to belong to a period now for some time past; nor indeed are the people willing to submit to an improper use of power, even if their superiors were inclined to exert it. If the southern traveller imagines that he sees the spirit of feudal government still hovering over the dead body, he will also see that it has long lost its hold over the minds of the people.

A suggestion has recently been made, which would remove one inconvenience frequently represented to strangers in their visits to this country. It relates to the collection of taxes. The produce of these being so small, no collector is appointed to receive them on the spot, and they must therefore be paid at the county town, which in the case of the island now under review, is Inverness. The inconvenience that may hence arise, in the case of errors, is obvious. It has been proposed to place the collection in the hands of the officers of excise, whose leisure, and residence on the spot, would enable them to perform this additional duty with ease to themselves and the people, and at a very slight expense.

Inconveniences also arise from the difficulty of communication which results from the deficiency and imperfection of roads, ferries, and post offices. With respect to the former, much has been done recently to improve them, but more is yet wanting. It would be too much to expect universal satisfaction where so many jarring interests are concerned, and where misrepresentation must sometimes inevitably defeat the best intentions of the government. There can be no doubt, that its interest is concerned, in promoting for the general wealth, those improvements which the individuals are, in districts so poor, unable to undertake. If its intentions are occasionally obstructed by the particular views or imaginary interests of proprietors, it is no great matter of surprise. The tedious and limited communication by posts is often injurious, by preventing an early knowledge of the fluctuations of prices in the articles of export. Thus speculators in kelp, cattle, or wool, frequently profit by the ignorance of the producer. Where agriculture has a character so commercial, the freedom of communication cannot be too great. If a small sacrifice of immediate revenue is made for this object, either by the proprietors or the government, it will be ultimately replaced by the improvement of the country at large.

A few remarks of a different nature remain to be made on the fisheries. They have been productive of advantages to the proprietors, and consequently to the country, in a way which does not appear to have been originally foreseen, however well it is now understood. These advantages consist in the increase of value which the lands have undergone by their extension, even where the extension is still limited to a partial domestic supply. Hence arise the chief benefits of the crofting system, the most efficient and profitable changes of this nature having been the allotments of small farms on the sea shore. Rents have thus been obtained for farms of a division so minute as to have been nearly incapable of paying any from their surplus produce. In a similar manner a revenue has been derived from tenements which produce no surplus, the rent being here analogous to that which arises in the vicinities of commerce and of manufactures; a price paid for the accomodation requisite in the fisheries, and a portion of the wages of labour. A superficial view of the limited produce and of the apparently high rent of many Highland farms of this nature, has thus been often made a ground of ill-founded censure on the proprietors; who perhaps have not been sufficiently careful in rendering the nature of this operation intelligible to their tenantry; if indeed it be possible to render intelligible to them what their better informed neighbours are so often incapable of understanding. It is no small matter in this case, as in that of taxation, to prevent a confusion of the semblance and of the reality. The grievance of a tax exists too often when the real tax is levied on an individual very different from the imaginary sufferer. An instance of an injudicious attempt at this distinction occurs in one of the islands under review. Here, the proprietor levies a rent on each boat employed by his tenantry in fishing. The consequences are obvious; grievous complaints are made of oppression and of injustice.[1] Yet this is a case not of rigid justice merely, but of mistaken lenity, since he whose indolence or incapacity prevents him from fishing is exempted from that rent which the land alone would not allow him to pay without inconvenience or ruin. The regulation is, however, in

1 And rightly so.

every respect inconsiderate, since it not only creates an imaginary evil, but operates as a discouragement to the fisheries, on which the proprietor must in a great measure depend for his rent as the tenant also must for his subsistence.

Economy

A stranger who for the first time sees the miserable cultivation which is carried on by the smallest class of tenantry among rocks and bogs, will be surprised to find that any rent can be paid from the produce of such possessions; in other situations they would pay none, or rather they would not be cultivated, since they could not repay the expense of cultivation so as to leave any profit to the occupier. Here, the great and increasing competition for land necessarily generates a rent which the habits of the farmer and the small quantity of food and accommodation he requires enables him to pay.[1] Such rents are in many instances called oppressive. In this view it may truly be said that any rent is oppressive; but even the abandonment of a rent, which in the case of the small tenants rarely exceeds £3 per annum, would not remove the evils under which this country labours. The fault lies deeper, and is compounded of the excess in the quantity, and the defects in the distribution, of the Highland population.

It is this also which constitutes the chief obstacle to the proper improvement of the land. It cannot be said that there is a want of industry or a deficiency in the labour bestowed on this object, when we examine the spade cultivation by which the small farms are generally conducted, and which was already noticed in treating of Tirey. There is, in fact, a super-abundance of labour applied to it, which under the proper direction of capital would effect useful and permanent improvements; it is lost because it is wasted in the pursuit of those which can only be temporary. There is no want of industry, but it is misdirected. Here again the proprietors suffer under the unjust censure of impeding improvements by with-holding leases. But a lease to him who has no capital is nearly useless, while the only security which the landlord can retain for the productiveness of the soil, is the power of withdrawing the farm from him who neglects it, and bestowing it on some other of the craving competitors who are surrounding him, and who come with the double claim of equal wants and greater industry.[2] When the system shall change by the

1 In other words, land-hunger is taken advantage of to raise the rents and depress the standard of living.
2 Or with the even more pressing claim of an offer to pay a higher rent.

enlargement of farms and the introduction of a superior class of tenants, the proprietor will naturally dispose of his land with the same regard for his own interest as his Lowland neighbours; that interest and those of his tenants, as well as of the community at large, being seldom at variance. Before quitting this subject, it is however not unin-structive to remark, that although there can be no question of respecting the improvements of waste lands daily making by the new classes of small tenants under separate holdings and securer leases, yet the ultimate value of these improvements appears to have been over-rated by speculative persons. They are generally on too small a scale to be of future advantage when the advance in the state of farming shall cause larger tracts to be occupied. That rough land which from its nature has been necessarily cultivated by the spade, must be thrown into pasturage when more perfect and economical cultivation by the plough[1] shall have been introduced. Under any circumstances but the present crowded population, and low value of labour,* the cultivation of such land must cease altogether; and it will cease when labour shall become disposable under capitals less divided; and when these, directed to more legitimate objects, shall seek for employment in the breaking up of new lands.[2] These small holdings will therefore be eventually abstracted from the permanent mass of improvement, and those writers who consider the present changes as both the commencement and indication of legitimate and effectual improve-ments have consequently misled themselves. A small addition of improved pasture may remain, but the system is temporary, and so far from being the first stage of general improvement, is merely an amelioration of the old imperfect and imperfectible one. It is evident, on reviewing the effects of this system, that if the same quantity of labour and expense which have been bestowed on small improve-ments in these islands had been directed to great ones, they would here, as in Isla, have brought extensive tracts into a regular and permanent system of cultivation. But the present practice is inseparable from the present state of the population and the holdings

1 *i.e.*, not runrig.

* It must be remarked, that the low price, or rather value, of labour mentioned here and on other occasions as the result of excessive population, is virtual only; it is not marketable labour that is meant. On the contrary the price of hired labour in these districts is excessive, or rather, the article is not to be procured. Hence the peculiar state of the kelp manufactory, besides numerous other evils which impede the progress of agricultural improvement. The causes must already have been too obvious to require detail.

2 What this laboured argument really means, is the degradation of crofters and small tenants to the status of farm-labourers.

of farms. Capital is wasted since it produces neither permanent change, nor accession of capital, nor augmentation of the means of future progress, but must always be renewed; and it may fairly be said that the wretched Highland crops are raised at an expense much greater than their value. The introduction of capitalists and the enlargement of farms are the true foundation of the improvement to which this country must look.

The arable land of Barra[1] bears a small proportion to its pastures, and it may, I believe, be safely stated, that every thing arable or capable of permanent improvement is already in a state of cultivation. In any other circumstances indeed, the cultivation of Barra would be judged excessive and injudicious. A change of system, such as in many instances might be productive of advantage, would therefore in Barra only tend to diminish the number of occupants, by diminishing both the quantity of produce capable of being immediately consumed on the soil, and the labour required for the cultivation of that land which ought to be maintained in agriculture. In the present state of the island, moreover, a large proportion of the population is supported by the produce of a very active fishery, as I have already shown. Could this fishery be indefinitely increased there would of course be no limit to the increase of population. But this cannot be done precisely as is required to meet the additional demand for employment and food; perhaps it cannot be done at all. In the mean time the people of Barra have exceeded the demand for this and every other employment, and have entirely occupied all the land capable of cultivation. They are therefore redundant, and as a sufficient practical proof of such redundancy, it is only necessary to state that there is a considerable village at Kilbar for which no land is to be found; land, which in a country without markets, forms so indispensable a requisite in the economy of a Highland family. A single acre has by the humanity of the proprietor[2] been given to this community for the cultivation of their potatoes, and a wretched existence is thus worn out by them, partly by this resource, partly by the fishery in which the men are engaged; both of which being insufficient, the women and children are constantly employed in digging cockles[3] on the sandy shore, offering a spectacle of poverty which is painful even in this country where it is daily seen in all its modifications.

1 The following paragraph is inserted from p. 106 of the same book as the rest of the account.
2 Colonel Roderick MacNeill, who died in 1822.
3 Which must be pointed out are an excellent food and still both consumed locally, and exported to England.

Soil and Alluvia

A small fresh-water lake is to be seen at the southern end of this island, containing the ruins of a tower;[1] the residence of some ancient chief, or a place of refuge for his family. There are no other lakes of any note, and not a single permanent stream of water exists in the country.[2] A few dry channels of water-courses are visible on the sides of the hills, where an occasional shower falls, but which are speedily drained on its cessation. Springs are almost equally deficient, a character which will be found very general throughout the remainder of the islands connected with Barra, other general features, as will hereafter be seen, pervading the whole.

The deficiency of water arising from the want of springs is, in an economical view, a source of much inconvenience, not only to the inhabitants, but to the shipping which frequent the harbours. None can be obtained in summer except in the small cavities which the roughness of the ground leaves in the winter water-courses, and this, being the drainage water of the surface, is impregnated not only with peat, but often with less innocent matters. In a geological view some peculiarities seem to originate from the same cause. No banks or deposits of alluvial matter are to be observed in the flat parts of the island or on the sea shores; nor are there any beds of clayey soil in situations where they might be expected. There is indeed very little soil in the island, if we except the hill above Kilbar. In general the peat lies almost immediately on the bare rock in the higher parts; while on the western side many feet in depth of sand are accumulated by the incessant blowing up of that which the sea rejects. The intermediate land offers the best soil for agricultural purposes, being composed of such a mixture of peat, earth, and sand, as might be expected from its situation; the one or the other being predominant in proportion to the vicinity of the sea or of the mountain; or the greater or less facility with which the sand drift is enabled to sweep it. The small quantity of clay which enters into these soils is sometimes found forming very thin beds under the peat, which is however in general much too deep to admit of this matter being reached by the agricultural processes in use, so as to be brought into action.

As there are no beds of the usual alluvia of flat lands in Barra, so there is none of the mountain alluvial matter so common in hilly countries, which consists of mixtures of angular stones with clay. The

1 Loch St Clair and Castle St Clair.
2 This is absolutely incorrect. There are at least four or five permanent streams in Barra.

gneiss of these islands appears to be of a very refractory matter, undergoing little change from the action of the atmosphere. The surfaces are smoothed as if from the very slow effects of air and water, but in general the angles are tolerably sharp, and the traces of fissures penetrate to no depth. Everything appears in its place; the precipices which result from the fall of rocks are rare, few fragments are scattered about, and those which are have an integrity and freshness rarely found in any other class of rocks in Scotland. A spectator cannot help being struck by the aspect of obstinate durability which they display. If we compare this gneiss with granite, with mica slate, with quartz rock, with limestone, or with trap, its superior powers in resisting destruction will be strikingly apparent; while the imagination is lost in reflecting on the slowness of those changes by which many parts of the rocky globe were first made fit for the habitation of plants and animals.

The difficulty with which this rock decomposes into earth, is the evident cause of the nakedness of the surface. If the lichens find a hold, it is true that they are followed by their usual attendants, the mosses, the rushes, and the grasses, which in the end produce a body of green covering wherever they can effect a lodgment. But this covering is only peat. The peat is laid on the naked rock, and the vegetation is one generation of Scirpi, or sphagnum is followed by that of others in endless succession, without change or amelioration. The cause of the extreme resistance of this gneiss is not apparent. In composition it exactly resembles granite; and in the disposition of its parts it differs but little; yet where most granites are covered with a dense coat of gravel, of clay, and of mixed vegetable soil, this rock is bare even to the very level of the sea. The absence of precipitous faces and of the marks of violent fracture will be found to arise from the same cause to which the want of springs is owing, namely, its freedom from fissures. There is no place in which water can lodge, nor consequently where the power of frost can be brought into action; that agent from which the violent fractures of rocks seem almost entirely to originate. Hence arises that peculiar character of the hills which predominates in a greater or less degree throughout the whole range of the Long Island. No serrated outline, no spiry summits, no angles nor abrupt faces vary their appearance; one rounded and tame line separates them from the sky. A few parts only of Harris and of Lewis offer an exception to this general rule. Nothing indeed can well be conceived less interesting in a picturesque view, than the whole of this chain of islands. Much amusing display of a sort of ichnographic scenery, arising from the labyrinthine disposition of the land and water, may be seen by ascending the hills, but there is scarcely anywhere a subject for the pencil. While the mountain outlines are tame, their groups are without complication. No trees occupy the valleys, no water-falls sparkle along the declivities, the cliffs have neither magnitude of parts nor breadth of disposition,[1] the shores of the numerous bays are uniformly low, and the sea rocks have neither elevation nor form to compensate for the dullness of the interior scenery.

Geology

The rocks of Barra offer nearly as little instruction to the geologist, as they display attractions to the lover of landscape. Gneiss is the universal substance, and with but little exception it will be found to predominate throughout the whole of the Long Island.

The rock here is so irregular that the beds can rarely be traced for more than a few yards together in a straight line. They are commonly bent and occasionally much contorted, while their inclinations to the horizon are so irregular and inconstant, that no consistency or order can be perceived among them. Still, their leading position approaches the horizontal one; unlike those of the southern parts of Coll, which not only are elevated at high angles, but show a considerable rectilinear tendency. In composition and structure they vary almost everywhere, the principal differences being produced by the presence or absence of hornblende, or of mica. The micaceous varieties are, however, rare, and the compounds of felspar and mica only, are seldom found to occupy any great space. They rather form the occasional laminae of a fundamental mass containing hornblende in various proportions; that substance causing the laminar appearance and fissile tendency of the rock. Occasionally this gneiss passes into common hornblende schist, while in certain situations the laminar tendency so far disappears that it assumes the characters of a common granite.

Granite veins abound as usual in this gneiss, and they have in Barra a character similar to that which they possess in Coll; the red colour however is predominant.

In weathering, these rocks acquire a uniform rough surface with a slight convexity, which, together with the fissures that cross each other at considerable angles, and the occasional exposures of the veins, give to the whole an appearance resembling granite very apt to mislead an

1 This is certainly not true of the cliffs of Barra Head, Mingulay, and the south-west of Barra itself.

inexperienced eye, particularly from a distant point of view.

Trap veins abound in the gneiss, attended with some unusual appearances. In many places there are large rents filled by loose matter and vegetable soil, but appearing to have once contained such veins, of which the exposed portions have been washed out. But those which render the gneiss of Barra remarkable are of very small size, and distributed in a manner of which no corresponding examples have occurred to me in any part of Scotland but the Long Island. They are subdivided into branches of extraordinary tenuity, traversing and reticulating the gneiss or the granite veins in the most intricate manner, was either of these happens to lie in their way. However small these veins, even though reduced to the diameter of a thread, they maintain their distinctness from the including rock, never diffusing themselves throughout its substance, or entering into any compound with it, but always remaining defined by a determined boundary. They are readily distinguishable on a fresh fracture; and when the rock is exposed to the weather, it is equally easy to recognize them by their rusting and falling out, while the gneiss retains its refractory nature and aspect. In some places they are so abundant as to equal or exceed in quantity the rock which they traverse. Of this there is a remarkable example at Cuire. The original rock is a dark gneiss containing much hornblende and intersected by veins of grey granite. The trap veins are so numerous as to have separated the rock into small irregular fragments, so that the whole has at first view the aspect of a conglomerate consisting of fragments of gneiss and granite embedded in a basaltic paste. Where it has been exposed to the weather, these have been so unequally acted on that it puts on the appearance of a tufaceous lava. I must add, that the matter of all these veins, whether great or small, is invariably identical, and is a very compact fine-grained black basalt. No large vein of basalt is to be observed in the neighbourhood of Cuire.

VATERSA, SANDERA, PABBA, MULDONICH, MINGALA, BERNERA[1]

These islands, together with a few islets of little note, form an irregular group to the south of Barra; the latter, which is the southmost point of the Long Isles, being popularly known by the name of Barra Head. As the composition of the whole is similar, and as they present but little interest, a very brief notice of them will suffice.

1 A footnote of MacCallum's, in which wrong derivations are given for all these names, is here omitted. For their proper or most likely meanings, see p. 227-8.

Vatersa is a small island consisting of two distinct hills connected by a flat sandy bar where the opposing seas nearly meet. This small tract exhibits the broken remains of sand hills standing to mark the changes which the land has undergone by the gradual and alternate accumulation and dispersion of these banks. There is nothing here opposed to the junction of the two seas, and the consequent division of Vatersa into two islands, but this bar, which the westerly swell perpetually throws up and which is again dispersed by the winds over the surface of the land. The separation of Vatersa from Barra is effected by Chisamil Bay, and by a narrow strait to the westward which affords passage only to small boats and is occupied like all the shores of this country by two or three small islands, of which Eorsa and Snoasimil are the most conspicuous.

These islands are all composed of gneiss, differing in no way from that of Barra already described. Vatersa offers perhaps more conspicuous examples of contortions and instances equally beautiful of the reticulations of the trap veins; while, as in the little island of Fudia, oxidulous iron is occasionally to be seen in the granite veins.

Sandera is nearly connected with Vatersa, with which it also corresponds in materials and disposition; forming a single hill of gneiss and attaining, like that, an elevation of 800 feet or thereabout. Although the islands of Fladda and Linga protect it in some measure both from the action of the western swell and that of the prevalent winds, it is covered by sand to a much greater height than either Barra or Vatersa; in consequence of some peculiarity of its shape which directs the current of wind high over its eastern end. This sand which, partly by its calcareous nature, and partly by its mechanical power in overcoming the tenacity of peat, has produced such excellent effects in Barra and many of the neighbouring islands, is here in such excess as to overwhelm and exclude vegetation altogether. At a distance the island appears as if covered with a coating of snow. Although small it is inhabited.

I may add that Pabba like Sandera, consists of a single hill of similar elevation and materials; having a somewhat precipitous face towards the west, and being inhabited by a few fishermen at its flatter eastern end.

Muldonich is also a single hill of 6 or 700 feet in elevation, and like the neighbouring rocks it is composed of gneiss.

As I had no opportunity of landing either on Mingala or Bernera, I can only conclude from the general characters and disposition of the rocks, and from their continuity with Pabba and Vatersa, that they also consist of gneiss. Judging from their appearance as seen from the sea and neighbouring islands, their elevation does not appear to reach 1000 feet. Each exhibits a precipitous and rugged face, Mingula to the west and Bernera to the south.

Some future geologist will perhaps fill up the blank which I have unwillingly left, if indeed there be anything in those two islands but what I have conjectured to exist. He will be fortunate if he is not compelled to leave much unseen, and to supply somewhat from conjectures. Though like the philosopher in Rasselas he were to find the winds and waves obedient to his word, he would still have much to encounter. He cannot ride in a land without roads, since his horse can neither tread the bogs nor scale the rocks. Though he may walk with the strength of Antaeus, and like the Arab live on the 'chameleon's diet' it will avail him little, unless with the wild duck, the proper tenant of this amphibious region, he can also traverse the lakes and swim the firths. The dependence which he may place on the maritime habits of the islands will be overthrown at every step by the mis-arrangements common in this country which display so strikingly some of the characteristics of the Highlander; an almost unsurmountable indolence, and a content which is either satisfied with an expedient or submits to inconveniences of its own creating as if they were part of the necessary career of his life. Poverty is not always the cause of these inconveniences. If the poor fisherman has no rudder to his boat, no yard to his mast, or no sheet to his sail, his richer neighbour is often equally in want of them.[1]

ERISKA, FUDIA, HELLESA, GIA

Numerous islands lie in the strait between Barra and South Uist, and on the eastern shore of the former, one small chain of which separates the harbour Ba Hirivah from Ottervore road. The composition of the whole is precisely the same.

Eriska is the boundary of Ottervore toward the north, and is separated from South Uist by a narrow and rocky sound, being of considerable extent when compared with the neighbouring islands. On a detached and high rock at its southern end are to be seen the remains of a square tower,[2] the ancient residence of some turbulent chieftain. This island offers also a circumstance of historical interest,

1 See p. 92 for an incident which MacCulloch here relates in a footnote.
2 Caisteal a' Bhreabadair.

having been the first place on which Prince Charles landed while on his voyage from France to Arasaik, where his disembarkation took place.

Although the gneiss of Eriska presents no features deserving of particular notice, that of Fudia is somewhat distinguished by the magnitude and number of the granite veins which it displays. Lumps of granite, apparently independent of veins, are also seen embedded in it. From these as well as from the larger veins there proceed branches anastomosing and diverging in a very capricious manner, which the great continuity and extent of the naked surface gives ample opportunities of examining. The felspar of these veins is remarkable for its purple hue, and it is found in large concretions, as is usual in the granite veins which traverse gneiss. Large masses of confusedly crystallized horneblende are also found dispersed throughout the gneiss.

A few veins of quartz are seen traversing the rock. These are of small dimension, not exceeding two or three inches in breadth, yet they present circumstances of some importance in the history of gneiss. It has been generally supposed that the quartz veins of this rock as well as those of mica slate, were of contemporaneous origin with the substances in which they lie, or, at least, that they have been formed by a secretion of quartz into cavities produced by the shrinking of the adjacent parts during the process of induration. But these veins are here attended by a distinct shifting of the rock which they traverse; a circumstance sufficient to prove their posteriority, and the forcible dislocation of the parts which bound them, at a period more recent than that at which the rocks acquired their form and disposition. In the instance under review the changes in the gneiss belong to two distinct periods, since it is first displaced by the intrusion of the granite vein, while the gneiss and the vein together are subsequently shifted by the quartz.

The last circumstance in Fudia worthy of notice, is the existence of oxidulous iron in the granite veins. This is accompanied by black mica, and forms detached masses of the size of an apple, or thereabout, protruding from the surface of the rock.

Although Hellesa and Gia correspond in every respect with Barra in structure and character, they exhibit one of the most striking features of that island in a still more accessible form. This is the passage of the trap veins through the gneiss. It is difficult, perhaps impossible, in Barra to trace the reticulations of the basalt to a principal mass: a geologist therefore, limiting himself to that island, might easily pass over the whole without remarking the phenomenon, or, if he observed it, remain unable to explain it for want of a clue. It is one of these recondite appearances in the disposition of rocks which points out the necessity of rigid and minute search combined with the more general view of broad and leading characters. On the shores of these small islands the larger trap veins are seen in various places, and they are easy of access. They are in general distinctly pointed out by the vacuities which the action of the sea has caused. The water gradually insinuates itself, not only between the walls of the veins and the body of the rock, but among the traverse rifts of the veins themselves, detaching them in masses which the waves wash away, leaving open rents and semi-cavernous appearances. These veins vary much from three to six feet in thickness, and are generally in an upright position, but affect no particular direction. It is not difficult to pursue their ramifications, which penetrate the adjacent rock, often to a considerable distance, producing the appearances already described in speaking of Barra. It will hereafter be seen that this phenomenon occurs in many other islands in this chain.

I may here add that as Wia, Fladda, and the smaller neighbouring islands, perfectly resemble these, as well as Barra, in structure, it is superfluous to make further mention of them.

KELP-MAKING[1]

Having mentioned the kelp of Loch Maddy, I may extend the remarks on this manufacture for a few lines; since it is almost the only one which may be said to exist in these islands, and since its establishment, although but recent, has made so material an addition to the value of these estates, and to the demand for labour. The total produce of the Western Islands in kelp varies from 5000 to 6000 tons, of which two thirds are the produce of the Long Island; the result of its highly indented shores, and of the consequent extent of surface, as well as of the superior tranquillity of the waters in which the plants grow. The variations in the price of this article, resulting from the varying competition of foreign commerce, are very considerable; and as the total expense of manufacture has been estimated on the average of £5 a ton, a considerable deduction must, in calculating the profit, be made from the market price, which at the time of my last visit was £10.

1 *Description of the Western Islands*, Vol. I, p. 120. Though this occurs in the chapter on North Uist it is relevant to Barra as kelp was also made there. It is now only made in South Uist.

That price has occasionally varied even to £20, causing differences of serious amount in the value of these estates. A great increase in the supply of foreign barilla, or the discovery of the long-attempted problem to decompose sea-salt by a cheap process, would destroy this most precarious source of profit;[1] since the interests concerned in it are too few, and the total advantages too insignificant, to claim the protection of restrictive laws. In general, it may be remarked, that the kelp is reserved by the proprietor, and manufactured on his account;[2] a very questionable piece of policy in some points of view. A large portion of the population is employed for the three summer months in the manufacture, which is so laborious and severe as to have no parallel in this country; certainly, at least, not at the same rate of wages. This labour has been called compulsory, and in one sense it may be considered a servitude, since it is generally the condition of tenure and either the whole or a portion of the rent by which the tenant holds his farm. If he were a free labourer, it is often said, he would not engage in so disagreeable a task. But this, although abstract-edly a painful view, is a false one, and is unjust as it regards the proprietors of estate; though casual visitors may sometimes be inclined to think that Highland proprietors have not yet forgotten their ancient habits of unrestricted sovereignty. It is a case of competition, and is the natural result of excess of population, combined with the absence of that proper and necessary division in an agricultural system which creates a class of independent labourers. The tenant must pay a fine for his farm, and he knows the price which he has to pay. That rent which he cannot procure by his surplus produce, he must pay by his labour, and as the system does not admit of a steady demand for work, he must labour when he can obtain it. An efficient and steady demand for labour might indeed affect the rate of wages, but it would scarcely leave the labourer the choice of refusing to work in the manufacture of kelp, when called on. He might imagine himself free, his wages might possibly be greater, but still he must work wherever there is work for him. It is plain moreover in this case, that as the surplus produce of his farm does not enable him to pay the rent, and he must find the money for it by his labour, no advantage is gained if he is merely to repay the money with one hand which he has received with the other. He may in fact be considered as a cottar, subject to the calls of his

1 The reduction of the duty on barilla in 1822, and the discovery of the Leblanc process of making soda from salt in 1823 fulfilled this prophecy.
2 This is still the case in South Uist.

employer, not so well situated perhaps, yet still as well as the state of the country admits.[1] It is even to be doubted whether, in many cases, anything short of this apparent compulsion could overcome the natural indolence and aversion to labour which, from whatever causes, is a strong feature in the character of the unimproved Highlander.[2]

As far as relates to the details of this manufacture, they seem to have been for some years past in a state of rapid improvement, and to have attained on many of the estates, in consequence of the attention of the proprietors or their agents, all the perfection of which they are susceptible. The time occupied in it, as I before remarked, is about three months, namely June, July and August. Driftwood, thrown on the shores by storms, and consisting chiefly of *fucus digitatus* and *saccharinus*, is used to a certain extent when fresh and uninjured, but the greater part is procured by cutting other plants of this tribe at low water. The method of landing the weed after cutting is simple and ingenious. A rope of heath or birch twigs is laid at low-water beyond the portion cut, and the ends are brought up on the shore. At high-water, the whole being afloat together, the rope is drawn at each end, and the included material is thus compelled at the retiring tide to settle on the line of high-water mark. The differences in the declivity of the shores therefore, as well as their linear extent, and the greater or less rise of the tide, together with more or less shelter from the prevalent surge, constitute the chief bases of the variations of a kelp estate. Soda[3] is well known to abound most in the hardest *fuci*, the *serratus, digitatus, nodosus,* and *vesiculosus.* On some estates they are cut biennially, on others once in three years, nor does it seem to be ascertained what are the relative advantages or disadvantages of these different practices. The weed is burnt in a coffer of stones, a construction which, however rude it may appear, seems fully adequate to the purpose.

Attempts have been made to introduce kilns of a more refined construction, which have failed from the most obvious cause, the expense of fuel necessary for their support; the inventors appearing to

1 MacCulloch's reasoning is not convincing. If the tenant is compelled to make kelp by a condition in this lease, he is clearly engaged in a servitude which would not be tolerated to-day. If the rent of his holding cannot be paid out of its surplus produce, then the rent is too great.
2 Since the seaweed from which the kelp was made was considered the property of the landlord, and since the tenant was forced on pain of losing his holding to work at the kelp during a time when he would have been far better employed on his croft, and since nearly the whole profits of the kelp went to the landlord, it is not surprising that the Highlanders did not take readily to this kind of labour.
3 Kelp is now burnt for iodine, not soda.

have forgotten that the substance in the ordinary mode of treatment formed its own fuel. The number of these fires which during summer are forever burning along the shores, give an interest and a life to these dreary scenes; recalling to the spectator's mind the activity of society in regions where all other traces of it are nearly invisible. The poet who indulges in visions of the days of old, may imagine the lighting of the war-fires, and fancy that he sees the signals which communicated the news of a Danish descent through the warlike clans.

The quantity of seaweed required to make a ton of kelp is estimated, as I have already noticed, at 24 tons, but varies according to the state of its moisture, and hence a conception of the labour employed in this manufacture may be formed, since the whole must be cut, carried on horses, spread out, dried, and stacked, before it is ready for burning.

It is a subject of frequent dispute whether the estates would gain more by the conversion of this material into manure, than by the kelp manufacture, but it is a question of too complicated a nature to admit of a ready answer. If it be admitted, as I believe the fact is, that there is at present a sufficiency of this and other manure already at the disposal of the small cultivator, the question is fruitless. If it be supposed that the mere diversion of the whole seaweed to the land would bring a larger portion of that into cultivation, it will then be easy to put the question, and to enter upon the calculations necessary to answer it. But this is not a correct view of the case. A different distribution of capital, population, and employment is required before large tracts of land can be effectually improved; and the diversion of the seaweed to this purpose is but a small part of that which is requisite to effect this object. When such alterations shall take place in the state of capital, population, tenure, and the division of lands, as will doubtless arise in the gradual course of improvement, it will be time enough to examine this question;[1] and the solution will probably not be very difficult. In the mean time, while there is no such demand for it existing, and while the price of labour, however that labour be obtained, is such as to render it an object of profit to the landholder, it is futile to say that the making of kelp is not of advantage to the community. As a manufacture it furnishes employment to a half-employed population, and forms thereby a steady addition to its

1 Which is as much as to say that the large farmer shall be permitted the use of seaweed as manure, but not the small one.

means. What remains of the argument respecting the relative claims of kelp and agriculture on the seaweed, must necessarily be a mere question of the market price of the former compared with the price of production.

But another doubt has been started, of a more refined nature and of far less easy solution. It has been asserted that from short-sighted views respecting the profits of this manufacture, the proprietors have imagined they had an interest in a crowded population, by means of which the wages of labour were lowered, and a ready supply of it reserved for the purpose of making kelp. The consequences of such a policy, if it exists, would be to lower the rent of land as well as the price of labour, since a superfluous tenantry is here identical with an inadequate rent. As this proposition appears to contradict the common axiom respecting the effects of competition, it is proper to explain the cause. There is a point where, in this country, it ceases to have its usual effect and beyond which that effect becomes negative. From extreme subdivision arises bad cultivation, land imperfectly stocked, bad live stock, and consequent general poverty and inability. This result, if it were not everywhere apparent, would be proved by the increase of rent which has followed the consolidation of small farms, or, a diminution of competitors, such as these small competitors are. It is besides obvious, that the landholder who would increase his population for these ends, can only do it by offering his land on better terms than his neighbours.[1] In this way, the landlord who is proprietor of the land as well as the kelp, would lose on one side what he might gain on the other. It is plain that if the two properties were separate, the kelp-maker would have a correct view, of his own interest at least, in wishing for a crowded population, which, as far as they are separated, he actually has. Whether the proprietor of both has or has not is a mere question of contingency. In him, the practice of crowding the population, admitting it to be a fact, is a mere commercial speculation in which he sacrifices a given sum in the shape of rent, for the contingent acquisition of another in the shape of profit on kelp. He cannot well be so blind as not to perceive that he is paying the price of labour in two distinct shapes, and it is clearly his interest to ascertain the price at which he is the manufacturer of the

---

1 In this involved argument, MacCulloch gets tied up and contradicts himself. He has already stated that the Barra fisheries permit the landlord to let holdings which would otherwise be unletable (p. 98); the same was true of the kelp industry. It was a double source of profit to the landlords, and undoubtedly fostered overpopulation.

merchandize in which he deals. If his avarice or his ignorance are such as to render him a loser by his speculation, it is scarcely a subject for the interference of others:[1] like other speculations it has a natural tendency to rectify itself if wrong, and must be left to that freedom which ought alone to direct all the movements of commerce. It will I believe be admitted by many of those who are acquainted with these islands, that there are tracts of land now occupied by small tenantry at an inadequate rent and under inefficient management, which if well managed would return a considerably greater profit to the landholder, and possibly exceed that which under the present system he makes by his kelp. But the changes required for this improved management of the land are such as cannot occur under the present state of population, if we consider either its number or its distribution. To produce these changes by violent measures is difficult, as various attempts have proved; were we even to leave out of consideration the painful moral effects which follow all those sudden and violent changes, that operate on the state of population in a country. The changes have however commenced, and they cannot fail to spread. For the total benefit of the community, it is to be desired that they should, but it is also to be wished that they should take place with the least possible inconvenience and suffering to those who must, to some extent at least, be displaced.[2] When the land shall have been raised to its adequate value, and to the state of improvement of which it is susceptible, a class of independent labourers will naturally arise to accompany the change; and the manufacture of kelp, which has perhaps already been dwelt on too long, will be subjected to a new calculation.

1 No matter who else may suffer in consequence.
2 This laudable wish was unfortunately not fulfilled.

CHAPTER 10

The MacNeill Letters, 1805-1825

*

The following twenty-six letters,[1] which are here published for the first time, were written by Colonel Roderick MacNeill of Barra (c. 1755-1822) and General Roderick MacNeill of Barra (c. 1788-1863), the last two MacNeills of Barra, to the Rev. Angus MacDonald, parish priest of Barra from 1805 to 1825, and subsequently head of the Scots College at Rome. These letters possess very great interest. They were written at a time when the Highlands were beginning to undergo great social and economic changes, many of which were for the worse, and show, more vividly than any history could do, the difference between the attitude of the old and the new type of Highland chief towards his clansmen.

It is necessary here to give an account of contemporary conditions in the Highlands. As is well known, the defeat of the Rising of the Forty-Five had resulted in the complete overthrow of the old social system, with the result that the whole country had been reduced to a state of dejected aimlessness, stagnation, and discontent. The memories of the clan system remained strong as long as the generation that remembered them lived, but as soon as that had passed away, the scene was set for a rapid deterioration while the old ways were becoming forgotten and the new ones but imperfectly learnt. Much voluntary emigration took place under these conditions between 1760 and 1790, and later in Barra, where Colonel MacNeill deplores "the loss of so many very decent people" in 1817.[2] He was the last proprietor of Barra to express regret at the emigration of his tenants.

It is not easy to bring home to the modern reader how much a change of this kind involves. Forcible conquest and assimilation is not a very congenial process for the conquered. It meant in this case the enforced uprooting of centuries-old habits and customs, and the violent alteration of a traditional outlook and way of life. It meant that there was neither hope nor future for any who followed the old ways or held to the old loyalties. Apart from the humiliation of defeat, the transition from clan to private ownership of land entailed profound social and economic dislocation. That shrewd and penetrating observer, Dr Johnson, whose sympathetic insight into the social

---

1 Now in the possession of the Rev. Dr Donald Campbell, Dalibrog.
2 See p. 126.

conditions of the Highlands in 1773 has not gained the appreciation of Highlanders that it deserves, describes this change as follows:

> "The Chiefs, divested of their prerogatives (i.e., the rights of hereditary jurisdiction) necessarily turned their thoughts to the improvement of their revenues, and expect more rent, as they have less homage. The tenant, who is far from perceiving that his condition is made better in the same proportion as that of his landlord is made worse, does not immediately see why his industry is to be taxed more heavily than before. He refuses to pay the demand, and is ejected; the ground is then let to a stranger, who perhaps brings a larger stock, but who, taking the land at its full price, treats with the Laird upon equal terms, and considers him not as Chief, but as a trafficker in land. Thus the estate perhaps is improved, but the clan is broken."[1]

Barra was very fortunate in that this deterioration in the relations between chief and clansmen (or proprietor and tenants) did not begin until 1822, fifty years after Dr Johnson wrote, and even after the Clearances had started in Sutherlandshire. Colonel Roderick MacNeill, the grandson and successor of the MacNeill who was imprisoned in 1746 for his Jacobite sympathies, is shown by his letters, as well as by the testimony of the Rev. Edward MacQueen[2] and the Rev. Alexander Nicolson,[3] to have been a chief of the old type, warmly attached to his tenants and his property. His relationship between him and them was still personal and not commercialized.

At this time, the chief industries in Barra were fishing, agriculture, and kelp-making. As far as the small tenants were concerned, the agriculture in Barra as in other unenclosed areas in Scotland was conducted on the runrig system.[4] That is, the arable land was held in common by the tenants of the township, who cast lots periodically for the assignation of the various shares. No person had a title to any particular piece of land; but each tenant in the township had a title to a certain proportion of the arable area. These portions were often divided into smaller portions which were situated in different parts of the area, the whole being divided up in a very complicated way. The advantages of the system were, that every tenant had land of approximately identical quality as apart from quantity; labour could be done communally,

1 *Journey to the Hebrides*, p. 129 (1925 edition).
2 See pp. 57 and 66.
3. See p. 163.
4 See Alexander Carmichael's account of runrig in the Outer Hebrides in *Celtic Scotland*, Vol. III, by W. F. Skene.

and every one had an interest in the welfare of the township. *The drawbacks were, the lack of enclosures with consequent straying of stock on to the cultivated land, the difficulty of keeping the land cleaned of weeds, the difficulty in developing new rotations of crops, and the frequent necessity for one cultivator to cross his neighbours' patches on his way to his own. It was a complex system, of which the social advantages were probably outweighed by the agricultural drawbacks. It was rapidly being abandoned on the Mainland at this time, and in Colonel MacNeill's letters there are several references to the desirability of enclosing and dividing the cultivated land, showing that he was anxious to adopt what was then the principle agricultural improvement.*[1] *The exact date that runrig ceased in Barra is not ascertainable, though Michael Buchanan, aged 40 in* 1883, *the chief Barra witness to the Crofters' Commission, told the Commissioners that runrig had been practised in his grandfather's time. Colonel MacNeill was obviously much interested in farming, and his remarks about the desirability of giving security of tenure to small tenants were very much in advance of the opinions of his contemporary proprietors.*

Kelp-making, which was introduced into the Highlands and Islands in 1765, *was for about fifty years highly remunerative to the proprietors, and in a much lesser degree profitable to their tenants. How profitable kelp must have been to the proprietors can be judged from the fact that the tenants, who were bound by a condition of their tenure to make the kelp, were receiving for their labour about £2, 5s. a ton at times when the kelp was selling at from £16 to £22 a ton, practically the entire difference, less freightage, representing profit to the estate.*[2] *Moreover, on the basis of this new profitable employment, the proprietors were actually able to raise the rents, thus making a double gain. Dr Johnson writes* (1773):

> "*They have lately found a manufacture considerably lucrative. Their rocks abound with kelp, a sea-plant, of which the ashes are melted into glass. They burn kelp in great quantities, and then send it away in ships, which come regularly to purchase them. This new source of riches has raised the rents of many maritime farms; but the tenants pay, like all other tenants, the additional rent with great unwillingness; because they consider the profits of the kelp as the mere product of personal labour, to which the landlord contributes nothing.*"[3]

In 1794 *Colonel MacNeill was paying £2, 12s. 6d. a ton for kelp from the*

1 See pp. 127 and 134.
2 *Public Administration in the Highlands*, p. 85.
3 *Journey to the Hebrides*, p. 110.

THE BOOK OF BARRA

people's own shores, "the highest price given in the Highlands."[1] This is a tribute to his generosity as compared with others, but with 200 tons of kelp which fetched "the best price that is given for any that is sent from any part of the Highlands"[2] leaving Barra annually for Leith and Liverpool, his profits must have been considerable. The price of kelp began to fall in 1814. In 1817 the reduction of the duty on salt—a benefit for the fishing industry—depressed it further. In 1818 Colonel MacNeill complains of his losses on kelp. In 1822 the industry was deliberately abandoned, with the direct results to the Highlands, by the reduction of the duty of barilla. The development of the Leblanc process, which was started in England in 1823, finished kelp as a source of soda.[3]

General MacNeill succeeded his father in 1822. Colonel MacNeill, though a benevolent landlord, does not seem to have been a good business man, for his heir complains bitterly of debts and a settlement in favour of the younger children that was beyond the estate's means to support, and says later that he got the estate in a heavily burdened condition.[4] If this were the case, it is clear that General MacNeill must have found himself in a very difficult position. It is hardly likely that his difficulties were lightened by his attitude towards his people, which was not the traditional attitude of a chief towards his Clansmen. General MacNeill marked the new order of things in Barra. The worst was still to come; but from being a happy community organized on the system of combined autocracy and communism of the clan system, Barra became a commercialized estate, soon to be owned by absentees and managed by factors and other inter-mediaries, many of whom were strangers to the Highlands, and some of whom do not seem to have been too particular about their trust, if the stories told to the Crofters' Commission in 1883 have any foundation. In common with much of the rest of the Highlands Barra was to enter in 1822 an era of poverty and depression from which it did not even begin to emerge for two generations; and the principle cause of this poverty was that the high rents charged when the kelp industry was paying were not reduced after the industry had collapsed.[5]

It is difficult for a Highlander to write about these times with perfect objectivity. Under the prevailing economic theory of laissez faire, next to nothing was done by the Government at Westminster to promote the welfare of such comparatively remote and unprofitable regions of Scotland as Barra. In the absence of any popularly-elected Scottish Legislature, the emancipation of the

---

1 See p. 57.
2 See p. 66.
3 Kelp is now burnt as a source of iodine, though not in Barra.
4 See p. 135.
5 See p. 164.

Highland crofters was forced to wait upon the slowly flowing tide of English public opinion. In such circumstances even the most progressive and patriotic of Highland landlords could do little to enable his people to achieve permanent prosperity or assist them to develop a sense of independence such as is to be found today amongst the peasantry of Norway. Secure for a long time from State interference, the Highland and Island estates were in fact administered like little kingdoms; where no security of tenure existed, the threat of ejection could obtain obedience to the most oppressive of estate rules and regulations.[1]

In times when there were no old age pensions, no unemployment insurance, no free education, no Government grants for roads,[2] piers, or schools, and no loans for building, a Highland proprietor like General MacNeill had to make his property pay or run the risk of having a destitute population left on his hands after a series of bad years, for whose welfare he would be almost entirely responsible. Had the principle of State aid been established as early as 1840, it is certain that many proprietors would not have resorted, as Colonel Gordon later did, to enforced emigration in order to solve the problem of destitution caused by the potato famine. The solution of such problems was beyond the power of individual proprietors, however well disposed and patriotic.

General MacNeill's expressed intention to secure himself "an ample harvest" came to nothing. He had come into kelp on a falling market, and in 1827, five years after succeeding to the property, became bankrupt. Trustees took over the administration of Barra, which was sold in 1838 to Colonel Gordon of Cluny. In the year of his bankruptcy General MacNeill left Barra, never to return, and no proprietor of the island has ever resided in it since. Between 1821 and 1831 the population of the island fell from 2303 to 2097, though the Protestants, who were all strangers, increased from 60 in 1813 to 380 in 1840. It is evident that General MacNeill had partly carried out his threat to replace Catholic by Protestant tenants. Some indication of the regard in which he was held is given by the fact that the Rev. Alexander Nicolson, who warmly praises his father, is most guarded in his references to General MacNeill; and one of the witnesses who appeared before the Crofters' Commission in 1883, John MacPherson from Kentangaval, tells a striking story of extortions committed by the General's estate officers. Today, General MacNeill is remembered in Barra as heavy-handed and irascible, though not without a certain regard as the last of a long line of native chiefs and proprietors. Doubtless the recollection of the later Gordon Clearances and absenteeism has

---

1 See Appendix A of the *Report of the Crofters' Commission*, pp. 297-300, where the Estate of Reay Regulations in force in 1826 are given.
2 Military roads had been built in parts of the Mainland, but that was all.

benefited General MacNeill's memory by comparison. For all that, his letters cannot commend him to any impartial reader.

*

I

Chester the 23 November 1805.

Dear Sir,

I with much pleasure embrace this opportunity of answering your favor a considerable time since. As to the business of your house: the rash and inconsiderate conduct of a predecessor of yours, rendered necessary for me to be carefull of my rights.[1] Any house built on my property is of course at my command. I am sorry that at Gariemore[2] was not better on your arrival.

I am not disposed, in the least, to doubt the sincerity of your intentions to curb vice: at same time you will excuse my recommending a very particular caution in not interfering with the Laws of the Kingdom which are fully adequate to all punishments, beyond Church censure. It will give me pleasure to be in good habits with you, as with those more worthy, of your predecessors. The late Bishop M'Donald, I considered as my particular friend, as well as the worthy man Mr Allan Mor his Brother: both men of enlightened understandings and liberality.

The Clergyman in yours as in all situations, has it in his power to do much good. I hope your influence will be employed in promoting the happiness of your paritioners, by recommending morality, the habits of sobriety and industry, with loyalty and a proper sense of the blessings enjoy'd under our happy constitution. Pray excuse these hints such matters are apt to be overlook'd in remote situations.

I congratulate you on our late glorious success:[3] purchased however at a dear rate, by the life of the renowned Neilson. His last victory has given security to his native Country, even influenced the affairs of Europe.

So far from my wish to check any comforts you can have in your

---

1 This, as well as the remark in the second paragraph 'with those more worthy, of your predecessors' refers to the Rev. James Allan MacDonnell, priest in Barra from 1784-1805, with whom Colonel MacNeill was on very bad terms. See *The Clan Macneil*, p. 147.
2 Near Borve.
3 Trafalgar.

present situation: it will give me pleasure to contribute towards them.
I am Dear Sir, yours most sincerely

Roderick M'Neil.

*

II

The Rev. Mr Angus M'Donald
Garriemore
Barra
Dunvegan, Carinish
N. Britain.

Prospect Place near Liverpool[1]
the 20th April 1809.

Dear Sir,
I received your kind favor of the 9th November, I need not say long
since, various matters prevented my making an answer for some time:
and latteraly the necessity of my going to attend my son[2] at
Portsmouth.

You will be pleas'd to know, that tho: in a dangerous state on his
return from Spain, he is now as well as to be able to travel and is now
with his grandfather[3] at Fassfern.

As I do not propose being in the Country early, it would give me
pleasure that you the Parson[4] and Watersay[5] meet at Borve and make
such Regulations as seem to you best, as to the subject you mention:
Ewen M'Donnel of course will be with you.

Dogs are a great Nuisance, but to this there is an easy remedy, as
such as choose to keep them will have to pay the Tax for Dogs which
at present I pay for the whole Country.

1 Colonel MacNeill's writing so frequently from Liverpool may perhaps be explained by the fact
that his kelp was in part shipped there. See p. 66.
2 Roderick MacNeill, his heir.
3 Sir Ewen Cameron of Fassfern.
4 Rev. Edmund MacQueen. See p. 54.
5 Donald MacNeill, tacksman of Vatersay.

The season has been very fair over all England. In haste to overtake the Post.
Yours sincerely

Roderick M'Neil.

*

III

The Revd. Mr Angus M'Donald
Barra.

Liverpool the 6th June 1816.

My Dear Sir,
It is now some considerable time since I heard from you. Reports have of late come to me, of a spirit of Emigration from your Parish; but having no hint from you on the subject, I paid little attention to them. Matters, however, are now so far settled: a considerable number having signed (as it is called) with a Mr Fraser.[1]

It is no doubt distressing to my feelings, that People to whom I am so much attached, should leave me: but if it is was for their good, I should regret it the less.

From the terms, this man has made with the people, I must think, they are far too high: freights and provisions are very low. I have not a doubt much better terms, could be made: this very day, I learn, that Vessells are going out to America in ballast. The saving of two, or three pounds, for each passenger, would amount to a very large sum for a family. Were it agreeable, I would with pleasure do all that was possible to save the small means of those people, and so, let their situation be better, when they get to America. Mr Fraser, acts as a job to get money, and his profits would be better in the pockets of the Passengers.

I shall make the proper enquiry, and be prepared in a few days to write you by Post, what they are.

I am not quite decided, as to going home this season: but if I can be of use to these people, whether my own business requires it or not, I will not hesitate to go.

1 See p. 59. Emigration agents were active in the Highlands at this time; they had an interest in securing passengers, who in some cases were induced to go by baseless promises.

The People may be quite easy as to their signing, with this man: he has no legal claim on them. The mark, if not before a Justice of Peace, and two wittnesses, is of no avail. I shall be anxious to hear from you.— With my best wishes I am, Yours truly

Roderick M'Neil.

If I recollect, some of the people lost money by this very Mr Fraser, some time since—John M'Kinnon late of Nask.
Please say where the Emigrants wish to go in America.

*

IV

The Revd. Mr Angus M'Donald
Priest, Barra.

Liverpool the 25th June 1816.

My Dear Sir,
I received your favor of the 13th May some time since: it justifys the opinion I had, and which I expressed to you by letter some little time since, that when there was anything going on in the Country, that I should be acquainted with, I might depend on hearing from you.

In the building a Chapel, I will with pleasure accede to what you think but[1] for the accomodation of your Parishioners. As to the *Glebe*, there is nothing in the Island of Barra, will give me more pleasure, than to see it: the least portion, but the best cultivated.

I have made enquiry here, and at other places, and at Clyde and the East Country as to the terms on which ships can be engaged for Passengers. The answers made me, are, that it is much too soon for any thing of the kind, for some time to come, as the freights may change, from various causes: but that at present freights are exceeding low, as well as provisions and consequently the terms must be very reasonable. From this it is clear to me, that Mr Fraser, in his bargain with the people, must make *very high terms*, as in the event of war, or any disturbance of any kind, that may tend to raise the freights, it will otherwise be impossible for him to fulfil his bargain, without help: in

1 *i.e.*, only.

which case disappointment to the poor people is the certain consequence. Had these people (or did they still) apply to me I would save them Mr Fraser's profit: for they cannot but believe me more ready (for many good reasons) to serve them for *love*, than Mr Fraser. As to the threat of penalty he has employ'd to secure himself profit: there is no one, so ignorant, as not to know that a signature by Mark not made [before a][1] Justice of Peace and two witnesses has no force in Law.

It will give me pleasure to have the Country news by the kelp Vessell in case it is not my fortune to be in the Country this season. Yours truly

Roderick M'Neil.

*

V

The Revd. Mr Angus M'Donald
Craigston, Barra
by Dunvegan, Carinish
North Britain.

Liverpool the 8th August 1816.

My Dear Sir,
Having been in Chesshire for some time, on my return here I found your favors of the 8th, and 24th July, both of which are now before me. The interest you take in the wellfare of your Parisioners does you much credit: it is what I would have expected from you. I would have made the Poor a further allowance, but that I had accounts of the Jolly Major[2] having left Greenock at the time I received your letter.

How soon I understood that a portion of the Emigrants were Redemptioners,[3] I doubted I would be of no use to them. You are aware, it would not answer me or any one not in America to interfere

---

1 Letter torn.
2 Major MacDonald, afterwards factor of Barra. See p. 73.
3 Emigrants who received their passage to America on the condition that their services there should be disposed of by the owners or the master of the vessel, until the passage-money and other expenses were repaid out of their earnings. (*Oxford English Dictionary.*)

with such: indeed such traffic is not congenial to my feelings. I confess I am hurt, that any man in Barra, should want confidence in me, much more, think me capable of abusing his confidence. To such, all I have to say, is that I wish them much good fortune with their favorite.

However willing to give myself trouble and incur expense, for these good people, they cannot expect that I should feed them with false representations and delusive hopes: I leave that art to others. Now it appears that they would have come forward generally, I would have thought it my duty, to go to the Country immediately and done for the best according to their wishes, as far as lay in my power: but their suspitions are so revolting to me, that I must for the present decline any interference whatever. I can at no time have any thing to do with wild plans: but if at a future period a proper number come forward in a temperate manner, my wish to please them is such, that I would do all in my power to forward their views.

As to Country arrangements, you may be assured much attention, will be paid to your recommendations, but some time hence, those matters may be spoken of, and in the mean time, nothing rash or hasty will be done. I have at all times been willing to come forward for the protection of the people of Barra, nor will their having sign'd make any change in me: the threats made use of are idle and ridiculous. When the extent of matters is known, I will be glad to hear from you: the merits of those y[ou][1] mention are known to me: Hector M'Kenzie Glen[2] and his family, I am very much inclin'd to serve, I know their attachment to me which has been at all times steady.

Independent of matters of greater moment, it will give me pleasure to hear from you, as to the state of your *Glebe* and Country news.

Yours at all times, truly

Roderick M'Neil.

You will see by the Papers the general state of distress everywhere.

*

1 Letter torn.
2 Near Castlebay.

VI

The Revd. Mr Angus M'Donald
Barra.

Liverpool the 28th May 1817.

My Dear Sir,
I have no recollection whither I heard from you or wrote you last. I could not think of losing so good an oportunity of sending a bill of health. My concerns are much as usual: Roderick[1] has been dangerously ill, but thank God he is better for some little time, and is now at Cheltenham, in a convalescent state.

I am sure you are heartily tired of Emigrants concerns: the loss of so many very decent people, is much to be regretted: at same time, those who remain, will in time, be much better: this reflection always offers us something consolatory, when one reflects, he has seen for the last time, those he has been accustom'd to from early infancy. I promise myself much pleasure in seeing your territory but I regret circumstances, I cannot command, will prevent my being home before the middle of August.

This is the third Vessell, that will be in the Country waiting kelp: so hope all exertions will be made to send them off.
Yours truly

Roderick M'Neil.

A supply of different matters (of which I have, but imperfect information) goes to the Country: you with Mr Nicleson,[2] the Factor, and Watersay will arrange as to Poor.

Roderick M'Neil.

*

1 His son.
2 Church of Scotland minister in Barra; see p. 149.

VII

The Revd. Mr Angus M'Donald
Barra.

Liverpool the 1st September 1818.

My Dear Sir,
I have your letter of the 8th July from Glasgow, long since, and I take the oportunity of my young Nephew[1] to write you. I do not recollect if I acquainted you with my Son's marriage:[2] it gives me pleasure to say it is entirely to my satisfaction: the family is most respectable: the Father has a large fortune (15000 a year) the portion is not large (6000) but there is a prospect of more. Her elder brother is Member for Armagh.

That your Glebe is in the best order possible gives me pleasure to think, and it would seem to me as if what you do begins to be noticed by the Country, and to have influence. I am entirely of your opinion as to the bad effects of the precarious tenure[3] of his little portion the Tenant has his land.

Things of that kind, only require beginning, and might come but from the Tenants themselves. It seems to me desirable, that all the hay grounds, and as much as possible of the ground for labouring were divided, in large portions, so as to encourage the clearing of stone, enclosing etc.

What you have done is clear to all: could you influence your neighbours it would give me pleasure. Should any thing of this kind be done, to any considerable extent, and represented to me: the division should be permanent to any one, who clear'd or enclosed.

My wish is that the Factor may accomodate you as to timber as far as possible: I would have written him to this effect, but that I know he is now, on his way south.

I fear we shall be short of kelp this year, but the price will make up in some measure.

Many many thanks for your kind letters; I assure you, they are most

1 Not identified.
2 To Isabella, daughter of Lieutenant Colonel Charles Brownlow of Lurgan, County Armagh, who himself married MacNeill's daughter Jane as his second wife in 1828, and was created Lord Lurgan of Lurgan in 1839.
3 See p. 85.

acceptable: nothing gives me more pleasure than to hear from friends, and particularly, from that little corner.
Yours truly

Roderick M'Neil.

My friend Mr James M'Donald of this place often talks of you: I believe he thinks well of you and your Glebe; he mention'd something to me, and I request you may make yourself easy, on the subject: you will not doubt I will do all that can be done with propriety.

Roderick M'Neil.

*

VIII

The Revd. Mr Angus M'Donald
Craigston
Barra.

Liverpool the 27th December 1818.

My Dear Sir,
I receiv'd your's of the 9th November only three days since, and your's of the 11 same month only yesterday. The account you give me of your little Glebe, gives me infinite pleasure. One would naturally suppose such an example would do much, but alas, I fear a Clergyman's example may be treated as that of others: *it is easy for them*: in your case however I earnestly wish it may be the other way. Your Brother shall have half of Bolinabodigh,[1] on a lease of seven years, on condition you engage for his good conduct, and endeavours at improvement: of course he will have your advice.

On the subject of a letter written by you for William M'Millan:[2] I have not the least idea that this Man can forward, or retard emigration: that depends on circumstances beyond his reach and mine and I should rather suppose he is an illiterate man, not likely to be trusted by (a) ship owner in any seaport town, and certainly not

1 Buaile nam Bodach, near Northbay.
2 See p. 196.

likely to make the necessary arrangements, so as to let others disposed to trust him have common justice. I have never come into any terms, with any man, in such circumstances: if I thought it right, which I do not, it is out of the question: you had no sooner, as you thought, brib'd one, than another starts up, wo . . .[1]

However, as you seem to take an interest in this man, if he makes an offer of proper terms by your interference, I will return you an answer: I shall judge of his views by his offer.

My loss this year is very great from neglect, I cannot say how much, I mean as to defitiency of kelp: I fear I have suffer'd loss, as to farming also: for some time a doubt has been on my mind. Had a late person indulged in drink, to your knowledge. I have given Mr Alexr. Nicleson[2] full power to do for me, in the meantime, as I cannot get home at this late season: I have directed him to cause the kelp shores to be survey'd by proper persons, I cannot think all has been right, in that particular: but the survey will do me justice.

When I get home, I will use every exertion, that the land, and hay, are permanently divided: those for and against it will show me, who I must look to and who not.

The season has been very mild here as yet. My worthy friend Boisdale[3] did not long survive coming South.

Yours truly

Roderick M'Neil.

Should divisions take place without my interference, it wont give me pleasure. When you have a spare hour, I shall be glad to hear from you.

1 Undecipherable.
2 See p. 149.
3 Alexander MacDonald of Boisdale, MacNeill's brother-in-law.

NOTE
The Rev. D.J. Rankin, Iona, Cape Breton, Canada, has very kindly given me information about the destination in Canada of the early emigrants from Barra. I quote his own words:—"In the year 1784 Barra people who had served in the War of the American Revolution settled at Arisaig, Nova Scotia (Antigonish County). They were MacNeils, and the Government got for them large grants of land, some of which is now occupied by their descendants. In 1801 several people from Barra came to what is now Iona, and later were joined by a great many others, till around the Bras d'Or lakes became all settled by people from the Island of Barra. Then they spread to St Peter's, Christmas Island, and Washahuck. There were also a great many people of Barra origin settled at Mabou among the Lochabar people there. The people who settled at Mabou Harbour came there about 1805, and probably 1808, and they were later joined by those who settled around the Bras d'Or lakes."

IX

The Revd. Mr Angus M'Donald
Craigston, Barra
by Dunvegan and Carinish
North Britain.

Liverpool the 22 February 1819.

My Dear Sir,
I duly receiv'd your's of the 18th December 1818, as also your's of the 28th January. I as always feel most thankfull for your kind communications from the Country.

As to your Brother,[1] all that is necessary, is to show my letter to our friend the Major, who you will be pleas'd to know, has accepted the management of my concerns in the Country; to whom I will refer you as to all other matters, till I come home, which will be early in summer.

I know the Major has much respect and regard for you, and I am sure, he will do all possible for him to accomodate you. I shall be most anxious to see your gras etc. on the Glebe, and you will not doubt I love to encourage good farming. Mr M'Lean had been recommended very much to me from different quarters: but the Major's acceptance, put this matter at rest. As to the man that offers for Flodda,[2] I refer to the Major, at same time, I confess, he seems to me to expect to be brib'd, which will not do: there would be no end to such matters.

Watersay mentions your great kindness and attentions during Mrs M'Neil's[3] illness. I have now only to request, you will offer the Major any thing that occurs to you: at same time I by no means give up your correspondence, on the contrary, I will be most happy to hear from you as often as your time admits.
Yours truly

Roderick M'Neil.

*

---

1 See p. 128.
2 Presumably a sheep farmer.
3 Mrs Donald M'Neil, wife of the tacksman of Vatersay.

X

The Revd. Mr Angus M'Donald
Craigston
Barra.

Liverpool the 26th June 1819.

My Dear Sir,
I thought to have answered your letter of the 5th May more at leisure, but I find I must content myself with giving you a bill of health for the present, I regret this the less, as I am sure my friend the Major will do all to your wishes: you and he are both very *wise* and reasonable and cannot but understand each other.

You will be pleas'd to know I have accounts of Roderick[1] from Milan of the 8th on his way to Florence. The other branches of my family all are as usual. I shall be most anxious to see *your* Glebe: I am glad the Parson is your rival and Watersay has lately made a park[2] to show, what he can do.

I owe you many thanks for your very kind attention to my Sister during her very serious illness. I hope to see you ere long.
Yours truly

Roderick M'Neil.

*

XI

The Revd. Mr Angus M'Donald
Barra.

Liverpool the 10th May 1820.

My Dear Sir,
It is long since I have had the pleasure to hear from you. My friend Mr M'Donald of this place proposes to pass some time in his native air: may I beg to recommend him to your kind civility.

1 His son.
2 *i.e.*, an enclosure.

My son Roderick has been about looking round him for some time; my last letter from him was from Rome: he then propos'd being in England in this month. My younger son Ewen was last winter at Edinburgh University and is just gone to Fassfern:[1] the other parts of my family are as usual.

You are well out of the way of Radicalism indeed there has been enough of that matter in other parts.[2]

If you will not give me Country news what would be most acceptable, you will say something of farming matters particularly your own. I have written Mr Niceson of this date beging to know as to his farming: it is not too much to say you and he are about the best Clergy farmers to be met with in most places, of which I am, I can assure you, not a little proud. What is Watersay doing: he has rather a better field than you have.

Yours truly

Roderick M'Neil.

*

XII

The Revd. Mr Angus M'Donald
Craigston
Barra.

Liverpool the 15th August 1820.

My Dear Sir,
I have your letters of the 30th May and 13th July before me.

Your accounts of Country matters are at all times most acceptable: am truly glad you are satisfy'd as to the Craigston Crofters. A Clergyman has it in his power to do much good in other places, besides his Church, and while instructing his unenlighten'd neighbours, to turn their land to the best advantage, it cannot be doubted his time is well employ'd. That you and the Parson, give each

1 Cameron of Fassfern was MacNeill's father-in-law.
2 There was a General Strike in Glasgow, followed by clashes between troops and strikers, in consequence of which 24 strikers were afterwards condemned to death and three were actually executed.

other the best example in farming, and indeed all other aspects, gives me pleasure: tho: it is not *absolutely* necessary, you should go the length of taking a wife.

In doing your motives in all you have done, all possible justice, I may assure you, I have every will to do what is reasonable. The person in whom I confide, is at this time, and will be for a few months on the Continent, so that I can do nothing decisif: in the mean time will you have the goodness at your leisure to state in precise words, your particular wishes, whether as fier, or melieuratier,[1] specifying the sum to which that is limitted. By the time my confidential man returns, I will have your answer, when, I will write you on the subject, and I have no doubt all will be arrang'd to your satisfaction. As to general news, you will have it better by the papers, than if I were to say any thing on the subject. We have at present fine warm weather.
Yours truly

Roderick M'Neil.

*

XIII

The Revd. Mr Angus M'Donald
Craigston, Barra
by Dunvegan & Carinish
North Britain.

Liverpool the 13th November 1820.

My Dear Sir,
I receiv'd your's of the 20th September long since, and am most gratefull for all the acceptable information contain'd in it; feeling much interest in all that concerns the Country, and your being my best correspondent. A year is no fair trial, and it will be seen next season, who is the most successfull, the Priest, Parson or Watersay; for it seems the Major has no chance: tho: I hope in time he may, at same time I cannot help confessing I am more anxious of his success in kelp, than farming.

1 Improver.

Will at your leisure have the goodness to state if the sums you mention are for what has been done, or for that, and what you propose doing. I will say nothing of what has occupy'd the general attention so long, your Papers will tell all.[1]

There has been much rain for the latter part of last month and first days of this month: for the last ten days the weather has been very fine and dry. I shall be anxious to hear from you the state of the harvest and Country news. I would have written before now, but that I was in hopes of an oportunity to save you postage,[2] which has failed. Yours truly

Roderick M'Neil.

*

XIV

The Revd. Mr Angus M'Donald
Barra.
From Capt. Hannah.

Liverpool the 9th August 1821.

My Dear Sir,
It is only by a letter from Watersay by Capt. Hannah that I learnt you were ailing, and the same letter to my great pleasure informs me you were better. I hope all that I will have to regret in this ailment, is the having deprived me of a letter from you, usually so full of informations I so much value, and that by this time you are reestablish'd in health. I hope by next trip Capt. Hannah will bring accounts of your crops and gras.

I am much pleas'd that Watersay reaps so much benefit, from his park, and I hope your example, Mr Nicleson's, and his, will at last have influence, and make the tenants wish to have a small spot they can call their own. The weather has taken a change here, and we have rain enough: I hope with you, a change may still benefit the Country.

I hope you have been comfortable in your home and that the

---

1 This probably refers to the troubles between George IV and Queen Caroline.
2 In those days the postage on letters was paid by the recipient.

advantages of your Cathedral are felt, as they ought. They are building a very large Place of worship here for those of your perswasion.
Yours as always truly

Roderick M'Neil.

*

Colonel MacNeill died in 1822. The remaining letters are from his son and heir, who became later, as he is called here, General MacNeill.

*

XV

London, October 27, 1823.

My Dear Sir,
Believe me your well meant advice so far from offending gave me pleasure; you were not aware how matters stood—no man aware of the (to me) ruinous nature of the Deeds executed by my late father could concientiously advise me to submit to them. With reference to his actual income and enormous debt, they were, to say the least, absurd; I was literally tied to the stake, having no alternative but to reduce them, or consign myself and family to penury—all that man could do, I did, to avoid the expence and vexation of a Lawsuit—I proposed arbitration, and offered provisions to the younger children far beyond my ability, as admitted by several of the Trustees, and all to no effect— evil counsel prevailed. In those of whom, from near connection I had a right to expect justice, if nothing more, I found only duplicity, and a want of candour quite incredible.

However, as I shall in all human probability be at Barra in the course of Dbr, shall say no more till we meet on the hateful subject, further than to inform you that beyond a doubt a very short time will put me in possession, when I shall not slumber in idleness.

Mrs Macneil I am happy to say is well and looking well, but being in an interesting situation I don't think it prudent that she should journey with me this time. My little girl is both healthy and funny.

Remember me to your brother Pastor and his fair Lady and all *friends.*

Tell the Major I shall write from Edinbro—I go by Liverpool. I remain, in haste, but yours truly

R. MacNeil.

*

XVI

London, October Twenty seven 1823.

Revd. Angus MacDonald
Barra
Inverness shire.
C. Brownlow.   N.B.

My Dear Sir,
Pray tell the Major with my compliments that if he has not written in reply to my last, by the time you receive these few lines, that he will oblige me by directing to me at Edinbro. My best regards to Mrs Macdonald and him. Shall not expect to hear from you, but when we meet must have a budget of news.

R.M.

*

XVII

The Revd. Angus Macdonald
Barra.

Edinburgh, 20th March 1824.

My Dear Sir,
Mr Macleod now factor for me at Barra, will put these few lines into your hands, and I have no doubt you will find pleasure in being of every possible use to him, unacquainted as he is with the Characters of the people he will have to transact with.

I very much regret I cannot repair to Barra now, but shall be with you in course of the summer to put matters to rights. I wish you to effect a *great* diminution in the number of holydays, and on my way to the Country I shall certainly personally explain my views to the Bishop of Lismore. My anxious wish is to make the people industrious and comfortable, but they *must* work or they will not do for me. Possessing as you do unbounded influence over your flock, I look to you for the most cordial cooperation.

You are the only person connected with my property, from whom I have experienced a friendly disposition during the time it was in other hands, this I cannot easily forget.
Believe me dear Sir, Yours sincerely

R. MacNeil.

*

XVIII

London, May Ten 1824.

The Revd. Angus MacDonald
Barra By Dunveggan
M. Forde. Inverness shire.

Address under cover to Charles Brownlow Esq.,
Clarendon Hotel, Bond Street, London, May 8th 1824.

My Dear Sir,
Before I proceed to notice the subjects successively on which you have touched, I must put you right as to Mr Macleod, who believe me does nothing without my approbation and acts entirely by my directions in everything. He tells me that he had derived from you the most cordial assistance—depend upon it he will not be turned from his duty to his employer, by *any monitors.*

The fishing as now carried on (or rather as it has been) if of little benefit to the tenants generally, and a decided loss to the Landlord— a great portion of the fisherman's time has hitherto been taken up in navigating his little bark to Glasgow, and upon arriving there he found himself compelled by necessity to sell at what price *the Huxters choose to give him.* I know also that several of my tenants made a practice for several years past of disposing of fish *to strangers* on the coast, for inferior and dear tobacco, and other articles in barter. I know too, that little or no *rent* has been paid (whatever other purposes the money may have been applied to) by the tenants with the profits of their fishing.[1] The tenants have always been very glad, nay even clamorous, to be supplied with meal and salt, why if they have such a fancy to go several hundred miles for what supplies they may require (rather than have their wants provided for on terms much more advantageous than they could make for themselves, and that too at their very doors)— Why, I say, did they not buy their meal and salt at Glasgow also? Do they mean to say to me, *you may* supply us with meal and salt, because we cannot bring it home in sufficient quantities ourselves, but we much prefer *spending our money at Glasgow* to paying you the rent *justly due* to you? This my good sir is the *plain English* of the case, and applies to the young men not holding land just as much as the others—those young men are the *sons, grandsons* and *Nephews* of the occupiers of the land, they are *fed and housed* by them, in short they are fed and housed on my land and pay me not a shilling. I trust you will now perceive that I know what I am about well enough to see the absurdity of the idea of what you call the spirits of the young lads being dampt, and dampt by what, by having the means of prosecuting useful industry supplied to them by their Landlord instead of having to paddle to a distance for them. And now my dear sir let me request you will immediately on receipt of this tell all your parishioners, that although sufficiently disgusted with the manner in which you say my first attempts have been met, *I will persevere.* Any one of my tenants who choses to take his fish to Glasgow, or dispose of it in barter to strangers on the coast is of course at liberty to do so. But then again they must recollect that I have an equal right to dispose of my lands as I may think most advisable; and they much deceive themselves, if they think that opposition or obstacles, (and I anticipate some) will turn me from what I conceive the best course—you will tell them all that any man who does not comply with my terms shall be turned off my Lands, and any of the young men, who think it proper to voyage to Glasgow may there remain, for I pledge *my word* they shall never again eat a potatoe on my property, be they ever so penitent. As to holidays I shall be very explicit; many of them are dispensed with in Catholic countries, this I know from having been a good deal abroad. The Bishop has power to dispense with many of them; particularly those that happen during the

1 See p. 66.

kelp and best fishing seasons might be omitted. They are peculiarly grievous in the summer and although I have the greatest respect for the Catholic faith I think it hard that I should suffer loss, and I must candidly tell you that if I don't experience *real and effectual* cooperation from the Bishop, and yourself, I will bring in *Protestant tenants*. If my plans cause you any loss in your own pocket say so candidly and I will make it up to you.

You will let it be distinctly understood that all my prohibitions as to the tenants and fishermen apply to *this year* as well as years to come. Yours very faithfully

R. MacNeil.

*

XIX

The Reverend A. Macdonald
Barra
Invernessshire
Scotland.

34 Montague Square,
19th July, 1824.

Dear Sir,
Keep your mind quite easy as to yourself *I* will take care of your interest, but I *cannot permit* any deduction on the fish account for you. You will understand that what I shall do for you is *quite between ourselves*. As I expect to be at Barra by the 10th of August at the latest I shall not now go into particulars, but depend upon it I will not suffer myself to be prejudiced against or for any one, but will judge for myself in all respects.

I write in very great haste but remain very truly Yours

R. MacNeil.

*

XX

The Revd. Mr Angus Macdonald
Barra
Invernessshire
By Carinish.

London Feby. 1st 1825.

My Dear Sir,
Both your letter with Mr MacLeod's have duly come to hand. I have desired him in no way to interfere with the conducting of the road, which is entirely under your superintendence and for the proper and judicious execution of which I hold you responsible: I have not the least doubt in my own mind, that you will fully justify the confidence that I repose in you.

I don't now go into particulars on any subject, but will write to you fully by Mr Parry who will be with you before the Ides of March. I have desired Mr McLeod to give over to you (taking your receipt) all the tools and wheel barrows for road making sent home from Greenock.

Mrs Macneil who is now getting very much better desires to be kindly remembered to you.
Believe me dear Sir, Very sincerely yours

R. MacNeil.

P.S.—Mr M'Leod says nothing of the Craigstone business from which I trust it is a mere rumour—indeed my very last injunction to him (repeated in my letter to him of to-day) was neither to *displace* or *place* any person on my property— I have again heard from our friend Kennichregan[1] but not candidly to the point. But depend upon it he shall not have *Eoligary* nor the *stock on it* one farthing under its value and as to any grazing in the South end, or Kielas,[2] there is none for him, *that being otherwise bespoke—*
R.M—L.

*

1 Donald MacNeill of Kenachreggan, who purchased Canna from Clanranald in 1828. He was married to a cousin of Roderick MacNeill.
2 Caolas, in Vatersay.

XXI

To Revend. A. Macdonald
Barra.

Windsor Barracks,
Feby. 7th 1825.

My Dear Sir,
I am to-day in receipt of yours of the 15th Dr., also yours of the 11th I
replyed to some days ago, and by the same post wrote to M'Leod to
give up to your charge and responsibility the road tools and barrows
sent from Greenock— they consist of ½ *a gross of Pick axes,* ½ *gross
spades, a gross shafts for pickaxes,* ½ *a gross for spades, 1 bar best steel—Also
a dozen wheelbarrows, with broad wheels.* Mr Parry who is here with me will
deliver this to you I hope in course of this month, he is charged by me
to take over from M'Leod all the accounts, and books, and responsibility as to everything till my own arrival. I made up my mind as to
poor M'Leod before I left Barra, indeed soon after my arrival I found
he would not suit me—I wrote to him from Edinbro to say that after
the 26th of March next, I should have no further occasion for his
services—his subsequent conduct even by his own account has fully
justified the propriety of the measure. I cannot afford to employ a man
after I find him of no use. Surely Robertson and the rest of the junta
are insane. Do they think I can suffer my property to be made the
theatre for their cabals and petty intrigues. Depend upon it your
triumph shall be compleat as the discomfiture of your clumsy
opponents. I have little dread of emigration. I certainly shall in all the
various ways in my power (and they are not a few) oppose it—You may
tell Alex McIntyre Tailor (*if he has signed*)[1] that although not another
man in Barra should sign, I will (after taking the uttermost far thing
due to me, and that without giving any time) land him in Arisaig—the
very few not in arrears are all liable for delapidations on the property,
that part of it in their hands. I saw how matters stood while at Barra—
some who did not relish any change at first, because they did not
understand it, held out emigration in terrorem—*others* again, to my
knowledge, encouraged Mr McNiven with the view of introducing
Protestants into the shoes of the deluded Roman Catholics. I myself

1 *i.e.,* Signed with an emigration agent for a passage to America.

dont like a divided house, and would much prefer rowing on in the same boat with the natives of the soil, and I have no doubt, if industrious, they may become a very comfortable and happy tenantry, it is quite clear to my mind that if not, it will be entirely attributable to inveterate sloath and pig headedness.

As probably the balance may be in favour of Mr M'Leod on his salary of *one hundred a year*, you will oblige me by advancing to Mr Parry what he may want for that purpose and I will settle with you.

I send some leather, tobacco, and a few other articles. I have no objections to a short credit for shoes, but tobacco being an article of Luxury must be paid for. I beg you will continue to write frequently and believe me at all time, Very faithfully yours

R.MacNeil.

*

XXII

To Revd. Angus Macdonald
Barra
favored by Mr Parry.

Windsor March 15th 1825.

My Dear Sir,
Your kind favours have all come to hand, also your letter to Mr Lunes enclosed to me. It was quite unnecessary, (unacquainted as he is with the local circumstances detailed in your communication) to urge him to represent to me anything on the subject. Be assured M'Leod can not plead ignorance in extenuation of his insane proceedings. I had quite made up my mind to have done with him, before I left Barra, and wrote him to that effect from Edinbro long before I heard from you. I had taken all the steps I thought requisite with regard to fishing tackle months ago. So you see that your apprehensions were groundless as well as the implied neglect on my part.

I had hoped *you* would have given me credit for more consistency and sincerity in following out my plans, than to suppose me capable of hesitating in their accomplishment as firmly and rapidly as circum-stances will admit.

I have directed Mr Parry to apply to you to put him on the way of warning every one in Barra holding Land as well Clergy as Laity.

I have resolved to leave here for Barra early in April to superintend every thing as to letting and so on. A substantial farmer accompanies me who is desirous of *looking* at both farms, and M'Lean says he will be in the Long Island about the same time—so you see we get into fassion by degrees.

I need not say how sincerely obliged I feel by the kind interest you take in every thing. I have not time for more having to scribe a letter to your brother Clergyman and remain,
Yours very faithfully

R. MacNeil.

All here unite in kind regards.

*

XXIII

To The Reverend Mr A. Macdonald
Garriemore.

May 19th 1825.

My Dear Sir,
I send your order and that of the Elders, which you ought yourself to enclose to Lunes; and also an order from Watersay to have *the Merks* lodged with him instead of Arnott. I shall be with you early on Saturday without fail. Pray don't forget to put on paper for me the *history of Shaw's Legacy*.[1] I also send two letters to be put in the Office *at Tobermory* by the Egg Merchant, also your own letter to Brownlow to be put in the post likewise. As the wind is not fair you perhaps may hear from Watersay before the boat sails, if not it does not signify as I shall see H. Macneil on Saturday.
At all times sincerely yours

R. MacNeil.

*

1 See pp. 65 and 166.

XXIV

Revd. Angus Macdonald
care of Mr A. Stewart
Factor
Barra
by Tobermory N.B.

London July 30th 1825.
34 Montague Square.

I am my dear Sir much obliged to you for your kind letter, and am particularly pleased to observe that you are alive to Mr Stewart's merits. He has always expressed himself favorably of you. I am sorry for the poor fellow at Brevick. I have sent very conclusive orders touching the contumacious Widow and others. I think it but fair candidly to tell you that the conduct and tone of the good people of Barra whom every days' experiences teaches me cannot be depended upon, from their fickleness, idleness, and stiff-necked prejudice, has produced in my mind a decided revolution. Every man my good sir has a right to do the best he can for himself in his own affairs—if one set of servants (tenants at will, are nothing else) won't do, the master must try others. I cannot afford the slow operation of waiting till John or Thomas or Hamish are pleased to be convinced that Macneil, after all, was right and could not have meant to cheat and ruin them. No, Mr Angus, I see my way sufficiently clear before me, but to ensure myself an ample harvest (which if I live I have no doubts of) I must have fishers and kelpers who will cheerfully do my bidding. Pray don't I request of you take the trouble of lecturing on my account, as I care not how many are on the wing. In the name of common sense abandon all idea of further condescensions (as you term it) on my part to your spoilt children, as it would give me pain to refuse a request of yours. So pray do not ask me as my resolve is not to be shaken. So if you mean to keep your flock together look to it. *I* can easily fill up the vacancies. I shall prosecute the Irish fishermen to the uttermost. I am quite aware of the state of the fish market at Glasgow and elsewhere. I will thank you to read aloud verbatim the following proclamation, after service, on the very first Sunday after receipt and *at Borve*—I have sent Mr Stewart a copy, that those who may not be at Mass may not pretend ignorance.

GENERAL MACNEILL OF BARRA, 1788-1863
[Reproduced from the copy of a portrait in the possession of
Mr. Donald MacNeil, Castlebay]

TRAIGH MHOR
[Photo J. L. Campbell]

ARDMHOR
[Photo Margaret Fay Shaw]

CASTLE KISMUL
[Photo Margaret Fay Shaw]

DUN BRISTE, BERNERA, AND BARRA HEAD LIGHTHOUSE
[Photo Margaret Fay Shaw]

RUINS OF THE CHAPEL AT KILBAR
[Photo J. L. Campbell]

PABBAY FROM MINGULAY
[Photo Margaret Fay Shaw]

CLIFFS ON MINGULAY
[Photo Margaret Fay Shaw]

GUILLEMOTS ON MINGULAY
[Photo Margaret Fay Shaw]

HERRING FLEET AT CASTLEBAY
[Photo Margaret Fay Shaw]

GUTTING HERRING AT CASTLEBAY
[Photo Margaret Fay Shaw]

CASTLEBAY
[Photo Margaret Fay Shaw]

EOLIGARRY HOUSE
[Photo J. L. Campbell]

SUNDAY AT NORTHBAY
[Photo J. L. Campbell]

THATCHED HOUSE, ARDMHOR
[Photo Margaret Fay Shaw]

Believe me my dear Sir (though out of humour) sincerely your friend

R. MacNeil.

Proclamation
1st.
You will tell the kelpers, that they have earned my utmost displeasure. They have not obeyed my orders—nor the orders of those by me set over them, which I consider as disrespectful to me, as it is disgraceful to them. However as they have worked, so shall they be paid.

2nd.
Say to the fishermen that their audacity and base ingratitude has quite disgusted me. That if they do not within eight and forty hours after this proclamation, bend their energies to the daily prosecution of their calling as fishermen, I shall turn every man of them off the Island were they steeped to the ears in debt—tell them also that since they have shown themselves so unworthy of that interest, which in my heart I felt for them, I shall follow out my plans without in the most trifling degree consulting their feelings or prejudices.

3rdly.
Say to those who are about to emigrate that I sincerely wish them well through it, and assure those who have signed and repented that their repentance comes too late— So help me God, they shall go, at all events off my property, man, woman, and child. Tell the people once for all, that I shall consider any act of inattention to the orders of my factor Mr Stewart as an impertinence to myself. Nor shall any one who dares even to hesitate to obey him and Mr Parry (in both of whom I have the greatest confidence) remain on my property should his, or their character been even so good previously. Lastly I shall exert myself to the utmost to crush all the disreputable trafficking and smuggling which has been too long tolerated.

R. MacNeil.

*

XXV

To Revd. Mr Angus Macdonald
care of Mr Stewart
Factor at Barra
by Tobermory.

London August 8th 1825.

My Dear Sir,

In order that I may not by any chance be misunderstood, I trouble you with a few Lines in addition to my last. It is desirable you should know my sentiments very distinctly. Upon succeeding to the management of the estate of Barra, I need scarcely tell you that I found it in a most deplorable state. Whatever it yielded was certainly not finding its way in to the pockets of the proprietor of the soil. I very soon however saw that it was capable of yielding a very handsome return. My plans once digested I naturally cast about to see how they could be most speedily fulfilled. The Priest, the adviser and guide of his flock, at once occurred to me. For although I was sensible that twenty years' residence on a remote Island, must have produced the usual effects of want of collision with the world, still I relied on the counteracting influence of education, and endeavoured to avail myself of the good offices of the Pastor with his flock. I candidly laid open to him my views, which he seemed to appreciate, even beyond my expectations— he proffered me his cordial cooperation—and certainly on several occasions has been of essential service to me. But to stop in the middle of the brae, my good Sir, never will do.

From old feudal feelings, I was desirous of effecting the object I had in view, by means of the natives of the Island. From my own observation, I saw that you possessed influence almost unbounded over your flock. You yourself did not hesitate to admit it, and I at once perceived that if you in good earnest set your shoulder to the wheel, the happiest results would be the consequence. What then am I to think, when I find the fishermen slothful, and negligent, to a shameful degree—so perverse, that Mr H. Macneil (but of this you are already aware, having of course been called in in consultation) has resigned his employment in disgust. The kelpers also are in a state of most disgraceful insubordination. What then, I repeat, am I to think— Why, one of two things—either you are not free from prejudice yourself, or your feelings lead you to encourage it in others. However, as I have already made known to all concerned, I shall now look to my interests without any further regard to obsolete prejudices. You will do well to advise your friends at Sandra, and all the Leaders as they are termed, to mind well what they are about, if they wish to remain at Barra. They are of little or no importance to me, whatever may be their value to you and if I don't on my arrival find them heart and hand engaged in fishing, *I pledge you my honor* they shall tramp, and the Land shall be this ensuing spring occupied by *strangers*. I am fully determined to hear no more of supposed Grievances—the only aggrieved person in the Island is the proprietor, and on my word, he will find a remedy. He may be thwarted, opposed, and disgusted, but not easily defeated in his endeavours to improve his property, and humanize his tenants. Pray don't take the trouble of writing again, as I leave here in a few days, and I shall soon be with you.

I hope you see John Bull regularly and that your health continues good. Mrs Macneil is quite well, and all the family.
I remain dear Sir, Very truly yours

R. MacNeil.

*

XXVI

The Reverend Mr A. M'Donald
Garimore.

Eoligarry October 18th 1825.

My Dear Sir,
It is perfectly correct that I gave instructions to render a small piece of road at my new village passable for carts, and Mr Stewart accordingly gave the necessary instructions to Neil M'Kinnon the ground officer to whom he pointed out the line to be followed.

I am quite grieved that you should have been at the trouble of going out of your way so unnecessarily. Although at all times ready avail myself of your good offices, and obliged to you at the same time, I really cannot think of trespassing too much on your valuable time. Indeed it would not be fair and certainly not necessary; considering as

I do that my present Factor is perfectly capable of superintending all the concerns of my little property with credit to himself, and advantage to his employer. I shall be engaged at this end of the Island for a few days, and shall be glad to see you. Should you know of any opportunity to Watersay say to Mr H. Macneil his presence if convenient, is requested here.

With great regard I remain, My dear Sir, Yours very truly

R. MacNeil.

CHAPTER 11

Barra in 1840

PARISH OF BARRAY

PRESBYTERY OF UIST, SYNOD OF GLENELG

*

THE REV. ALEXANDER NICOLSON, MINISTER[1]

I. TOPOGRAPHY AND NATURAL HISTORY

Name

Some have supposed that the parish derives its name from St Barr, who was always considered by the natives as the tutelar saint of Barray, to whom the principal Romish churches in the island are dedicated, and called Killbar in honour to him. Nothing can show better the estimation in which this personage was held in the eyes of the people than their having set apart a day annually as a holiday to his memory. On that day (25th of September), all the Roman Catholic population convene in their chapel in the forenoon to hear mass, from whence they set off to Killbar, each man riding his small pony, with his wife or favourite lass mounted behind him; who, after riding thrice round the sacred edifice, return to the place from whence they set out. The females provide, before-hand, quantities of wild field carrots for this occasion, with which they treat their partners. This superstitious ceremony, which has been adhered to for ages, is still countenanced by their priests, although they acknowledge that the Roman calendar has never been honoured with St Barr's name. But it must be observed that, by the intermixture of strangers with the natives, this ceremony is falling greatly into disuse. With due respect for St Barr, it is much more probable that the name of Barray was originally derived from its particular situation or bearing, *i.e.*, from Ay or I, an island, and Bar, a point or top; Barray forming the point or top island of the Hebrides.

Boundaries, Extent, Etc.

The parish is formed of that cluster of islands lying at the south-west

1 N. S. A., Vol. XIV, pp. 198-236. The Rev. Alexander Nicolson was Church of Scotland minister in Barra from 1813 to 1847. He wrote this account of Barra for the *New Statistical Account of Scotland*. He is frequently mentioned in the preceding chapter.

end of Lewis Islands, or the Western Hebrides. It is bounded on the north by a channel of six miles, separating it from South Uist; the islands of Canna and Rum are the nearest lands to it on the east, distant about twenty-six miles; the islands of Coll and Tyrie, are the nearest lands to it on the south, distant about thirty miles; and on the west it is bounded by the Atlantic Ocean. The parish consists of the main island of Barray, properly so called, besides several other islands of considerable size, amounting in all to upwards of twenty. About ten of these are inhabited, and the others used as grazings. The main island of Barray is about 12 miles in length, but varying in breadth from 6 to 3 miles, being much indented by bays and arms of the sea, principally on the east side. The other islands vary in extent from 4 acres to 1800 acres. Those to the south-west stretch out in one line from the mainland to Berneray or Barray-head, about 15 miles. The currents and tides run with great rapidity between these islands, increased by the immense swell from the Atlantic Ocean, so as to render the intercourse betwixt them and the other islands not only hazardous, but at times impossible.

Topographical Appearances
Although Barray cannot boast of high mountains, yet there are some of considerable height, yielding fine pasture to their very tops, with very little heather intermixed. And though, at first sight, the aspect of the island appears rocky in the eyes of a stranger, yet, upon a more minute examination, it will be found interspersed with pleasant and fruitful hollows and valleys, together with some low rich meadow land. Indeed, the whole island, as well as its numerous appendage islets, yield to no other place of their extent in the Highlands of Scotland for pasture of every description. The west coast of the island, with the exception of two or three sandy bays, is defended against the powerful attacks of the Atlantic billows by a barrier of immense rocks, many of which are, by the constant action of the waves upon them, excavated into a variety of deep caves and dreadful fissures, some of which are so very steep as to render it impossible for any person, not possessed of strong nerves, to look down from the top of the rock to the frightful gulf below. The islands of Berneray and Mingalay are particularly distinguished for the height of their rocks. That immediately below the light-house, erected a few years since, at Berneray or Barray-head, is about 700 feet[1] above the level of the sea, and there is another rock

1 628 feet on Ordnance Survey.

in the adjacent island of Mingalay reckoned to be 1400 feet[1] of perpendicular height. The extent of the parish from Scirrival, the most northerly point of the main island, to Berneray, the most southerly island belonging thereto, may be estimated about 28 miles, including the different channels intervening. On the east shore, the land is rocky, with heath and moss, with the exception of one great bay, which is sandy, as also some of the land to the north. The west shore is both rocky and sandy. The principal bays are on the east side, and constitute excellent and safe harbours for shipping, such as Bayhierava (or inland bay), Uilevay, Castlebay, Watersaybay, Flodday sound, and Ottirvore. All these are entered from the east. The principal headland in Barray is Berneray or Barray-head, from whence many ships steer their course for America. The names of the larger islands of which the parish of Barray is formed, and which are mostly inhabited, are as follows: Watersay, Sanderay, Pabbay, Mingalay, and Berneray to the south; Flodday, Hellisay, Gighay, Uidhay, and several others of a smaller description, not inhabited, to the east and north-east.

Meteorology
The most prevalent winds in Barray, as well as in the rest of the Western Isles, are south-west and north-west. The most violent gales that blow are generally from the south-west, and their dreadful effects are visible on such parts of the islands as are composed of loose drifting sand, and exposed to the Atlantic gales. There, the sand is driven to and fro by every successive gale, leaving nothing behind but the rocky skeletons of granite or whinstone, where once the ground was clothed with a beautiful variety of red and white natural clover. The same wind carries along with it great quantities of rain during a part of the autumn, and most of the winter; but in the month of March, the wind occasionally veers round to the east, with cold dry weather. Due north and south winds are not very frequent, and rarely continue above two or three days at a time.

Although the climate is, in general, variable and fluctuating, yet it is far from being unfavourable to the human constitution, as instances of longevity have occurred here, as frequently as in any other part of Scotland; and there are still to be found in the parish a few who have exceeded a hundred years, with all their mental faculties unimpaired. The quantity of rain that falls cannot with any degree of accuracy be ascertained, as no regular meteorological tables are kept; but the

1 891 feet on Ordnance Survey.

quantity that falls in Barray is in general far less than what falls in any of the adjacent islands, perhaps owing to the lowness of its hills. The climate is, upon the whole, mild, from its being surrounded by the sea, and the reflection of the sun upon the sandy soil, of which a great part of the island is composed, to which also may be ascribed the early vegetation and ripening of corn and grasses. Sown hay has been cut down here in the month of June, and barley sometimes as early as the latter end of July or beginning of August; and instances have been known of barley sown on the 20th of June being cut down ripe in September. Snow and frost are little known in this island, and when they appear, seldom continue more than a few days at a time. The diseases most prevalent are rheumatism, fevers, croup, asthma, bowel-complaints, cutaneous eruptions, sore legs in consequence of frequent immersion in salt water during the boating and fishing, and such other diseases as are the usual concomitants of poor living, want of cleanliness, and destitution of clothing. Besides the other various evils to which the inhabitants are subject, the want of a medical practitioner among them is not the least; neither is there any of that profession within twenty miles, to whom they can apply for advice, under the most distressing circumstances. The consequence is, that people are often cut off in the prime of life, who, under the management of a skilful medical man, might be spared to their families.

Rainbows, halos, and polar lights are seen often in this quarter. It is universally admitted that the aurora borealis or polar lights make their appearance much more frequently in our hemisphere now than ever they did in former times, and in much greater splendour. They generally prognosticate a change of weather from good to bad, or from bad to good. The halo about the moon indicates in summer rain, and in the winter snow or frost. As the south-west and north-west are the prevailing winds, when the atmosphere thickens to the west, it prognosticates rain and bad weather; but while the west keeps clear, no change of weather is apprehended.

The Island of Berneray (anciently denominated the Bishop Island), and the adjacent island of Mingalay, are particularly distinguished (as already observed) for the height of their rocks, and their romantic appearance in every other respect; but what adds greatly to the splendid scenery of these precipices, are the innumerable tribes of aquatic fowls by which they are inhabited during the whole of the summer season.

These birds pay their first visit to the rocks on the 1st day of

February, early in the morning, when they clean out the rubbish of last year's nests. Betwixt that period and the month of May, they pay cursory visits to the rocks. Early in the month of May, they lay their eggs on the shelves of the rocks, so close to each other that it appears wonderful how they can distinguish their own eggs from those that surround them. Each of these birds has but one egg, and as soon as the young one is hatched, and gathers strength about the end of July, the old bird gets it upon its own back, and throws itself and the young one headlong into the sea below, from whence it returns no more that season. Of these fowls there is no great variety visiting the above rocks; but few as they are, each tribe keeps possession of a certain division of the rocks, which its neighbours dare not approach. Thus from the bottom to the top of the rock, each keeps its own division. Nothing can possibly exceed the grandeur of beholding the myriads of these aquatic fowls standing erect on the ledges of these precipices, sometimes three and four deep, with their white breasts and red bills, resembling files of soldiers standing at ease, and so very tame that a person might catch them with his hands were he able to approach them; and when roused from their slumber by the firing of a shot, they rise over your head like a cloud of locusts, deafening by their cries, and darkening the sky by their numbers. The natives, at very great risk, descend into the rocks, and not only rob the poor birds of their eggs, but kill them for their carcase and feathers. The first they reckon good eating, and the feathers they sell for beds. This desperate robbery has cost some of the natives their lives. No less than two melancholy instances of this kind have occurred within a few years. It is hardly possible to point out a scene more worthy of being visited for grandeur and variety than that of these rocks, particularly during the months of June and July. St Kilda, so often resorted to by strangers, Coruisge, Cuiraing, or any other place on the coast of Scotland, cannot come in competition with the scenery of the southern isles of Barray during the period above mentioned.

Hydrography

There are only four fresh-water lakes in the island, none of which exceed half a mile or a mile in length, or deserve any further notice than that they abound in small black trout and eels, and have each an old dun built upon one of their small rocks or islands. Neither are there any rivers or streams of consequence, as in a place so confined, and so intersected by arms of the sea, rivers of any considerable size cannot be formed. Although the island abounds in springs of excellent fresh water, yet there is none of any medicinal quality.

Geology and Mineralogy

The rocks in this parish are generally of coarse granite:[1] but in the Island of Berneray a quarry of granite has been discovered of a very superior quality, beautifully marled, and said to be inferior to none of the kind in Scotland. Of this stone the lighthouse and its appendages are built. It bears to be dressed and polished in a superior style. The soil of this place is of different kinds and qualities, such as moss, light sand, light black soil, and meadow land.

Zoology

Barray can boast of no species of animals peculiar to itself, nor any birds but such as are common along the whole coast of the Western Isles. Deer appear to have been inhabitants of it at one time, from the number of their horns still found buried in the earth. No part of the west coast of Scotland abounds more in fish of every description than Barray, such as ling, cod, tusk, hake, turbot, flounders, together with the various other kinds that frequent the western isles; and the coast is frequently visited by immense shoals of herrings, which the inhabitants seldom take the advantage of catching, for want of proper tackling. The grub-worm often proves destructive to the labour of the farmer, more especially in cold wet weather, and the caterpillar no less hurtful to that of the gardener. Various means have been resorted to for their destruction, but none has proved effectual. With regard to shell-fish, no place on the western coast abounds more in this article of food than Barray. Here are to be found lobsters, crabs, clams, razor-fish, mussels, welks, limpets, and the still more important shell-fish the cockle, constituting, in scarce years, a principal part of the subsistence of the inhabitants. Cockles are to be found in the sands of Barray in such immense quantities, that scores of horse-loads may be taken up during a single tide, and the people consider them the most nourishing shell-fish on their shores. Sometimes they eat them when boiled, out of the shell, at other times, such as have milk, boil it and the cockles together, making them into soup, which they consider a very nutritious diet. They commence the use of them in times of scarcity in April, and continue the use of them till the beginning of August. The people allege that the quantity of this fish found on the shores is much greater in scarce seasons than at any other time.

This is wrong; the rock is nearly all gneiss. See p. 104.

Botany

Under this head, little or nothing can be said, as there is no herb or plant in Barray but such as are common to every other parish on the Western Hebrides. Barray is as defective in the article of timber as any of its neighbouring isles. It is said that wood will not grow in any part of the Long Island, but the truth is that no trial has ever been made. It is beyond doubt that these islands were once clothed with woods, from the innumerable trunks of large trees still found under ground, even some of them below high-water mark. Certain it is, however, that young plantings will not thrive very close to the west shores, exposed to the sea spray; but there are many sheltered spots in every island, where there is hardly a doubt that trees would thrive. As a proof of this, Colonel Macneil, the late proprietor of Barray,[1] had a spot on the east side of the island planted with various kinds of trees which grow in a few years as well as could be expected anywhere; but the proprietor transplanted them to the ground about his mansion house,[2] where they had not the same shelter, and where the soil was light sand; in consequence of which, they pined away; whereas, had they been left where they were originally planted, they might in a few years have been large trees. This limited trial proves that it is not impossible to rear trees in Barray, by proper care.

Fruit trees when lined to garden walls, thrive well, and yield excellent fruit, but not otherwise.

II. CIVIL HISTORY

As this parish was only disjoined from that of South Uist in 1733-34, there can be no historical account of it previous to that date, but as connected with South Uist.

[Here the writer quotes from Dean Munro's account. See p. 33.]

This parish was surveyed in 1820-21, and plans drawn, when the superficial contents were found to be about 22,000 imperial acres, including the several islands connected with it. Colonel Macneil is the only owner; but the property is now under sequestration[3] and in the hands of creditors.*

1 Colonel Roderick MacNeill, who died in 1822.
2 Eoligarry.
3 Since 1827.

* Since the above was written, the whole estate of Barray has been purchased by Colonel Gordon of Cluny.

Family of Macneil

The family of the Macneils have held possession of Barray from time immemorial. Martin says that when he visited this place in 1703, the Highland chroniclers alleged that the Macneil then in possession was the thirty-fourth lineal descendant from the first who obtained it. Whether this account be correct or not to the full extent, it is certain that the Macneils possessed these islands for a great length of time. In the Register Office a charter may be seen by Alexander Lord of the Isles and Earl of Ross, giving to Gilleownan, the son of Rodrick, the son of Murdoch Macneil, not only all the lands of Barray, but also Boisdale in South Uist, on condition of assisting the Lord of the Isles, as well in peace as in war, against all enemies whatsomever, men and women, by sea and land. This charter was given at Finlagan, in Islay, in 1427; and was confirmed by King James IV at Stirling in 1495, after the power of the Lords of the Isles had been broken down. The Macneils were of old a great terror to their neighbours, as, being expert seamen, they carried their depredations to every creek in the Western Islands, which might be a powerful reason with the Lord of the Isles for making them his allies. One of them in particular was remarkable for his activity and turbulence (called Ruary an Tartair) or the noisy or troublesome Rodrick, who spared neither friend or foe, until at last he committed piracy on one of Queen Elizabeth's ships, when a reward was offered for his apprehension, which was at length accomplished with very great ingenuity by the tutor of Kintail, as may be seen more fully detailed in the former Statistical Account.[1]

Parochial Register

There is no parochial register kept in this parish, nor can we learn that any was ever kept. This may be accounted for by the parishioners having been, till of late, almost all Roman Catholics, over whom the minister could exercise no control.

Antiquities

There are several ruins of religious houses in Barray, some of which appear to be of ancient structure. The principal ones are at Killbar. Each of these has an altar of rough stones in one end, and the pedestal of a cross stands at a short distance from the buildings. These churches were dedicated to St Barr; and of old a wooden figure of the saint was stuck up for the adoration of the deluded people. This figure was

1 See p. 59-60. A quotation from Martin, already printed (p. 41-2), is here omitted.

dressed up in its best habiliments on the saint's anniversary, and we are credibly informed that it was customary for persons proceeding on a journey to make some present to the saint, of clothes or linen, to insure prosperity to their undertakings. No trace of this figure is now to be seen.[1] Numerous watch-towers are over the whole of the island of Barray,—as also Duns upon every lake in the place, supposed to be built by the Scandinavians, when in possession of these islands. There are likewise many Druidical circles, as they are designated; but a Danish gentleman, who lately visited these parts as historiographer to the King of Denmark, maintains that they are of Scandinavian origin, and were intended by these people as places for their heathen worship. In several of the islands are to be seen immense heaps of human bones; and we have been credibly informed by a gentleman of some information, and a native of the place, that he had seen, on the island of Watersay, the entire skeleton of a trooper and his horse, where they had fallen side by side on the sand, with some pieces of the armour pretty entire, where the sand-drift had exposed them to view. Although the gentleman's veracity cannot be doubted, it is difficult to account for the fact. There are several tumuli over the country in which, when opened, were found human bones along with deer horns.

The most entire and regular ancient building in Barray is Kismull Castle, the ancient residence of the Macneils of Barray. It is built upon a small rock in the middle of a beautiful bay (Kilelerin of Dean Munro). The whole rock is covered by the sea at high water; the castle is of an irregular figure, strongly built, with anchorage for small vessels on every side of it. It is about 60 feet high, with a square tower in one corner, overtopping the rest of the wall by many feet. Tradition says that delinquents were let down by a rope and confined there. Immediately over the entry to the castle, the gockman or watchman stood all night, repeating some rhyme to keep himself awake, and throwing stones down over the outside of the gate through a hole made in the wall for the purpose, to prevent a surprise. On the area within the walls, the dwelling-houses were built, which, if we may judge by their size and appearance, must have afforded but very indifferent accommodations.

In the centre of the area a large circular well is sunk; but it is doubtful whether it was used as a reservoir for rain-water, or sunk for the purpose of raising water from beneath. The well is now filled up with stones thrown into it by the natives, in order to prevent accidents.

1 See p. 42-3.

Attached to this castle, at the entrance to the gate, there is a dock built for the galley, adapted to the exact length and breadth of the boat, and defended on the west by a strong wall from the action of the sea. Martin says that the natives informed him, that the castle was 500 years old when he visited the island, and that it had then its regular officers and guards, keeping watch upon the walls to prevent surprise.

Both coins and arms have often been found in Barray, but none of them have been preserved. About three years ago, in trenching the clergyman's garden, a gold medal, nearly the size of a half-crown-piece was dug up. It was cast for the coronation of Augustus, the second King of Poland; but how it found its way to this distant corner is not easily understood, unless we suppose that it belonged to some person on board of a Dutch ship which was wrecked on this coast, when on her way to Batavia, about the beginning of the last century, when every person on board was lost, including several people of rank. As the bodies of these men were washed ashore, it is more than probable that this medal was found upon one of them.

Modern Buildings

The mansion-house of Barray at Eoligarry, built by the late proprietor,[1] is a most commodious building, situated in a sheltered place, and surrounded by fields of fine improvable lands, not inferior in quality or appearance to any in the Western Isles. The manse, which is very commodious, was built in 1816, but stands now in need of some repairs. A church was built a few years since, and can accommodate 250 sitters in the ground area, and is fitted for galleries to accommodate 200 more, if necessary. There are three other excellent farm-houses slated and in good condition. A mill has lately been erected for grinding of corn, on a better construction than any that had been there before. There is likewise an extensive soda manufactory,[2] which has been working for several years, but it was found at last necessary to discontinue it, after it had involved the proprietor in such expenses as obliged him to sequestrate his whole property for behoof of his creditors, and now to advertise it for sale. Of late, a most splendid lighthouse has been erected on the island of Berneray or Barray-head, the farthest south of all the Barray isles, with that beautiful granite found upon the island itself. The roof of it, as well as the houses built for the keepers, are all covered with sheet-lead.

1 Colonel MacNeill, 1763-1822.
2 At Northbay.

III. POPULATION

According to the church records the population of the parish in	1750 was 1285
Dr Webster's return	1755 was 1150
Dr Walker's return	1771 was 1395
Sir John Sinclair's Account	1791 was 1604
Government census	1801 was 1925
Government census	1811 was 1969
Government census	1821 was 2303
Government census	1831 was 2097

The increase in the population would have been very great, owing to early marriages, and the reluctance of the people to leave the country for work in the south,—had not emigration to Cape Briton and Nova Scotia carried off the island a great many almost every year. In some years, several hundreds leave it for those places. At present, there are 278 families who possess lands, and 93 families who hold no lands whatever. Of the last, 70 persons are upon the poor's roll; 3 are fatuous; 4 deaf and dumb; and 2 blind. The average of births, deaths, and marriages, cannot with accuracy be ascertained, for want of a parochial register, and from the great majority of the population being Roman Catholics.

Very few attain the age of thirty before they marry, and sometimes they enter into that state at twenty. This may account for the fewness of illegitimate children born in the parish;—instances of which are very rare.[1]

Habits, Etc. of the People

The inhabitants are of the middle size, patient and hardy in enduring cold and fatigue. They are expert seamen, and considered the best boatmen in the Western Isles. No instance has occurred of a Barra boat being lost for upwards of twenty years, although boats are generally at sea both summer and winter. Gaelic is the language universally spoken, and it is very pure and still unmixed with many English words. The English language has made little or no progress, because schools have been wanting. The people of Barray have no games or amusements but what are common to the surrounding islands. Dancing, with music of the bagpipes, is a favourite pastime. They are not remarkable for cleanliness in their habits or dress in

1 It might indicate more probably the influence of the Catholic Church. M. C. M.

general, yet on holidays their appearance is decent enough. The men dress in jackets and trowsers of home-made or south country cloth; the women wear clothes made by themselves, and, at times, south country droggets or prints. They wear a handkerchief about their head instead of a cape, and a petticoat about their shoulders for a cloak. The women are slovenly in their manners, and not very active or cleanly. The people are so very poor that many of them are destitute of bed-clothes.

Their ordinary food consists of barley-meal, potatoes, and milk, and at times fish, with which those placed in the more favourable situations are abundantly supplied. All the fishermen export their cod and ling to Glasgow and other markets, and reserve such fish as is not marketable for the use of their own families. In very scarce years, such as 1836 and 1837, they subsist, in a great measure, upon cockles and other shell-fish, with very little bread and milk. Under all these destitu-tions, it is surprising how contented they are with their lot. With regard to their intellectual powers, little can be said. Their want of education, together with their seclusion from the society of other countries, must confine the exercise of their intellectual powers within very narrow limits. Still they are shrewd and inquisitive, but too indolent and indifferent to provide for themselves or families any of those comforts or necessaries of life which, by a little more exertion and prudence, they might easily acquire. They are extremely addicted to the use of both spirits and tobacco-smoking. There are more spirits consumed in Barray than in any other place of its extent in the Western Islands. In point of religion, the natives, who are mostly Roman Catholics, are not worse than their neighbours of the same persuasion. They are regular in their attendance on their own worship, without, perhaps, bringing forth those fruits which such attendance should naturally produce. As soon as the congregation is dismissed, the inn is their common resort, where they drink to such excess as often ends in a quarrel. The Protestants, who are comparatively few in number, and mostly strangers from other parts of the Highlands, are, with few exceptions, sober and industrious, and in their religious attainments, are noways behind their neighbours in the adjacent islands.

IV. INDUSTRY

Agriculture

By a survey made of this parish in 1820-21, it was found to contain 22,072.943 imperial acres, distinguished into arable, machir or sandy ground, hill-pasture, moss or meadow, as follows:

Arable.	3921.9377
Machir or sandy.	1540.453
Hill pasture.	16139.5089
Moss or meadow	470.9938
Total	22072.943

As all the lands in Barray are let either in farms or in crofts, consisting of arable and pasture ground intermixed, it is not possible to ascertain the exact rent of an arable acre.

Rent of Land
The average price of a cow's grass depends much on the quality of the pasture, which varies much in different parts of the parish. It may, however, be stated at £1, 10s. or £2 per annum; that of a sheep, from 2s. to 2s. 6d. per annum.

Rate of Wages
Farm-servants receive from £4 to £7 per annum, exclusive of maintenance; and women from £2 to £3 per annum besides maintenance. Daily labourers receive 1s. 6d. in summer, and 1s. in winter, per day, without maintenance. Masons receive 2s. 6d. per day; house carpenters 2s.; and all country artisans, such as tailors, shoemakers, weavers, charge according to the quality of the article wrought, or the labour bestowed upon it. The black-cattle of Barray are very good. The stock reared by the proprietor himself was considered as one of the best in the Highlands.[1] The small horses reared by the crofters are much esteemed, both for their symmetry and hardiness; of these they keep too many, to the detriment of their black-cattle, at the same time they find them exceedingly useful for the manufacture of their kelp, and for leading seaweed from their shores for manure, although a much fewer number might serve them for every useful purpose. No regular sheep stock had been introduced into this parish until last year, and those who are the best judges are of opinion that no place in the Highlands is better adapted for the

1 See p. 57

rearing of sheep than Barray.[1] The prices of black-cattle have been, for a few years back, less than they formerly were, and have varied so much every year that it is hardly possible to state an average price. Corn, meal, and potatoes, are all sold here by measure; never by weight. The boll of meal consists of twenty pecks; the peck contains 51/2 pints English liquid measure; the country people, however, have a measure among themselves, used nowhere else, which they call an omer, containing two pecks. Potatoes are sold by barrel measure, containing 35 English gallons. Meal sells at 1s. per peck, and potatoes at an average of 2s. per barrel. The imperial measure has not as yet been introduced into this parish, except in the case of spirits or other liquids.

Husbandry

As the parish is better adapted for grazing than agriculture, it cannot be supposed that the latter has made much progress. There are but few farms fit for a regular system of agriculture, and these are now let to graziers, who seldom crop much of their ground. The chief part of the lands is let to small tenants in crofts, from year to year; and it cannot be supposed that much improvement can be carried on in clearing or inclosing land, under such a precarious holding. Notwithstanding all the disadvantages under which they labour, they now turn their small patches of ground to much better purpose than they formerly did; for every crofter has his own small plough and couple of ponies, with which he turns up his ground with much more ease and in a better style than under the old system with the machine called "crom-na-gadd," which required the labour of four men and three horses. By simplifying their agriculture, the people are now enabled to raise a sufficiency of corn and potatoes for their own consumption, unless in very unfavourable seasons, such as the two last, when the most part of the Western Highlands suffered a destitution similar to what they experienced. They plant their potatoes, in general, with the plough, when the ground admits of it; and when it does not, they plant them with the dibble, and have returns of from fifteen to twenty. The principal manure is seaweed, which they lay upon the ground at all periods from November to the end of May; but the earliest laid on always yields the best quality of potatoes. After their

1 We can at least be thankful that the entire population of Barra was not cleared off to make room for sheep, as happened in the case of the neighbouring Island of Rum in 1826, where 400 people were forced to remove for a sheep farmer, his servants, and 8000 sheep.

potato crop, crops of barley and oats succeed.

Without giving the tenants a more permanent tenure of their lands by leases, making their crofts larger, and encouraging them in clearing, draining, and enclosing and following a more regular system of crofting than what has been hitherto pursued,—it is impossible to expect that any great improvement in their management can take place. The common buildings or dwellings of the peasantry are of a most miserable description; the wall is formed of loose undressed stone, without mortar of any kind, the centre being filled up with common earth, roofed and covered over with divot and straw, bound together by heather ropes. There are neither windows nor chimneys. For the first, they have round holes in the thatch for admitting the light; and one or more holes on each side of the house, which are opened or shut, according as the wind blows; and a hole in the roof for emitting the smoke of their peat-fires, which are placed in the middle of their bare earthen floor. In one end of this miserable habitation they live, with their cows and horses in the other, during the winter and spring seasons. The natives have little or no idea of cleanliness or comfort. They have seldom much furniture to boast of; sometimes not a chair to sit upon; a bed to sleep on, or bed-clothes to cover them from the severity of the night air; yet these very people resort to the dram-house as often as they can spare a shilling for that purpose. There are, however, some exceptions from this, in the conduct of those who have come to Barra from other countries. These have built for themselves more comfortable dwellings. They are more cleanly in their habits and dress, and far more industrious and of more sober habits than those they found on the spot; and it is hoped that their example in this respect will have a salutary influence on the manners, habits, and industry of their neighbours. Under the late proprietor of Barray, the people enjoyed every comfort consistent with their rank and situation in life.[1] He was remarkable for his kind treatment of them. Another great obstacle to the improvement of their lands is the manufacture of kelp, at which the people are bound by their holdings to labour during the summer season, and even sometimes to the end of August, the fittest time for the improvement of their lands, and attending to the management of the crop in the ground. Although this article of manufacture was a source from whence the Highland proprietors derived great benefit while it sold at high prices, and employed the people at remunerative wages, yet it has

1 See p. 116.

turned out in the end ruinous to both proprietors and tenants,—whose dependence had been placed much upon it. The tenantry have thus been reduced to the utmost poverty; and are unable to pay their high rents, and still less able to betake themselves to any other country by emigration.

Colonel Macneil, the late proprietor, while he resided in the parish (which he did for some years), made some useful improvements in the farm of Eoligarry, which he kept in his own possession, by draining and inclosing.

Fisheries
Barray is perhaps one of the best fishing stations on the west coast, and might prove, were proper means taken, a considerable source of wealth. The people at present are too poor to carry on fishing on an extensive scale, from their inability to purchase or build boats capable of encountering the boisterous seas they have to contend with, or to provide sufficient materials for their fishing; yet, under every disadvantage to which they are subject, they generally employ from 20 to 30 boats, of about three tons each, in the fishing, with five men to each boat; but, from the smallness of their size, they are often unable to put to sea, or to carry on the employment systematically. They are, in some seasons, however, pretty successful when the weather is favourable: and then they go with their own boats to Glasgow or Greenock, with what ling or cod they take. The people of Barray were in former years very successful in harpooning "cearbans" or sail-fish, from which they extracted a good deal of oil, and received a premium from the Board of Trustees for Fisheries; but this productive source of wealth has been discontinued, from their inability to provide the necessary tackling; and although hundreds of these fishes appeared last season on the coast, no one was in a condition to take advantage of the circumstance. Barray was in former times much frequented by great shoals of herrings; but its lochs are now almost entirely deserted by that useful fish.

Produce
The average amount of raw produce raised in this parish cannot with any degree of accuracy be ascertained, as the most part of the lands (as already stated) is let in small lots to tenants who require the whole crop they raise for their own consumption.

Kelp

The only manufacture now carried on in this parish is that of kelp, in which all hands, young and old, are employed for about eight or nine weeks, at £1, 15s. or £2 per ton, but for which they formerly received £4, 4s. per ton. Kelp, which on former occasions, sold at from £16 to £20 per ton, is now reduced to £2, 10s. or £4 per ton at market, from barilla and salt being used as substitutes for it.

There are only four vessels belonging to this place, there being little or no trade to employ more.

V. PAROCHIAL ECONOMY

Market-Town

There is no market-town in the parish. The nearest to this is Tobermory, in the county of Argyle, distant fifty miles by sea.

Means of Communication

The only means of communication by post with Barray is by Dunvegan, in the Isle of Skye, where the nearest post-office is established. There is, however, a receiving house at Lochmaddy, from whence the packet sails to Dunvegan once or twice a week. A letter from this must of course pass by the ferry from Barray to South Uist, through the whole length of South and North Uist to Lochmaddy receiving-house, and from thence by the packet to Dunvegan Post-Office, a distance by sea and land, including ferries, of not less than 100 miles. The Commissioners for Lights employ a small vessel from Barray-Head Lighthouse, to sail to Tobermory once a month with the monthly returns, as a quicker conveyance than by Dunvegan. The country boats, too, ply at all seasons of the year to Glasgow with fish and such other articles as the country produces; so that the communication with the mainland is pretty frequent.

The harbours in Barray (as already stated) are extremely commodious and safe, which should be a great inducement to the prosecution of the fishing upon a more extensive scale than has been hitherto attempted.

Ecclesiastical State

The parochial church, which was built only a few years ago, is situated in the very centre of the parish, pretty close to the manse. It is about six miles from each extremity of the main island; of course, convenient for the attendance of all the parishioners resident on the main island.

All the seats are free. The manse was built in 1816, with offices and garden. The glebe is a grass one, sufficient for the grazing of sixteen soums[1] of cattle. It is of considerable extent; but much broken up by rocks and stones. The present incumbent has, however, converted a good deal of it into excellent arable land, which yields good crops. Its value at present may be about £40 per annum. The stipend is one of those augmented by Government to £150, exclusive of £8, 6s. 8d. for communion elements. There is one Roman Catholic Chapel[2] in the parish; the bishop under whose jurisdiction it is resides in Greenock. The number of Protestant families in the parish is 65; the number of families attending the Roman Catholic Chapel is 306. Divine service is pretty well attended in the Established Church, as also in the Roman Catholic Chapel. The number of communicants in the Established Church may average about 70. Owing to the poverty of the people, no contributions are made for charitable purposes; neither are there any collections in the church.[3]

Education

The parochial is the only school now in the parish. English and writing only are taught there at present, although the teacher is qualified to teach Greek, Latin, arithmetic, book-keeping, and geography; but as the school has but lately been opened, there are no scholars as yet advanced farther than English reading.

The salary of the parish schoolmaster is £26, exclusive of £2, 2s. in lieu of a garden. No schoolhouse has been built as yet, but the school is accommodated in the meantime in a house which is not fitted to accommodate any tolerable number of the parishioners. The fees generally exacted are, 1s. 6d. for English; 2s. for English and writing; reading, writing, and arithmetic, 2s. 6d.; Latin, etc., 3s. per quarter.

The number of scholars at last examination amounted to 40.

The clergyman keeps a private tutor for his own family, who teaches the highest branches of education. There was formerly a school in the parish supported by the Society for Propagating Christian Knowledge, which has for some time back been suppressed, for want of requisite accommodations. There was likewise a female school from the same Society; but it is not taught at present, as the mistress has been superannuated for some years back. To

1 See p. 66.
2 The present parish church of Craigston.
3 Yet the much poorer Catholics had to support a priest without a Government stipend, a large manse, and a large slice of the best land in the island. M. C. M.

accommodate the people of this parish with the requisite means of education, three schools are required.

Few of the natives can either read or write. Most of the Protestants who came from other places, are, however, able to read the Scriptures, either in English or Gaelic. The number of Protestants in Barray, when the present incumbent came to the parish, did not exceed 60 souls; now they amount to about 380.[1] There is not, perhaps, a single parish in Scotland in which the minister is put to so much trouble and expense in attending to his ministerial duties.[2] The Presbytery seat is about forty miles distant, exclusive of fords and ferries; he has to travel about 100 miles to the seat of Synod, besides ferries; and the expense of travelling in the Highlands is very great.

Poor and Parochial Funds

The average number of poor upon the roll is about 70. The only fund in the hands of the kirk-session for the relief of these, is the interest on an heritable bond of £400, left by two tacksmen, natives of Barray, which is distributed among them annually, according to their necessities. There is no church collection made, nor has there been any assessment for the support of the poor as yet resorted to. The people are, in general, very kind to their poor, who live in small houses of their own, where they are supplied by those around them with the necessaries of life, and thus they are prevented from begging from door to door, or even leaving the parish for subsistence. They, however, show no reluctance in applying for relief, nor do they consider it as any ways degrading to do so.[3]

Markets

The only markets in Barray are held in the summer and autumn seasons, for disposing of the surplus cows and horses to dealers from the mainland, who carry them to the southern markets.

Inns

There are no fewer than three inns in the parish, where a great quantity of spirits is sold, the effects of which on the morals of the people are most pernicious.

1 So apparently General MacNeill had carried out his threat, at least in part. See p. 138.

2 And no parish where he received so much for doing so little. M. C. M.

3 This sententious remark, which rather betrays the writer's attitude towards the people of Barra, was made at a time when there was probably less unemployment in Barra than there is to-day. M. C. M.

Fuel

The only fuel used in Barray is peat, which is procured from a distance at great expense and trouble.

MISCELLANEOUS OBSERVATIONS

The face of the country has undergone a material change for the better, since the former Statistical Account was written.

There are now excellent roads made through the greatest part of the Main Island, where a horse could then hardly walk.[1] These roads were executed by the country people, under the Statute Labour Act:[2] and they form an improvement of the highest consequence, as without roads no other improvement can be carried on.

The state of the natives is truly deplorable, when compared with that of every other place, where education has found its way. The introduction of strangers into the parish has, however, given a spur to industry[3], to which the old inhabitants had little or no inclination, their time having been chiefly occupied by boating and fishing during the best part of the spring season, and the tillage of their lands having been left to the women and children; in consequence of which, the proprietor had annually to import a large quantity of low-country meal to support his people during the summer season, so as to enable them to manufacture the kelp:[4] they now raise as much corn and potatoes as will supply themselves, unless in very scarce years.

The only way to render the people comfortable and industrious would be to grant each tenant a larger portion of lands than what he presently possesses, as he could manage that with the same number of hands, and the same number of horses which he requires for the small lot; and to grant the tenants a more permanent holding of their lands, by leases of nine or ten years, with stipulations for improvements, and other regulations. Rents should be paid in money instead of services, and such services as the landlord requires ought to be commuted for an adequate sum in money, and every shadow of vassalage done away. Rents should be reduced to a conformity with the real value of the lands, and adequate compensation given at the end of their leases for

1 See p. 140.
2 An Act passed by the Scots Parliament in 1669, empowering the Sheriff and J.P.s to convene tenants and cottars for labour on the roads, six days a year man and horse for the first three years, and four days a year afterwards. J. P. D., p. 314.
3 Agriculture is meant.
4 The people could hardly be expected to attend to agriculture and kelp at the same time.

every useful and permanent improvement.[1] The tenants should be encouraged to build more comfortable houses for themselves, and their cow-houses should be separated: and each tenant should have a kitchen-garden attached to his house, well fenced round with stone wall. Another great benefit to the parish would be the establishment of a more constant communication with the mainland, by means of a regular packet boat—which would enable the people to hold more regular intercourse with other countries, and so to have some insight into the manners, habits, and industry of other people. Were these improvements attended to, and due encouragement given to prosecute the fisheries, there is hardly a doubt that this small portion of the Western Islands might rival in wealth and happiness any country of the same extent in the Highlands of Scotland.

January 1840.
Inverness

1 This extremely sound advice remained unheeded for nearly fifty more years.

CHAPTER 12

Gloomy Memories –
Barra in 1851

*

DONALD MACLEOD

Donald MacLeod was a native of Strathnaver in Sutherlandshire, where he was born about 1795. The notorious Sutherlandshire Clearances were begun in 1807, under the administration of Young and Sellar. MacLeod soon became known as a bitter critic of the estate policy, and as such, a man marked down for removal. In 1827 he was summoned in respect of a debt which he had already paid, to a court itself presided over by the local factor; he refused to pay, and appealed to Mr Loch, then chief factor of the Sutherland estates, but with no success. In 1830 his family was violently ejected from his home during his absence, and it became impossible for him to live in Sutherlandshire any longer.[1] He went first to Wick and later to Edinburgh, finally emigrating to Canada where he spent the rest of his life.

MacLeod was the first Highlander to protest publicly against the Clearances which disgrace the nineteenth-century agrarian history of Scotland. In a series of letters published in the Edinburgh Weekly Chronicle *in 1840-41 he wrote with courage and ability against methods of estate management which to-day can find no defenders. At a time when few Highlanders, apart from the landlords and the clergy—and many of the Church of Scotland clergy, as in Barra, supported the policy of the Clearances—had more than a smattering of English, the crofters were almost completely without access to English or Lowland public opinion. Moreover, the Scottish Conservative press took the view that the Clearances were justified in the name of the rights of private property. It is an interesting commentary on the state of public opinion at the time, that the Sutherland family employed Mrs Harriet Beecher Stowe, the American anti-slavery propagandist, to answer MacLeod's criticisms of the Clearances. Having only the most superficial knowledge of the question, and no Gaelic at all, Mrs Beecher Stowe scarcely did herself justice on this occasion.*

Gloomy Memories, from which the following chapter is quoted, was first published in 1841 as a pamphlet containing MacLeod's letters to the

---

1 His own account.

Edinburgh Weekly Chronicle; *in later editions, published in Canada in* 1857 *and in Glasgow in* 1892, *more material was admitted. The desperate destitution and misery which prevailed in Barra in* 1851 *under the Gordon régime can be further illustrated by the following incident:*[1]

"The Secretary of the Royal Patriotic Society stated in January 1851 that there were then 50,000 persons in the Western Highlands and Islands very nearly destitute, if not entirely so. This was probably an exaggerated estimate, but one incident will suffice to show how acute the distress was in certain districts. In February of that year, sixty-one destitute folk arrived in Inverness from Barra, and sat down in front of the Town House to see what the authorities would do for them. Two-thirds of the party were sent to the poorhouse, and the rest were accommodated in lodgings. After a few days they drifted eastwards, hoping to find employment in the Buchan fisheries. Later on, other parties arriving, the Inverness inspector attempted to recoup the expenses of their sustenance from the Barra parochial board,[2] but the latter pointed out that they were not responsible for the able-bodied, and demanded that the impotent, if any, should be sent back to the island. The Board of Supervision admitted that the attitude of the Barra board was legally correct, whereupon the Inverness board declined to give the wanderers any further help, and what eventually happened was that, since the exiles refused to return home, the colony remained in the town living in great poverty and supported by the charity of sympathizers."

Between the censuses of 1841 *and* 1851, *the population of Barra fell from* 2363 *to* 1873, *or by about* 21 *per cent, a figure lower than that of* 1801. *During this period Colonel Gordon offered to sell the island to the Government for a penal colony, but the offer was fortunately refused.*

*

To follow these investigations a little further,[3] we cannot do better than by giving the following well-authenticated communication received

---

1 *Public Administration in the Highlands*, p. 100.
2 This Board consisted of three tacksmen, the Church of Scotland Minister, and the Factors. There was only one Catholic, and no representatives of the crofters on it.
3 1892 edition, pp. 138-141.

from a gentleman who had resided for some time in Barra, and was an eye witness of the enormities perpetrated there during the summer of 1851:

"The feeling and deceitful conduct of those acting for Colonel Gordon in Barra and South Uist last summer, cannot be too strongly censured. The duplicity and art which was used by them in order to entrap the unwary natives is worthy of the craft and cunning of an old slave-trader. Many of the poor people here were told in my hearing that Sir John MacNeill[1] would be in Canada before them, where he would have everything necessary for their comfort prepared for them. Some of the officials signed a document binding themselves to emigrate in order to induce the poor people to give their names; but in spite of all these stratagems many of the people saw through them and refused out and out to go. When the transports anchored in Loch Boisdale the tyrants threw off the mask, and the work of devastation and cruelty commenced. The poor people were commanded to attend a public meeting at Loch Boisdale where the transport lay, and according to the intimation, anyone absenting himself from the meeting was liable to be fined in two pounds. At this meeting some of the natives were seized and in spite of their entreaties were sent on board the transports. One stout Highlander, named Angus Johnstone, resisted with such pith that they had to handcuff him before he could be mastered; but in consequence of the priest's interference his manacles were taken off and (he was) marched between four officers on board the emigrant vessel. One morning, during the transporting season, we were suddenly awakened by the screams of a young female who had been recaptured in an adjoining house, having escaped after her first apprehension. We all rushed to the door and saw the broken-hearted creature with dishevelled hair and swollen face, dragged away by two constables and a ground officer. Were you to see the racing and chasing of policemen, constables, and ground officers, pursuing the outlawed natives, you would think, only for their colour, that you had been by some miracle transported to the banks of the Gambia on the slave coast of Africa.

1 Author of a report on the condition of the Hebrides in 1851.

"The conduct of the Rev. H. Beatson[1] on that occasion is deserving of the censure of every feeling heart. This 'Wolf in sheep's clothing' made himself very officious, as he always does when he has an opportunity of oppressing the poor Barramen and of gaining the favour of Colonel Gordon. In fact, he is the most vigilant and assiduous officer Colonel Gordon has. He may be seen in Castlebay, the principal anchorage in Barra, whenever a sail is hoisted, directing his men, like a gamekeeper with his hounds, in case any of the doomed Barramen should escape, so that he might get his land cultivated and improved for nothing. They offered one day to board an Arran boat who had a poor man concealed, but the master, John Crawford, lifted a hand-spike and threatened to split the skull of the first man who would attempt to board his boat, and thus the poor Barramen escaped their clutches.

"I may state in conclusion that two girls, daughters of John MacDougall, brother of Barr MacDougall whose name is mentioned in Sir John MacNeill's report, have fled to the mountains to elude the grasp of the expatriators, where they still are, if in life. Their father, a frail old man, along with the rest of the family, have been sent to Canada. The respective age of these girls is 12 and 14 years. Others have fled in the same manner, but I cannot give their names just now."

Let us now follow the exiled Barramen to the "new world" and witness their deplorable condition and privations in a foreign land. The *Quebec Times* says:

"We noticed in our last the deplorable condition of the 600 paupers who were sent to this country from the Kilrush Unions. We have to-day a still more dismal picture to draw. Many of our readers may not be aware that there lives such a personage as Colonel Gordon, proprietor of large estates, South Uist and Barra, in the Highlands of Scotland. We are sorry to be obliged to introduce him to their notice under circumstances which will not give them a very favourable opinion of his character and heart.

"It appears that tenants on the above-mentioned estates were on the verge of starvation, and had probably become an eyesore

1 Church of Scotland minister in Barra from 1847 to 1871.

to the gallant Colonel. He decided on shipping them to America. What they were to do there was a question he never put to his conscience. Once landed in Canada, he had no further concern about them. Up to last week, 1100 souls from his estates had landed in Quebec, and begged their way to Upper Canada; when in the summer season, having only a morsel of food to procure, they probably escaped the extreme misery which seems to be the lot of those who followed them.

"On their arrival here, they voluntarily made and signed the following statement:

"'We, the undersigned passengers per *Admiral*, from Stornoway, in the Highlands of Scotland, do solemnly depose to the following facts: That Colonel Gordon is the proprietor of the estates of South Uist and Barra; that among many hundreds of tenants and cottars whom he has sent this season from his estates to Canada, he gave directions to his factor, Mr Fleming of Cluny Castle, Aberdeenshire, to ship on board of the above-named vessel a number of nearly 450 of said tenants and cottars from the estate in Barra—that accordingly a great number of these people, among whom were the undersigned, proceeded voluntarily to embark on board the *Admiral*, at Loch Boisdale, on or about the 11th August 1851; but that several of the people who were intended to be shipped for this port, Quebec, refused to proceed on board, and in fact absconded from their homes to avoid the embarkation. Whereupon Mr Fleming gave orders to a policeman, who was accompanied by the ground officer of the estate of Barra, and some constables, to pursue the people who had run away among the mountains; which they did, and succeeded in capturing about twenty from the mountains and islands in the neighbourhood; but only came with the officers on an attempt being made to handcuff them; and that some who ran away were not brought back, in consequence of which four families at least have been divided, some having come in the shipes to Quebec, while other members of the same families were left in the Highlands.

"'The undersigned further declare, that those who voluntarily embarked did so under promise to the effect, that Colonel Gordon would defray their passage to Quebec; that the Government Emigration Agent there would send the whole party free to Upper Canada, where, on arrival the Government Agents would give them work, and furthermore grant them land on certain conditions.

"'The undersigned finally declare, that they are now landed in Quebec so destitute, that if immediate relief be not afforded them and continued until they are settled in employment, the whole will be liable to perish with want.'

(Signed) Hector Lamont and 70 others.

"This is a beautiful picture. Had the scene been laid in Russia or Turkey, the barbarity of the proceeding would have shocked the nerves of the readers; but when it happens in Britain, emphatically the land of liberty where every man's house, even the hut of the poorest, is said to be his castle, the expulsion of these unfortunate creatures from their homes—the man-hunt with policemen and bailiffs—the violent separation of families—the parents torn from the child, the mother from her daughter—the infamous trickery practised on those who did embark—the abandonment of the aged, the infirm women, and tender children in a foreign land—form a tableau which cannot be dwelt on for an instant without horror. Words cannot depict the atrocity of the deed. For cruelty less savage the (slave) dealers of the South[1] have been held up to the execration of the world.

"And if, as men, the sufferings of these our fellow creatures find sympathy in our hearts, as Canadians their wrongs concern us more dearly. The fifteen hundred souls whom Colonel Gordon has sent to Quebec this season have all been supported for the past week at least, and conveyed to Upper Canada, at the expense of the Colony; and on their arrival in Toronto and Hamilton, the greater number has been dependent on the charity of the benevolent for their morsel of bread. Four hundred are in the river (of St Lawrence) at present and will arrive in a day or two making a total of nearly 2000 of Colonel Gordon's tenants and cottars whom the province has to support. The winter is at hand, work is becoming scarce in Upper Canada. Where are these people to find food?"

1 The Southern States of the U.S.A.

We take the following[1] from an Upper Canadian paper* describing the position of the same people after finding their way to Ontario:

"We have been pained beyond measure for some time past, to witness in our streets so many unfortunate Highland emigrants, apparently destitute of any means of subsistence, and many of them sick from want and other attendant causes. It was pitiful the other day to witness a funeral of one of these wretched people. It was, indeed, a sad procession. The coffin was constructed of the rudest material; a few rough boards nailed together was all that could be afforded to convey to its resting-place the body of the homeless emigrant. Children followed in the mournful train; perchance they followed a brother's bier, one with whom they had sported and played for many a healthful day among their native glens. Theirs were looks of indescribable sorrow. They were in rags; their mourning weeds were the shapeless fragments of what had once been clothes. There was a mother, too, among the mourners, one who had tended the departed with anxious care in infancy, and had doubtless looked forward to a happier future in this land of plenty. The anguish of her countenance told too plainly those hopes were blasted, and she was about to bury them in the grave of her child.

"There will be many to sound the fulsome noise of flattery in the ear of the generous landlord, who had spent so much to assist the emigration of his poor tenants. They will give him the misnomer of a benefactor, and for what? Because he has rid his estates of the encumbrance of a pauper population.

"Emigrants of the poorer class who arrive here from the western Highlands of Scotland, are often so situated, that their emigration is more cruel than banishment. Their last shilling is spent probably before they reach the upper province (Ontario)—they are reduced to the necessity of begging. But again, the case of those emigrants of which we speak, is rendered more deplorable from their ignorance of the English tongue. Of the hundreds of Highlanders in and around Dundas at present, perhaps not half-a-dozen understand anything but Gaelic.

"In looking at these matters, we are impressed with the

---

1 The rest of this chapter is taken from Mackenzie's *Highland Clearances*, 1883 edition, pp. 259-261.

* *Quebec Times.*

conviction that, so far from emigration being a panacea for
Highland destitution, it is fraught with disasters of no ordinary
magnitude for the emigrant whose previous habits, under the
most favourable circumstances, render him unable to take
advantage of the industry of Canada, even when brought hither
free of expense. We may assist these poor creatures for a time,
but charity will scarcely hide the hungry cravings of so many for a
very long period. Winter is approaching, and then—but we leave
this painful subject for the present."

CHAPTER 13

The Visit of the Crofters' Commission to Barra, 1883

*

J.L. CAMPBELL

On March 17th 1883, after prolonged agrarian discontent in the Highlands and Islands, which culminated in serious riots in Skye and elsewhere, in consequence of which warships were sent to the Minch, the Crofters' Commission consisting of Lord Napier and Ettrick, K.T. (Chairman), Sir Kenneth S. Mackenzie, Bart., Donald Cameron of Lochiel, M.P., Charles Fraser-Mackintosh, M.P., Sheriff Alexander Nicolson, D.L., and Professor Donald MacKinnon,[1] was appointed by the second Gladstone Government to "inquire into the condition of the Crofters and Cottars in the Highlands and Islands of Scotland, and all matters affecting the same, or relating thereto."[2]

Some of the events which indirectly led to this belated intervention of the Government have been described in previous chapters.[3] At the bottom of the trouble was the lack of security of tenure which in effect gave the estate management complete power over the lives of its small tenants, together with a fundamentally unstable economic situation whereby large farms, often the creations of earlier clearances, marched with overcrowded crofting townships where the tenants were sometimes wretchedly short of land. In South Uist and Benbecula, for example, out of the 1883 land rental of £5983, 18s. 4d., thirteen tenants paid £2763, 2s. 6d. while the remaining £3320, 15s. 10d. was paid by 787 crofters. Land hunger, not agricultural value, fixed the crofters' rents; lack of security of tenure and the right to compensation for improvements made it valueless or nearly so for the small tenant to attempt to improve his holding or his house, since all such improvements became automatically the property of the estate. Moreover, it was dangerous for him to criticize the management of the estate in any way, for such criticism could be met with the threat of

1 Professor of Celtic Literature and Languages in the University of Edinburgh.
2 *Report of the Crofters' Commission*, p. 12.
3 See pp. 135-148 and 170-177.

ejection. It is only right to add that when the Commission sat in 1883 and the majority of the crofter witnesses refused to give evidence until promised by the estate that what they said—most of which was exceedingly plain-spoken, sometimes even a little coloured—such promises were only refused in two cases, on estates in Orkney and Islay, and only three evictions followed the sittings of the Crofters' Commission. Perhaps public opinion prevented others. In any case, the existence of such powers as those the estates legally possessed over the lives of their small tenants, however little they were used in fact, were felt to be an anachronism and a constant source of irritation.

The outcome of the work of the Crofters' Commission is described on page 269. The Commission travelled all over the Highlands and Islands, including Caithness, Orkney and Shetland, in the summer and autumn of 1883, and had an exciting moment when its boat was wrecked off Tiumpan Head in Lewis. The Commission took evidence in Barra at Castlebay on Saturday 26th May 1883, having sat at Portree on the 24th May. The first and principal witness who gave evidence before the Crofters' Commission at Castlebay[1] was Michael Buchanan, crofter-fisherman of Borve, forty years of age. Buchanan had been elected by the crofters of Borve to make a statement of their grievances; he did not actually hold a croft himself, but lived in that of his brother, with whom he worked and whom he aided to pay the rent. It is notable that out of the six representatives that were chosen by the Barra townships to appear before the Commission two were cottars and two others did not have crofts of their own, which suggests that the people chose as delegates men whose interests could be least adversely affected in consequence of any statement they might make.

In a brief statement Buchanan outlined the Barra crofters' case:

"The people are complaining of the smallness of their holding and its inferior quality, of the up-handedness of the factors, and the oppression of landlords.

"Before the year 1827[2] (when the first large farm was made) the island of Barra was almost always occupied by crofters, who lived comfortably and contentedly in possession of reasonably large crofts, the population being then about 3000, and at present it is only 2000."[3]

1 *Minutes of Evidence*, p. 543.
2 The year General MacNeill went bankrupt. See p. 158.
3 This is an exaggeration. In 1821 the population of Barra was 2303, and in 1881 it was 2161.

Buchanan then went on to enumerate particular grievances, which can be divided into two classes: grievances against the Estate and its managers, past and present, and grievances against the tacksmen, or large tenant farmers, of which there were then two, Dr MacGillivray at Eoligarry and R. McLellan at Vatersay.

Complaints against the Estate

1. That forty years previously most of the horses and cows of the crofters in Barra had been taken away by ground officers and estate officials.

2. That thirty-seven years ago stirks and two-year-olds had been taken by ground officers and estate officials, in the name of rent, and sold by private bargain to their own friends, for prices ranging from half a crown to 6s. 6d.

3. That the use of receipts had not been always properly understood, and that there had been cases up till about twenty years previously when rents had been paid and then demanded again.

4. That the factors showed partiality towards the large farmers at the expense of the crofters.

5. That cattle were forcibly taken in the name of rent, sold, and the proceeds not always credited to the tenant.

Buchanan expressed this very vividly:

> ". . . their cattle were forcibly taken away from them, and in many cases after selling these cattle some of the men did not get any credit for the proceeds. I refer to the cattle taken away in those days."

LORD NAPIER. "You mean the cattle that were purchased by the factors or the ground agents?"

BUCHANAN. "They were taken away by the ground agents and factors."

LORD NAPIER. "And no payment made?"

BUCHANAN. "For a nominal price, and in the name of rent, and in many cases afterwards the people never got credit for the money proceeds. The inhabitants of the island being reduced to such poverty, the consequence was that they were not able to pay rent, and could scarcely ask for land. Consequently the best and the most of the land fell into the hands of large farmers,[1] and the poor men were huddled

1 The whole of the north of Barra, including Ardmhór, Ardmhinis, Greian, Cliat, and Allasdale; Garrygall; Bentangaval; and Vatersay, had been in the hands of large farmers.

together, the one lessening the holding of the other; and that was on the most worthless and useless patches of land that could be found within the marches of the parish of Barra. Labouring under such disadvantages, they were obliged to apply to Dr M'Gillivray for some ground, for which they paid sixty days' labour per acre of sandy, inferior, and exhausted soil. About six years ago there were letters down from the English market desiring the natives of this island to gather every kind of shell-fish, particularly cockles, which were and are very abundant, and to be found on the strand lying adjacent to Dr M'Gillivray's farm. Dr M'Gillivray tried to prevent any collection of this shell-fish. The people did not pay very much attention to what he said. Then his brother-in-law, being at that time head ground officer on the estate,—or, at least, he was called so—drew up a paper with orders that it should be posted up on the chapel door,[1] threatening the gatherers of this shell-fish with certain penalties. The officiating clergyman of that chapel did not give his assent to this proceeding, and told his congregation that he considered it an illegal act. Being baffled, those two gentlemen, as justices of the peace, ordered policemen to watch for fear that any of the shell-fish should be laid down above high-water mark."

LORD NAPIER. "Was Dr M'Gillivray a tacksman or a proprietor?"

BUCHANAN. "A tacksman. He is the largest farmer on this estate. His brother-in-law, to whom I have referred, Roderick M'Lellan, then commenced to prevent the thoroughfare down to the shipping place, and even prevented the use of the steamer's boat to carry the cargo on board. Seemingly they were willing to deprive the poor inhabitants of the produce of the sea, as they were instrumental in depriving them of the produce of their native soil. They coveted, and succeeded in their attempts, and put us back in the precarious occupation of fishing, which limited our livelihood to an inferior condition. Another prevalent grievance is, that should I or any other man, particularly any other tenant who pays his rent honestly, say a word on behalf of another man, mostly all of the officials on the

1 The Catholic chapel.

estate are down on him, and consequently he is afraid to say much. The inhabitants of this island have every confidence in their present proprietrix. Lady Gordon Cathcart, that she would promote their interest and comfort were their cases properly laid before her ladyship, but the factor steps in and offers every possible opposition."[1]

Buchanan went on to say that as fishing was only possible at certain seasons of the year, fishing as a whole-time occupation was not practicable, but it was a great help combined with the land. The fishermen were very much hindered by poor postal communication (at that time there was no telegraph in Barra, and all the mails came by Dunvegan and Lochmaddy). Buchanan suggested that a fisherman should have seven acres to keep a cow and a horse—the cow for milk and the horse to carry peats— and potato ground; and that for the sake of the fish curers who gave much employment every summer in Barra the telegraph should be extended from Lochboisdale to Castlebay. He then mentioned two more grievances the crofters had against the tacksman; first, that if their horses and cattle happened to stray over the march they were pounded in a muddy pound, and sometimes intimation of pounding was not promptly given; and secondly, that to get bent (which grew chiefly on Dr M'Gillivray's farm) to thatch their houses they had to labour twelve days for two small cartloads, and sometimes were refused any bent. He added that the hope the crofters had had of getting larger holdings, on the falling in of the lease of Vatersay (held then as a big farm by Mr M'Lellan) had unfortunately been disappointed. This ended his statement.

Cross-examined by Lord Napier, Buchanan was asked to give examples of the compulsory seizure of cattle on rent account. He quoted the case of a widow in Earsary from whom a heifer had been taken against 30s. of arrears, and sold to a man on the island, the amount not being credited to her account. He quoted also the example of Donald MacKinnon of Tangusdale, from whom the same ground officer—one John M'Gregor—had taken a stirk. The ground officer then took the stirk to a house in the neighbourhood where, after several drinks, he asked the man of the house if he would buy the stirk for 7s. This was refused, but Donald MacKinnon's wife being in the same house, and within earshot, came in and herself bought back the stirk for 7s.

1 Lady Gordon Cathcart visited Barra once only during the fifty-four years she owned it.

Asked to quote an example of the exaction of a second payment of rent after loss or mislaying of a receipt, Buchanan quoted the case of Murdoch MacKinnon of Brevaig, about sixteen years previously, from whom a second payment had so been demanded by Mr Birnie, the factor; but by luck MacKinnon had eventually found the receipt and escaped having to pay his rent a second time. Questioned if these abuses had existed in recent years, Buchanan said that the compulsory seizure of cattle had ceased about twelve years previously but that mistakes over receipts still arose at times. The pounding of strayed cattle still continued.

Cross-examined by Sir Kenneth Mackenzie, Buchanan said that the Township of Borve had been founded about sixty years previously, and made then into fourteen crofts. It now contained eighteen crofts, of equal size but not of equal quality, and thirty-six families of crofters. He and his brother had half a croft, and grazed two cows, a heifer, and two working ponies on the common pasture.

The population of Borve had been very much increased by the bringing in of people from other townships at the time of the clearances thirty-five years previously; fourteen had come from Greian and Cliat, two from Craigstone, and three from Allasdale; this with the natural increase of Borve had left the township very much overcrowded. Greian and Cliat were now part of Dr M'Gillivray's farm; Craigstone and Allasdale were occupied by crofters. Allasdale had only just been re-let to crofters, of whom seven had gone there, including four men from Borve. Buchanan suggested that the superfluous population of Borve would be better at Poll or Killbarr, Scorrival or Vaslin, Cliat or Ardmhòr, or Orradh or Bogach-na-forla, or Ru-lis or Sandray, or Vatersay, or Uidh or Caolas or Bentangaval.

Questioned on the labour charged by Dr M'Gillivray for potato ground, Buchanan said that in rare cases female labour was taken at the same rate as male; the usual system was for eight men each to take the planting of a barrel, which came to an acre. In an ordinarily good season they would get a return of eight or nine barrels per barrel planted, in bad years scarcely double the quantity of seed.

Cross-examined by Lochiel, Buchanan repudiated the suggestion that the meeting which elected him a delegate had not been properly representative of the crofters of Borve.

Asked to produce further examples of the oppression of landlords and factors, Buchanan quoted the case of Isabella M'Lauchlin in Borve, who wished to resume some land she had sublet to another woman, who refused to go. The factor said that unless they settled the question themselves Isabella M'Lauchlin herself would be turned out. Subsequently her rent was refused and she was removed, but later reinstated in half of the croft.

Questioning Buchanan about the stirks, Lochiel went on to say:

> "Do I understand that the factor took the stirk away from the crofter and sold it on pretence that the proceeds would be credited to him for payment of the rent due, and that the proceeds were not credited to him for the rent due?"
>
> BUCHANAN. "I say he did."
>
> LOCHIEL. "Do you know whether it ever occurred to the crofter to put the matter into the hands of the procurator-fiscal?"
>
> BUCHANAN. "He did not do that. He was afraid that if he did so he would be worse off and only double his misfortune."
>
> LOCHIEL. "Does it not occur to you, if the statement you have made is correct, that it was more a question for the procurator-fiscal that it is for the Royal Commission?"
>
> BUCHANAN. "You know that best, your Honour, only I had to state it."
>
> LOCHIEL. "You said the horses and cows were taken away from you forty-two years ago, and the stirks thirty-seven years ago."
>
> BUCHANAN. "Yes."
>
> LOCHIEL. "Where did the stirks come from if the cows were taken away five years previously?"
>
> BUCHANAN. "There were some men whose stock was cleared completely away, and some men to whom perhaps a cow or so was left. There is a man in the township of Tangusdale from whom nine head of cattle were taken in that same year."
>
> LOCHIEL. "As a rule, do the crofters in this island not possess cows?"
>
> BUCHANAN. "A great many do not possess cows."

Buchanan went on to say that some of the crofters of Glen had applied for Mr M'Lellan's farm when the lease fell in, sending a deputation to Mr R. MacDonald, the chief factor of the Gordon Cathcart estates, at Aberdeen, but the farm was refused.

Questioned on the kelp industry, Buchanan said that it had gone on into Colonel Gordon's time (after 1840).

LOCHIEL. "Was not the cessation of the kelp manufacture the principal cause of the poverty of the people in the island?"

BUCHANAN. "I do not think it was; it was partly."

LOCHIEL. "To what do you attribute it, if it was not due to the disappearance of the kelp manufacture?"

BUCHANAN. "I attribute it to the following reasons: to the famine that followed the failure of the potato crop, coupled with the doings of the factors, studying not the interest of the crofters or cottars."

LOCHIEL. "Do you think the people could live by the island here entirely?"

BUCHANAN. "I think so."

LOCHIEL. "Do you think there is enough land here to support a population of 3000?"

BUCHANAN. "I can safely say there is."[1]

Cross-examined by Mr Fraser-Mackintosh, Buchanan recounted the history of the estate. Before 1827 conditions were favourable. In 1827 the property was let by General MacNeill; about 1840 it was sold (to Colonel Gordon of Cluny), and around 1847 the evictions began. There had been no evictions under the MacNeills, except that the tenants of Poll and Kilbarr had been moved to other townships.[2]

MR FRASER-MACKINTOSH. "May I take it that all the townships which you stated might be given back (to the crofters) were cleared?"

BUCHANAN. "You are quite safe in doing so."

MR FRASER-MACKINTOSH. "Were there circumstances of great hardships in connection with some of the evictions?"

BUCHANAN. "Heart-rending."

MR FRASER-MACKINTOSH. "Take the last one, which probably occurred within your own recollection?"

BUCHANAN. "I have seen with my own eyes the roof of the house actually falling down upon the fire, and smoke issuing."

MR FRASER-MACKINTOSH. "The houses were knocked down?"

1 The greatest recorded population of Barra was 2620 in 1911. The present (1931 census) population is 2250. No doubt if the smaller islands were re-settled, and the inshore fisheries properly protected and developed, the parish of Barra could support 3000 people.
2 To make the farm at Eoligarry.

THE BOOK OF BARRA

BUCHANAN. "Yes."

MR FRASER-MACKINTOSH. "Are you aware, in connection with the last eviction, that the people when they arrived in Canada were in a most miserable condition, dependent upon charity?"[1]

BUCHANAN. "I have seen that stated in public prints."

MR FRASER-MACKINTOSH. "Do the people here occasionally receive letters from some of those who were evicted?"

BUCHANAN. "Occasionally, but not very often."

MR FRASER-MACKINTOSH. "Do you know how they are getting on?"

BUCHANAN. "I believe two or three per cent got on pretty fair, but the rest we receive very bad accounts of."

Further questioned, Buchanan said that of old the MacNeills could bring out 200 fighting men, and their property extended as far north as North Boisdale in South Uist. He then gave the names of fourteen men who had been factors of the estate since Colonel Gordon bought it around 1840; of these twelve had been strangers, and ignorant of Gaelic. Mr Fraser-Mackintosh continued with questions about the big farms:

"What is the value of a day's labour here to a man if he gets a day's work to do?"

BUCHANAN. "The value of a man's labour here among big farmers is a shilling."

MR FRASER-MACKINTOSH. "Then according to that, Dr M'Gillivray gets (rent) at the rate of £3 per acre, being sixty days at one shilling a day?"

BUCHANAN. "Yes."

MR FRASER-MACKINTOSH. "Do you consider that a high rent?"

BUCHANAN. "I do."

MR FRASER-MACKINTOSH. "Have you any idea of the extent of Dr M'Gillivray's farm?"

BUCHANAN. "I suppose he occupies about 6000 acres."

MR FRASER-MACKINTOSH. "Has he a number of cottars?"

BUCHANAN. "He has seven shepherds besides his own domestic servants."

1 See p. 174.

MR FRASER-MACKINTOSH. "There will be about fifty altogether?"

BUCHANAN. "I cannot exactly say."

MR FRASER-MACKINTOSH. "What proportion does his farm bear to the whole island?"

BUCHANAN. "Pretty well on to the half of the island, and the best half."[1]

MR FRASER-MACKINTOSH. "And the other islands?"

BUCHANAN. "The other islands."

Questioned further about Vatersay, Buchanan said it had been crofters from Glen and Castlebay who wished to go there. There had been people on Vatersay before, and the reason given for not letting it to the crofters, that there was not enough water, was not supportable.

As for the bent, it grew naturally, and was not planted by Mr M'Gillivray; cutting could not harm it, as that only encouraged growth. The only reason he could give for M'Gillivray's charging so much for it was that he wanted his own work done at as little expense as possible.

Cross-examined by Professor Mackinnon, Buchanan said that the crofters had to pay for sea-ware, which was cast mostly on the strand adjacent to the big farm. The farmer's sheep often strayed on to the crofters' common, but were never pounded by the crofters, although the farmer pounded the crofters' sheep if they strayed over the march. The crofters would not dare to pound the farmer's sheep. It was the farmer who had objected to the cockles being taken, not the factor.

Cross-examined by Sheriff Nicolson, Buchanan said that the Barra crofters had not got their ideas from Ireland, and objected to having been called Fenians, as the local doctor had called them.

As to law cases, the people had to go to the procurator-fiscal at Lochmaddy, two days away, and most of them would prefer to be involved in small losses rather than have to undertake such a journey.

In reply to Mr Fraser-Mackintosh, Buchanan stated that the meeting which had elected him delegate was quite a spontaneous affair, and his election was perfectly regular. Buchanan's cross-examination concluded with the question from Mr Fraser-Mackintosh:

"Now, is it the case that, from the state of matters in this island, it is practically impossible for the crofters to do anything but submit to whatever the proprietor or factor may put on them?"

1 M'Gillivray did not have half of the island, but he had at least half of the cultivable ground.

BUCHANAN. "Owing to the position in which the people are, it was ever a very prevalent idea on this island that they would have to obey their superiors, particularly landlords and factors; and, I believe, should they wish to do anything, they could scarcely do it without consulting landlord or factor, whether to their own benefit or the reverse."

The next witness was Donald Campbell (57), crofter, of Craigstone, who read a statement setting forth the usual grievances of the crofters—overcrowding, poor land, and too high rents. Fifty years ago there were twelve families in Craigstone; now there were twenty-six on the same lands. Crofters evicted from townships cleared to make the big farm had been crowded in on them, but they had had no abatement of rent though the size of their holdings had been reduced. Since the potato famine (1846) the potato crop had been precarious; in bad winters they had no support except shellfish, and restrictions had even been made on the gathering of these, as Buchanan had stated. In the time of Colonel Gordon the young people had been forbidden to marry on the estate, or build houses on it, though since Lady Gordon Cathcart had come into the property, this prohibition had been removed.[1]

"If I allowed my son or daughter to remain even in the stable, they would deprive me of my holding, or threaten to deprive me of my holding.... They have left us so poor that when the children of the poor man grew up, not one of them could remain assisting the father. They would require to earn wages through the world. Perhaps the son would go away before he was of age, to earn wages, and never return. They sent away most of our relatives to America thirty-five years ago. They pulled down the houses over their heads, and injured them in every possible way. They valued the brutes higher than the men whom God created in His own image, and were more gentle with them, and all the respect we have received for fifty years has been from the present proprietrix. But it is difficult for her to improve our position."

1 This prohibition was enforced on a number of Highland estates before 1883 to prevent over-crowding and increase of population. It was intolerable in a place like Barra when half the arable land was in the hands of one farmer.

Cross-examined by Lochiel, Campbell said he could say nothing of the present proprietrix or the factor. They had not made the crofters worse off than they were before, but they had not made them any better. What the crofters wanted was land at the old rents, and assistance to stock it now they had grown so poor. He himself had five acres, half of which were rock, and two horses, a cow and a heifer on the common, for which he paid a rent of £2, 15s. a year.

Cross-examined by Mr Fraser-Mackintosh, Campbell said he had to buy meal every year to support his family. Milk was very scarce. A great grievance was the pounding of strayed cattle by the large farmers. The pounded cattle were not always well treated, and word was not always given that they had been put in the pound. If the crofters got suitable land they could raise good stock.

Cross-examined by Sir Kenneth Mackenzie, Campbell said he got one return of oats, two of barley, and six of potatoes. He sowed two bushels of oats and two of barley, and eight barrels of potatoes. Having given up fishing, he now made ends meet by labouring in the Lowlands every year. The Barra fishermen could do well if they had good boats, but they must have land too to support them in the stormy seasons.

Cross-examined by Lord Napier, Campbell said that the present proprietrix had shown her good intentions by allowing the young married people to build houses on the island, and by making a pier, but she had done nothing more.

John Mackinnon (69), cottar at Glen and formerly crofter in Tangusdale, the delegate elected by the people of Tangusdale, said that their grievance in Tangusdale was that they had had a third of their land taken from them sixteen years ago. Other land had been promised in return, but had not been given.

The land taken, about 80-100 acres, had been given to the then tacksman of Vatersay, Mr Archibald M'Lellan. After the land had been taken, no proportionate reduction of rent had been allowed. Since then they had not dared to protest for fear of being put out altogether.

In former days little meal was imported. Now the land was deteriorating with constant cropping. The principal tacksman, Dr M'Gillivray, had a good deal of arable land; altogether about half of Barra. He (MacKinnon) had had a croft in Tangusdale for about 13 years, but was summarily ejected by Mr Birnie, then factor, to make room for the policeman, though his rent had been paid. No compensation was given him. He was now a day worker with a house for which he paid 7s. 6d. a year, and a cow, which he grazed for a rent of about £1 a year.

John Macpherson (68), cottar, the delegate from Kentangaval, complained that the cottars were crowded on the crofters in Kentangaval, and wanted lands of their own. There were twenty-four cottar families in Kentangaval, who worked on the tacksmen's farms. A few of the cottars had cows, and some had patches of land on M'Lellan's farm. They got pasture from the crofters, for which they paid about £1 for a cow. He himself did not work on a farm, but acted as agent for fish curers in engaging female labour. The wages paid them by the curers were £1 of arles money in the winter, eight pence per barrel filled and packed, and three pence per hour of other work. They would make about £4 a season including the arles.

There were about twenty crofters in Kentangaval besides the cottars. His father had been a crofter, but his mother when a widow had been ejected in 1827 for trying to prevent the seizure of her sheep and cattle by General MacNeill's estate officers. There were no arrears to be settled at the time.

It was a complaint of the Barra herring fishermen that they were charged 7s. 6d. for net-ground on their own holdings.

Thomas Ross and Thomas Jenkins, both fish curers from Burghead, Morayshire, were the next two witnesses. Both complained bitterly of the lack of telegraphic facilities at Castlebay, which hindered them from learning the state of the markets, and from ordering salt for curing when necessary. The postmaster-general had been petitioned three times for an extension of the cable from Lochboisdale to Castlebay, but with no success.

Cross-examined, Ross said that the engagement the curers had with the fishermen was about 16s. to £1 a cran and a bounty of £50 per boat, also £1 or £2 of earnest money after that. In wages and purchases the fish curers spent about £1500 a year on Barra. There were thirty-three curers in Castlebay and twelve in Vatersay, each paying £5 for their ground to the proprietrix.

Thomas Jenkins, cross-examined, said that, in his opinion, fishing could not be carried on from Barra all the year round, owing to the weather. Barra fishermen had only recently started at herring fishing; there were eight Barra boats from Castlebay working that year. If the Barra people had good boats, they could make a living from the fishing; but they should have crofts and some grazing as well.

Allan M'Intyre (60), cottar and fisherman, delegate from Glen and Castlebay, described the overcrowding and impoverishment that had taken place in his own township. Castlebay in his first recollection had been tenanted by ten families, having each from two to seven cows. Now there were twenty-two crofters' families there, occupying the same place, with thirty landless cottar families amongst them. They all needed more land. Some of the crofters had had hopes of getting it on Vatersay, but these had been disappointed. His own father had had a croft. After he got it another man was put on it, and his fraction was too small to be worth anything. Most of the crofters had come from the other townships that had been cleared. They were very poor:

SHERIFF NICOLSON. "How do you make your living yourself?"

M'INTYRE. "By day's wages."

SHERIFF NICOLSON. "I suppose you buy all the meal and potatoes for yourself and your family?"

M'INTYRE. "It is six years since I ate anything that grew in Barra, whatever may happen with regard to the small patch that I planted this year."

SHERIFF NICOLSON. "You have no cow?"

M'INTYRE. "No."

SHERIFF NICOLSON. "Have any of the cottars cows?"

M'INTYRE. "One or two of them have a cow."

SHERIFF NICOLSON. "Where do you get your milk if you get any?"

M'INTYRE. "I know no such thing as milk. I don't know what it means for a number of years. There is not a place here where milk can be had. Can I get it from the man who has it not?—who requires it as much as I do?"

SHERIFF NICOLSON. "Then of course you are obliged to take tea, sugar, treacle and such things, instead of milk?"

M'INTYRE. "We are obliged to take gruel."

SHERIFF NICOLSON. "Are things worse than they were when your father was alive?"

M'INTYRE. "We are just able to live."

In reply to Lochiel, M'Intyre said that the cottars had a few sheep and stirks in very poor condition. They wanted land that would yield crops. The Castlebay tenants were of the opinion they could stock Vatersay if they got it.

Murdoch M'Kinnon (60), delegate from Earsary, said there were twenty-two crofters in Earsary, but only seven undivided crofts there. He himself had the fourth part of a croft, and a horse, a cow, a stirk and a heifer, which the croft could not, however, maintain. His rent was £2, 5s. He could not get a good price for his stirks as they were not well fed. He had between 1½ and 2 acres of arable land, and had not taken £1 worth of meal out of it in any year. His father had had the whole croft, of which he now had the fourth part, at a rent of £5. At that time there were five cottars in Earsary instead of twenty-two. Besides the twenty-two crofters there were also fourteen cottars in the township. Questioned by Lord Napier:

> "Is there any good land near your place which might be used to make the crofts larger?"
>
> M'KINNON. "There is a tack beside us, but perhaps it is too small for the man who holds it."
>
> LORD NAPIER. "What tack is that?"
>
> M'KINNON. "Oleas. If I had land that would yield half as much as the amount I pay for meal I would endeavour to make a living out of it. For eighteen years I paid on an average £20 to the merchant for meal and things to support my weak family. I was thirty-five years ago going to the east coast fishing. I believe I brought over £500 home. I spent the whole of that in meal and other things to support the family, all for want of land. If I had a good croft I would have some of that to leave to those I leave behind. If it were not for the local merchant here (Mr M'Neill), who keeps us all in provisions, no person would be alive in this place at all, and all the stock in the countryside is his to take if he chose to take possession of it—between himself and the proprietor."

When asked why, if he was short of land, he had not offered for a lot on Bentangaval when that was offered to the crofters that year in small lots, M'Kinnon said it was too far away (5 miles) and not suitable arable land in his opinion; also, it was believed that the Vatersay tacksman was retaining the right to put his cattle on it if his own pasture ran short.

He had been a fisherman, and used to get 7d. for ling and 3d. for cod from the curers, also 12s. a dozen for lobsters.

Farquhar M'Neill (61), crofter, the delegate from Brevaig, said that overcrowding was very bad in Brevaig and the land was exhausted by continuous cropping. "They got land for potato ground, and they pay dear enough for it, I think—3s. for the planting of a barrel of potatoes—and carrying seaware to manure that ground for 12 miles in small boats which will carry only a ton and a half each, so that the people are in a very sad plight, and if they could at all afford to get better lands they are much in need of them. The little stock that they keep upon the ground they have is not their own, but belongs to the merchant who keeps them in provisions."

In spite of an emigration thirty-two years or so ago, the township was still crowded. They needed more arable land rather than pasture.

Rev. Father James Chisholm (29) stated the grievance of the Catholics in Barra (nearly the entire population) in the matter of schools. There were three schools in Barra and one in Mingulay, but there was only one Catholic teacher in these schools.[1] There were school-board elections, but the people were under the fear of the factor's power, and the Catholics did not have a majority on the board—only two out of five of its members were Catholics.

Norman Maclean (48), Free Church Catechist in Barra, said that the people of his communion had improved during his residence of fourteen years in Barra, now possessing better houses, clothing, and stock. They had made no complaints about land to him. He could not say anything about the people belonging to other denominations.[2]

Replies by Tacksman and Factor[3]

D.W. M'Gillivray (74), surgeon and farmer of Eoligarry, commenced his statement by the remark that he only had less than a third of Barra, instead of a half, as had been said. He denied completely the assertions of Michael Buchanan and Donald Campbell that the crofters had been prevented or prohibited from taking cockles on the Tràigh Mhòr. No such prohibition had ever existed, in respect of cockles or any other kind of shellfish, though inquiries had been made to learn if they could be protected in the same way that oysters or mussels were, but it was found that that was impossible. What might have given rise to the idea was the fact that General MacNeill (1822-

---

1 This question was the subject of a considerable amount of correspondence in 1881 and 1882, which is printed in Appendix A of the Commission's Report, pp. 97-112. From it can be learned how completely the local politics of Barra were dominated by the factor at this time.
2 Canon Chisholm and Norman MacLean were actually the last witnesses examined in Barra. The order is changed here for the sake of clarity.
3 For the sake of clarity, Dr M'Gillivray's cross-examination is printed here after that of MacIntyre, MacKinnon, and MacNeill, though he was examined before them.

1838) had forbidden the digging of cockles in the line of road over which he used to drive to Eoligarry House.

With reference to the bent, that had always been readily granted, and the charge was three shillings a horse load, paid in labour done on his farm. The price of bent worked out at 4s. a cartload, or four short days' work. The assertion that twelve days' labour was charged was grossly exaggerated. Bent was a very good protection against sand drift, and was very good pasture.

As for the potatoes, he had given two hundred families[1] potato ground on his farm that year to relieve distress. The charge was two shillings per barrel planted, or two days' labour, and was nearly always paid in work. (This works out at sixteen days' work per acre.) Two thousand barrels were planted in a season. Often ground had been reclaimed in this manner, and much improved by this cultivation. The labour paid was used in making improvements.

LOCHIEL. "It has been suggested that when Buchanan mentioned sixty days' labour for the potato ground he intended to say sixteen?"

BUCHANAN. "No, I said it on good authority, and I have witnesses here."

LORD NAPIER. "The calculation is sixty days' labour per acre?"

DR M'GILLIVRAY. "Well, the way I calculate it is so much to plant a barrel of potatoes, and the people are quite willing to take it in that way."

LORD NAPIER. "It is a mutual benefit?"

DR M'GILLIVRAY. "Apparently so. They are better served; and when they are scarce of potato ground, they even come to me, and if I can give it I give it, and if not it is because there is a scarcity of it."

LORD NAPIER. "What is the benefit it confers on your ground?"

DR M'GILLIVRAY. "They say there are so many cottars and people of that description that potato ground is scarce among them."

LORD NAPIER. "That is the benefit to them, but in what degree does it improve your ground?"

DR M'GILLIVRAY. "It improves my ground so far, but it also obliges me to give it to them when they are in need of it. They work pieces of ground for me. They work, for instance,

1 This would be two-thirds of the families in Barra at least.

at drains, etc., and take this in lieu of money. This is far
more beneficial than money. Suppose I gave 2s. or 1s. 6d. a
day, this is far more beneficial to them than that."

Dr M'Gillivray went on to say that the crofters were getting numerous
because they intermarried and did not leave the island; that was the
ways subdivisions arose. There had been no evictions on his farm since
he got it. The people worked for him only in the winter, when the days
were short.

In his opinion, the condition of the cottars had improved of late,
since the fishing was now better conducted and Lady Gordon Cathcart
had helped them with boats. He thought more money was coming into
the island, for the people were buying more of his wool than they used
to buy. They wove and spun and dyed it themselves.

In reply to Sir Kenneth Mackenzie, Dr M'Gillivray said he had no
cottars on his farm, which he had now had for thirty-five years. It had
not been added to since he got it.

SIR KENNETH MACKENZIE. "You think the people have been
improving in their condition since you first remember
them?"

DR M'GILLIVRAY. "They are improving. They were nearly as
well off before the potato blight[1] as they are now, but the
potato blight put them far back. At that time there was an
emigration promoted by Colonel Gordon, which helped to
relieve the property pretty well. The people of South Uist
and Barra petitioned[2] in a body to be helped away, and
Colonel Gordon helped them away. He sent a vessel to
South Uist, and a vessel to Barra to take them. He also sent
clothing for scores of families."

SIR KENNETH MACKENZIE. "Are those the people of whom
we hear as having gone to Canada, and as having arrived
there destitute?"

DR M'GILLIVRAY. "Yes. I heard of a lot of people who went
from South Uist and Barra, and some of them have done
well, and some few have not done quite so well. They
sometimes get apples and fruit there, which brings on
disease of the bowels, and they die in consequence of that."

1 In 1846.
2 See p. 174.

In reply to Lochiel, Dr M'Gillivray said he did not know of any emigrants who had been landed in Canada in a state of destitution. It might have happened in the case of some induced to go over by an emigration agent named M'Neilan[1] before Colonel Gordon got the property. He thought the people might emigrate again if they were assisted, as they were becoming crowded in Barra again.

With regard to the bent, people often would work for bent when they would not work for money. He very seldom refused it.

Cross-examined by Mr Fraser-Mackintosh:

"Are you aware that Lady Gordon Cathcart sent some people to Canada from her estates?"

DR M'GILLIVRAY. "Yes."

MR FRASER-MACKINTOSH. "And she presented them with a large sum of money?"

DR M'GILLIVRAY. "Yes; I thought she was too liberal."

MR FRASER-MACKINTOSH. "About £100 each?"

DR M'GILLIVRAY. "Yes; that was more liberality than we had seen at any other time."

MR FRASER-MACKINTOSH. "Don't you think she might have expended £100 in improving their condition here?"

DR M'GILLIVRAY. "I don't think she would, because they were crowded, and this gives them a chance in a place where they are not so crowded. If more of that were done it would be a benefit for all parties."

MR FRASER-MACKINTOSH. "Don't you think that if she had made an arrangement with you and settled these families, or given them £100 to settle them on nice crofts on Eoligarry, that would have been as good as sending them to Canada?"

DR M'GILLIVRAY. "Yes, for a time; but it would become just like the east side of Barra. From the fact of their being a fishing population, and the people not going away, they have scarcely room upon it; and supposing my farm was cut up and them planted on it, it would be crowded in a few years."

MR FRASER-MACKINTOSH. "You have stated correctly that several parts of the island of Barra are crowded, but are you not aware that the population of the island is a good deal less than it was in former years?"

DR M'GILLIVRAY. "Yes, but there is not very much difference."

1 See p. 128, if it is the same person.

MR FRASER-MACKINTOSH. "Could Lady Gordon Cathcart
raise as many men as the old MacNeills did? We are told they
could raise 250 to 300 fighting men."

DR M'GILLIVRAY. "I don't know, they are not so much inclined
for that sort of thing now; they would rather go and fish."

Questioned further about the cockles Dr M'Gillivray said that if any
prohibition had been made it was without his knowledge. He did not
know if his brother-in-law Roderick M'Lellan, the other tacksman, had
done it.

His farm was not more than 5000 acres, including the small
islands. The rent was £550, and he had had three fourteen-year leases.
He had known General MacNeill well. The MacNeills had left Kismul
Castle about five or six generations previously and lived first at Borve,
then at Vaslin, finally building Eoligarry.

MR FRASER-MACKINTOSH. "Did you hear one of the
delegates mention a statement about the officers of the
MacNeills coming and taking away his mother's cow almost
by violence?"[1]

DR M'GILLIVRAY. "I have heard something of that sort but I
cannot speak with precision about it."

MR FRASER-MACKINTOSH. "Are you aware there were such
extortions?"

DR M'GILLIVRAY. "There were at the time of John MacNeill,
the fellow that lost his property."

LOCHIEL. "And took other peoples'?"

DR M'GILLIVRAY. "There was a sort of confusion, and the
officers went round."

MR FRASER-MACKINTOSH. "Then the story which this
man told about his sister meeting the officers with the cow
and taking it home, you have no doubt is accurate?"

DR M'GILLIVRAY. "I cannot say it is accurate. I heard of
some parties taking liberties—not the factor or the laird—
but some parties in the shape of ground officers, and there
was no law."

Dr M'Gillivray then went on to complain of the need of a Sheriff
Court, especially to settle cases of trespass. They had had Small Debt
Courts at one time, but they had been abandoned.

1 See p. 190.

MR FRASER-MACKINTOSH. "Is there any justice resident in this district except yourself?"

DR M'GILLIVRAY. "Yes, Roderick M'Lellan is a justice, too."

MR FRASER-MACKINTOSH. "Are these the only two?"

DR M'GILLIVRAY. "Yes, besides the factor. We used to have little courts for settling matters connected with trespass and injuring people's corn; we used to settle all that between ourselves."

MR FRASER-MACKINTOSH. "Why was all that given up?"

DR M'GILLIVRAY. "The factors who were coming after that were not justices, and the thing broke down."

Ranald MacDonald, Aberdeen, Factor and Secretary to Lady Gordon Cathcart, a native of Benbecula, in a heated and contemptuous statement denied that any grievances existed on the Barra estate, and attacked the characters of the delegates, particularly that of Michael Buchanan:

"I must say that those who have appeared to-day are not the people on whom I would place most reliance, and I have to explain to the Commissioners that, being desirable when they came to Barra to economize my time as far as practicable, I thought of asking the crofters in the different townships to meet openly and name three individuals among themselves who would give me full information regarding their circumstances, regarding anything which they thought it was possible or practicable to remedy, and that I should have the opportunity of making short explanations to the crofters from the different townships who met me. They did elect three persons in every township to give me information.... Now, I expected when the Commissioners came round, that some of those whom the crofters themselves selected in the open and unrestricted manner I have stated would have been among those who came forward to the Commissioners to give evidence. I wished to avoid the possibility of anyone saying that I interfered in the remotest way with the evidence that was brought forward, and I made no inquiry, and did not know who was to appear to-day. I confess I was a little disappointed—without reflecting in any way on those who came, because I wish to guard particularly against saying anything derogatory to them; but, at the same time, I must say that they are not the representatives to

give strangers an impression of the real state of affairs in Barra....
I only wish on the present occasion to reply to certain statements
which were made here to-day.... Several matters have been
brought before you as if they were a sort of general practice or
custom on the estate, of which I never heard the remotest whisper
until I came into this room to-day. I shall refer to a few of these,
and, in the first place, I shall refer to Michael Buchanan's
statements. He asked, in the way that he and others have been
tutored to ask, whether anything would be done to him in
consequence of his making certain statements; but no one knows
better than Michael Buchanan that, though his main employment
has been to go about and preach discontent among the people
here, no one connected with the estate would take the very
slightest notice of his doings. He knew very well that whatever he
did say to the Commissioners no notice would be taken of it. I am
sure the proper way to deal with a person of that kind is to take
no notice of him, because in the long run statements which have
no possible foundation in fact have no importance whatever, and
to take any notice of them would be to attach an importance to
the individual which sometimes is scarcely deserved.

"His first statement was about taking stirks and cows from the
tenants, and giving no credit for them. It is well known, and I say
it in presence of the Barra people, that such a custom does not
exist on the estate. In 1844 I find that, in consequence of the
destitute condition of the people of Barra, Dr M'Leod, who was
one of the most sympathizing factors they ever had on the estate,
was obliged to take ponies and horses, and cows and stirks from
the tenants in payment of arrears. I never did hear till to-day that
the people had any reasonable ground to suspect that either Dr
M'Leod or any other local factor on the estate of Barra ever
acted fraudulently or unjustly in connection with these matters."

MacDonald went on to say that if there had been any injustice, even
unintentional, he would have left no stone unturned to remedy it if it
had been brought to his notice. It was false to say, as Buchanan did,
that this system was carried on down to the present time.

With regard to receipts for rent, mistakes had sometimes arisen in
the past owing to there being several people of the same name in the
same township; now counterfoils were kept and such errors could not
arise. He denied absolutely that the taking of cockles had ever been

prohibited, or that the factor stepped in when matters were brought before Lady Gordon Cathcart, and offered objections.

As for the march between Dr M'Gillivray's farm and the crofters, there was a fence, but it was difficult to get all the crofters responsible for its upkeep to do their shares equally well. As for the condition of the inhabitants, he said:

"Some came forward, and Michael Buchanan was one of them, who said the inhabitants were reduced to poverty. He stated that in the strongest terms, and then there were others who came forward and said that the tenants of one of the townships are able to take a grazing requiring a capital of between £3000 and £4000 to stock it, so that these statements neutralize one another, and it is not necessary for me to say very much beyond what I do now. I don't know what may be the amount of debts due to the merchants, but judging from all the information I have been able to get, and I have endeavoured to get the most reliable information available, my conviction is that the general body of crofters are probably better off than they ever have been."

He then went on to say that compared to the East Coast, where "it is well known . . . that if a farmer has a capital ten times the amount of rent he pays he is considered to be in very good circumstances" the Barra crofters were very favourably placed. He gave the following statistics to justify his contention:

Number of Crofters in Barra	205
Stock of Crofters:	
311 cows at £7	£2177.0.0
188 six-quarter-old stirks at £5	940.0.0
184 stirks at £2	368.0.0
233 horses at £8	1864.0.0
79 colts at £5	395.0.0
1721 sheep / 716 young sheep	1000.0.0
Total value of Crofters' Stock	£6744.0.0

Stock of Cottars:

52 cows, 29 six-quarter-olds, 19 stirks, 56 horses, 15 colts, 188 old sheep and 140 young sheep, valued together at.	£1320.0.0
Value of crops (potatoes, barley, black oats, white oats and turnips)	£1720.12.0
Total value of Crofters' and Cottars' stock and crops (not including roofs of the houses)	£9784.12.0
Rent paid by Crofters (roughly 5.75 per cent on their capital)	£551.5.0
Arrears of rent outstanding	£2899.12.5$^{1}/_{2}$

"There are a few of the tenants who are not much in arrear, but there are others who are very deeply in arrear. Calculating the whole, and comparing the gross amount of arrears and the gross amount of rent, there are upwards of five years' rent in arrears, and some of them are upwards of ten; for instance, at Mingulay." . . . .

Mr MacDonald then went on to quote the rental of Barra from Whitsunday 1836 to Whitsunday 1837, the rental on which Colonel Gordon had purchased the estate from General MacNeill.[1]

1836 RENTAL

Crofters' lands	£1948.17.7
12$^{1}/_{2}$ Vacant crofts	97.0.0
Farms in General MacNeill's possession:	
Eoligarry grazing 4000 sheep.	
Vatersay grazing 1600 sheep.	
Hill of Bentangaval grazing 1100 sheep.	
Island of Sandray grazing 500 sheep.	
Island of Flodda grazing 200 sheep.	
Small Islands grazing 200 sheep.	
Grazing of 7600 sheep at 2s. 6d..	950.0.0
Total land rent of Barra	£2995.17.7

1 Barra was almost certainly over-rented at this time. See p. 169.

Kelp on the shores	£500.0.0
Alkali works	No sum
Mansion House and Fishing	£200.0.0
Gross Rental	£3695.0.0
Deducted as fanciful	£700.0.0
Net rent	£2995.17.7

PRESENT RENTAL (1882)

Crofters' rents	£551.0.0
Large farms	1621.11.2
Deducted for schools, churches and glebe	122.0.0
Net rental in 1882	£2050.11.2
Fall in Net rent since 1836	£905.6.5
Fall in Crofters' rents since 1836	£1397.12.7

The areas occupied by large farms and crofts were identical, except that in 1836 there had been crofters on the islands Fuday and Hellisay, and at Allasdale, for the last of which £140, 9s. a year was paid. These had been removed and the land added to Dr M'Gillivray's farm, but Allasdale had been re-let to crofters in 1882 at £110 a year. He could allow £400 or £500 a year rent for lands formerly let to crofters and latterly to Dr M'Gillivray (which would leave the reduction of crofters' rents made since 1836 to be about £950 instead of £1400). Castlebay had been rented at £169, 15s. in 1836; the present rent was £52, 11s. The rent of Craigstone in 1836 was £112, 17s. 7d.; now it was only £65.

Mr MacDonald said he could only account for this reduction in the total proportion of the rental paid by the crofters by the cessation of the kelp industry. It was also possible that the rental had been raised fictitiously by the MacNeills when they were about to sell, but he was not sure of that.

As for the petition that had been made for land on Vatersay, Lady Gordon Cathcart had thought that judging by Mingulay, where the people were upwards of ten years in arrears, Vatersay would not be suitable for small tenants.[1] Lady Gordon Cathcart thought it better

---

1 She depended entirely on the factor's advice in arriving at this judgment, which was quite erroneous.

that the fishermen should have as much land on Vatersay as would provide potatoes and maintain a cow, but not have crofts; he had since offered about 1700 acres of the grazing of Vatersay to forty-five fishermen on these terms, so that their stock of seven sheep and a cow each might graze in common there, but the people had not been able to buy the sheep. He did not think the fishermen should have crofts; they should fish all the time, as the East Coast men did. The cultivation of crofts interfered with the fishing.[1]

*

Since the sitting of the Commission at Castlebay left the last word with the Factor, it is necessary to point out in what respects his statement failed to meet the grievances of the crofters.

The attempt to discredit the character of the Barra witnesses who appeared before the Commission was not a very creditable action. Few of the other factors who appeared before the Commission elsewhere resorted to such a method. It was open to Mr MacDonald to refute the allegations and discredit the evidence as far as he could, which would have been best attempted without attacking the characters of the delegates themselves.

So far as the rents paid by the crofters was concerned, the comparison made by Mr MacDonald with the East Coast farms has no value. It is obvious that a very small holding in a remote district far from any markets cannot pay as proportionately high a rent as a middle-sized farm situated in an easily accessible district. So far as the fall of crofters' rents since 1836 is concerned, it is very surprising that Mr MacDonald did not mention the main cause for this, the potato famine, which not only caused great destitution at the time, but left the ground in very bad condition for a long period afterwards; indeed, according to Sir John MacNeill the value of the products of the crofts had been reduced by one-half in consequence of the failure of the potato. This, and the deterioration of the land through continuous cropping, and the failure of the kelp industry, fully account for the fall in crofters' rents, apart from any fictitious inflation of the rental that may have been engineered at the time the estate was sold. Nor was Mr MacDonald straightforward about the areas which had been taken previously from the crofters and added to the farm of Eoligarry. At a

1 This opinion was all very well, except for the fact that the crofters did not have, and could not afford, big enough boats to fish from Barra in all weathers.

subsequent interview with the Commissioners, at Edinburgh on 24th October 1883, Mr MacDonald was questioned by Mr Fraser-Mackintosh:

> "If emigration to any extent will now go on, such as has been begun by you,[1] it is Lady Gordon Cathcart's orders that the places they vacate be added to the neighbouring crofts?"
>
> MR MACDONALD. "Her most distinct and imperative orders."
>
> MR FRASER-MACKINTOSH. "That was not the case of old, I think, because, from a statement you yourself rendered, when some emigrants were sent away from Barra, their possessions were not given to the crofters that remained, but were incorporated into the farm of Eoligarry?"
>
> MR MACDONALD. "From my own knowledge I cannot say. It was long before my time."
>
> MR FRASER-MACKINTOSH. "This is what you stated yourself on 26th May—'I have made inquiries as to what changes have taken place since 1836 as to boundaries and otherwise, and I have noted the result of these inquiries in pencil on the original copy. I find that the following townships and islands then under crofters have been added to the large grazings, viz., Hellisay, Vuay, Nigh, Greian, Cliat, Fuday and Gigha,—in all, sixty-one crofters; rent £446,8s.'"?
>
> MR MACDONALD. "Yes; I made inquiries at your request, and gave you faithfully the result of my inquiries."
>
> MR FRASER-MACKINTOSH. "But no such thing is intended now?"
>
> MR MACDONALD. "No certainly not."

Mr MacDonald then went on to say that though Lady Gordon Cathcart was willing to assist the people to emigrate to Canada, she would not help them to migrate to other parts of the Highlands, or settle on the large farms in Barra.

So far as the poverty of the crofters and cottars was concerned, Mr MacDonald said at Castlebay that the evidence of Michael Buchanan and Allan M'Intyre about the poverty of the crofters "neutralized" one another; but at Edinburgh he made the remark, apropos of encouraging emigration, that "When I saw, in America, even the

1 The emigration arranged between Lady Gordon Cathcart and the Canadian Government in 1883. The scheme was a complete failure.

negroes, the descendants of those who came there as slaves, in a prosperous condition, it made me sad to think of the misery of the population in the Western Isles of Scotland." It is clear from the evidence that Mr MacDonald was concerned in vindicating himself and his employer before the Commissioners; unfortunately the evils the crofters complained of had most of their roots in the past, and though Mr MacDonald might claim that his management was not responsible for the people's condition, that neither lessened the grievances themselves nor removed the reproach that the estate management itself had been unable to alleviate them.

CANON CHISHOLM'S LETTER TO THE CROFTERS' COMMISSION[1]

Craigston, Barra,
October 1883.

The circular addressed to me by the Secretary of the Crofters' Commission invites me to express my views about the present state of the crofters residing upon this island.

As the grievances of the people have been set forth in their true light before the Royal Commissioners at Castlebay, I will not enter into particular cases.

Without giving way to any partial spirit, I must say that the entire bulk of the population of this island, with a very few exceptions, are compelled to drag out a very poor existence.

The cause of the prevailing poverty is easily arrived at; it is the want of land. The island is particularly hilly and rocky, yet there is enough of good land if it were divided among the people. But this does not seem, even to a superficial observer, to be the case. When we consider that the island is thickly populated, and when we advert to the fact that the best half of the island is held by large farmers, we must admit that the cry for more land is very reasonable.

At present the crofters are settled on very poor patches of land, which, from frequent cultivation, have a struggle to yield a few potatoes, or a thin crop of barley, and by no means do they return sufficient crops to compensate the labour expended upon them. As long then as the crofts are so small, and the townships so crowded, it will be impossible for the people to emerge out of their present

1 Appendix A of report, p. 96.

poverty. On this island no fisherman can live from the produce of the sea alone, owing to the tempestuous nature of the coast, and the want of a ready transit to the markets. Those, then, who follow the profession of fishermen should have as much land as would keep two cows, and those who live by the land should have their present holding greatly enlarged, and rented according to the value of the soil.

In order to remedy the sad state of matters, I would suggest that the large farms should be broken up and converted into smaller farms, with rents fixed by disinterested parties, and given to those who are willing and able to pay just rents.

I would also suggest that the crofters should get leases, for those who are tenants-at-will, and are subject to be turned out at any period, have, generally speaking, very little interest in the soil—that is to say, they would not enter into any expensive improvements, not knowing who might possibly reap the benefit of their labour. Compensation should also be given for improvements.

The people in their modes of living are frugal, and morally good.

We sincerely hope that some scheme will be devised to better our present condition, but such a one as would have for its object the removal of the people to some foreign country would be entirely opposed to the wishes of the people, and instead of being considered a benefit, would be looked upon as dangerous to their interests.

James Chisholm

CHAPTER 14

Barra in 1883

*

ALEXANDER CARMICHAEL[1]

Alexander Carmichael was a notable Gaelic scholar and collector of folk-lore. He was a member of the staff of the Inland Revenue, and collected songs and stories, hymns and incantations in the Highlands and Islands from 1856 to 1900. He wrote a valuable account of the agrarian customs of the Hebrides for W. F. Skene's History of Celtic Scotland, *and published a version of the story of Deirdre collected in Barra, as well as articles in the* Celtic Review *and other periodicals. His chief work, and that which brought him much fame, was his well-known* Carmina Gadelica, *a collection of hymns and incantations with many notes, which is one of the most interesting and best produced anthologies in Scottish Gaelic. Twenty-six out of two hundred and fifteen pieces in this book were taken down from reciters in Barra.*

This account of Barra is taken from an article entitled "Grazing and Agrestic Customs of the Outer Hebrides," which Carmichael wrote specially for the Crofters' Commission in 1883.

*

The islands of Barra form an oblong group. Of these islands, eight are inhabited. The Southern Isles of Barra were of old called the Bishop's Isles, because they belonged to the Bishop of the see. The head of this wild, precipitous chain of islands is called Bearnaraidh an Easpaig, Bearnarey of the Bishop, occasionally Barra Head—Gaelic, Ceann Bharraidh.

The Southern Isles of Barra are famed for birds. These are principally the Puffin, Razorbill, and the Guillemote—Gaelic, Buigire, Dui'eineach, and Langaidh. The Manx shearwater—Gaelic, Scrab, was extremely abundant there at one time; but since the advent of the Puffin, it is now practically extinct.

Both these last are burrowing birds. The Puffin is vicious to a

1 *Report of Crofters' Commission*, Appendix A, p. 456.

degree, his wonderfully strong, sharp, coulterneb bill cutting keenly as a lance.

Of old the crofters of Miuley[1] paid their rents in birds to MacNeill of Barra. These birds were principally the young of the shearwater, and called by the people, Fachaich, 'fatlings.'

The land was divided into crofts called Clitig, Feoirlig, Leth-Pheighinn, and Peighinn. The Clitig is half the Feoirlig, the Feoirlig is half the Leth-Pheighinn, and Leth-Pheighinn is half the Peighinn, 'Penny.'

The Penny Croft paid two barrels, the Halfpenny Croft one barrel, the Farthing Croft one-half barrel, and the Clitig Croft one-fourth barrel of Fachaich to MacNeill.

Probably not less than twenty barrels of the birds went to MacNeill yearly, and all from the small island of Grianamal, behind Miuley!

The proprietor came over to Miuley a fortnight before, and remained till a fortnight after Lammas Day—Gaelic, La Lunastain. The people were not allowed to go to the rocks till he came; when he left, they had the free range of the cliffs.

The people of the Southern Isles do not now kill many birds, being too much occupied otherwise.

The people of Miuley do not seem to have used ropes as they do in St Kilda, but to have clambered among the rocks like goats. The rocks are wonderfully grand. Mr Campbell of Islay and the writer measured the highest of these in October 1871, when the barometer showed nearly 800 feet above the sea. The place is named Aonaig, and this particular rock is called Biolacraig. The face of the cliff is as smooth and perpendicular as the wall of a house, and goes sheer down into the Atlantic.

This precipice was the crest of the ancient MacNeills of Barra, and 'Biolacraig' formed the rallying cry of the clan.

There is probably no more interesting island in Britain than this island of Miuley, with its wonderful precipices, long narrow sea galleries, several hundred feet high in the perpendicular sides, and marine arcades, winding their gloomy subterranean ways under the precipitous island. To boat through these galleries and arcades needs a calm sea, a good crew, and a steady nerve. The writer was the first to discover, and the first and last to go through much the longest, largest, and gloomiest of these wonderful sinuous sea arcades.

The MacNeills of Barra lived on a tidal rock called Ciosmal, in

1 Mingulay.

Baile Mhic Neill, now called Castlebay. There are two wells within the walls of this old castle. The people say that the water of these wells comes in pipes under the sea, the pipes being overlaid with large flags.

Some fifteen years ago the then Factor let the castle as a herring-curing station, when the principal well, in the centre of the court, was filled up,[1] and the chapel in the west corner carried away piecemeal as ballast for boats and vessels. The native people, who still fondly cling to the memory of their once proud chiefs, were grieved at the destruction they were powerless to prevent.

The site of Ciosmal Castle had been the site of a magazine, wherein the Norsemen kept war materials during the Norse occupation of the Western Isles.

Ciosmal was abandoned by the MacNeills during the first quarter of last century. They built houses in these (? three) other places, finally settling at Eoligearry, on the north end of the island. The family became extinct in the direct male line in Lieut. General Roderick MacNeill. It is said that so symmetrical in person was General MacNeill that 'no eye looked on him without looking at him again.' He was adored by his people, who, with the fidelity of their race, ruined themselves in trying to save him from ruin. They gave him their all.[2]

To Dr M'Gillivray, the people of Barra are much indebted, and this they gratefully acknowledge.[3] Since he became tacksman of Eoligearry, some forty-four years ago, probably he has given in one form or another some £7000 in work to the people of Barra, while his skill and his medicine are ever at the disposal of all. The eminent naturalist of that name was brother to Dr M'Gillivray.

A curious custom prevails among the people of Barra of apportioning their boats to their fishing banks at sea, much as they apportion their cows to their grazing grounds on land. The names, positions, extent, characteristics, and capabilities of these banks are as well known to them as those of their crofts.

The people meet at church on the first day of February—Gaelic, Là-Fhéill Brìde—the Festival of St Bridget; and having ascertained among themselves the number of boats engaging in the long line fishing, they assign these boats in proportionate numbers among the banks according to the fishing capabilities of each bank. The men then draw lots, each head-man drawing the lot for his crew, and the

1 The well had been filled up before this. See p. 157.
2 See, however, p. 138.
3 See, however, p. 180-81.

THE BOOK OF BARRA

boats are assigned to their respective banks for the season.

Should a bank prove unproductive, the boats of that bank are considerately allowed to distribute themselves among the other banks, the boats of which are then at liberty to try the deserted banks. The fishermen say that the ways and migrations of the fishes are as unaccountable as those of the fowls of the air—here to-day and there to-morrow. They say also that fishes resemble birds in their habits; some fishes, as the Cod and the Conger, in being solitary, like the Raven and the Skua; while some fishes, as the Saithe and Herring, are gregarious in their habits, and live in communities, like the Razorbill and the Guillemote. I am indebted to the intelligent and observant fishermen throughout those islands for much interesting and curious information regarding fishes and sea birds.

Having completed their balloting, the fishermen go in to Church, accompanied by fathers and mothers, brother and sisters, wives and children, and sweethearts. The good priest says a short service, wherein he commends those 'who go down to the sea in ships' to the protection of the holy St Barr, after whom Barra is named, of the beautiful St Bridget, 'virgin of a thousand charms'— 'Brìde bhòidheach òigh nam mîle béas'—on whose festival they are met, of their loved Mother, the golden-haired Virgin, and to the protection, individually and collectively, of the Holy Trinity. The people disperse, chanting:

"Athair, a Mhic, a Spioraid Naoimh,
Biodh an Trî-Aon leinn, a là 's a dh'oidhche;
'S air chùl nan tonn, no air thaobh nam beann
Biodh ar Màthair leinn, 's biodh A làmh mu'r ceann,
Biodh ar Màthair leinn, 's biodh A làmh mu'r ceann."

"Father! Son! and Spirit's Might!
Be the Three-in-One with us day and night;
On the crested wave, when waves run high
Oh! Mother! Mary! be to us nigh!
Oh! Mother! Mary! be to us nigh."

Having dispersed, the people repair to their homes, on the way thither eagerly and simultaneously discussing the merits and the demerits of their respective banks. To hear their loud and simultaneous talk, one would think that the people were quarrelling. But no, this is only their way—the Barra people being peaceable and gentle, and eminently well-mannered and polite.

This habit of the Barra fishermen of apportioning their fishing banks may seem antiquated to modern views.[1] The fishermen themselves advance good reasons for its retention, some of these being that it prevents overcrowding of boats on the banks, with the consequent entanglement of lines, resulting sometimes in the loss of temper and friendship.

In the *Inverness Courier* seventeen years ago or so, the writer suggested converting the strait between Barra Head and Miuley into a harbour of refuge, by throwing a break-water across the west end. A harbour there would be of inestimable benefit to shipping and fishing.

The arable land of the crofters of Barra is all divided into crofts, no part being in common.[2] The grazing grounds only are held in common, each townland being confined to its own grazing limits. The crofters of each townland have their own herdsman, and regulate their own townland affairs with no interference from without.

---

1 The habit would seem perfectly sensible to any impartial observer, especially when compared with some modern methods of fishing.
2 Michael Buchanan mentions in his evidence that the runrig system was in force in his grandfather's time; this is borne out by some of Colonel MacNeill's letters. See p. 117.

CHAPTER 15

The Subsequent History of Barra[1] 1883-1934

*

J. L. CAMPBELL

The coming of the Crofters' Commission in 1883 marked the turn of the tide in the fortunes of the crofters in Barra, as elsewhere in the Highlands. For some years previously public opinion had turned strongly against eviction as an instrument of estate management, and such scenes as are described in *Gloomy Memories* were not repeated; though impoverished, the crofters had become precariously secure on their small and often over-rented holdings.

The outcome of the work of the Crofters' Commission was the Crofters' Holdings (Scotland) Act of 1886, an act which has not unjustly been termed the *Magna Carta* of the Highlands. This Act granted security of tenure (subject to the fulfilment of certain statutory conditions), compensation for improvements done by the tenant, and facilities for the enlargement of holdings and the fixation of fair rents. The fixation of fair rents was delegated to a body of three Commissioners, of whom one had to be able to speak Gaelic,[2] and one to be an advocate of the Scottish Bar of not less than ten years' standing. This body, known as the Crofters' Commissioners, was the forerunner of the Scottish Land Court.

The Crofters' Commissioners visited Barra in 1890 and again in 1891 in response to requests to fix fair rents. On these two visits applications were considered from 278 small tenants—practically all the small tenants in Barra. The Commissioners found that the arrears of rent on these holdings came to £7583, 15s. 10d. Of this they ordered £6159, 16s. 10d. to be cancelled and the remainder paid. They found

---

1 The authority for much of the information contained in this chapter is the *Public Administration in the Highlands and Islands of Scotland,* by J. P. Day, D.Phil., an invaluable work for anyone interested in the economic history of the Highlands since 1746.

2 This is the only instance known to me when a knowledge of Gaelic has been *statutorily* required of a person holding a public appointment in the Highlands—an astonishing state of affairs.

that the rents totalled £814, 13s.; this they reduced to £532, 14s. as the total fair rent of the holdings in question.[1] Similar reductions were made on many estates, which largely justified the contention of witnesses like Michael Buchanan that the people had been impoverished by over-renting.

Another direct benefit from the Act of 1886 was the improvement of the crofters' housing conditions subsequent to the granting of security of tenure. Opponents of the Act had frequently stated that once security of tenure was granted to small tenants, nothing would restrain the crofter from allowing his house to dilapidate. With a very few exceptions, this argument was to prove groundless. According to J. P. Day:[2]

"Before the passing of the Agricultural Holdings (Scotland) Act, 1883, and the Crofters' Holdings Act, 1886, the tenant had no security that he would obtain at the end of his tenancy any compensation for the building which he had erected on his holding. It is rather curious that the Board of Supervision feared these Acts would check improvement in housing, because the change in the relation between landlords and tenants would, they anticipated, deter Highland proprietors in future from making any effort to improve the conditions of the dwellings on their estates. As a matter of fact, the security of tenure and right to compensation introduced by the 1886 Act led to a great improvement in the houses of the crofters."

The first report of the Local Government Board, which superseded the Board of Supervision, remarked (as quoted by Mr Day):

"It is quite remarkable what an impetus to improvement the Crofters' Act of 1886 has already been the means of producing. The feeling that there is a security of possession of the holding and that the rent thereof cannot be arbitrarily raised has, along with other causes, predisposed a great number of the crofting class to execute many improvements."[3]

1 I am indebted to the Clerk of the Scottish Land Court for this information. Judging by the arrears in 1890 and 1891, it appears that hardly any rent had been paid since the visit of the Crofters' Commission in 1883.
2 *Public Administration in the Highlands*, p. 295.
3 1894-95 report, Appendix A, 18. J. P. Day, p. 295.

Slowly but surely the economic condition of the island began to improve. In 1884 the long-demanded extension of the telegraph from Loch Boisdale to Castlebay was at last made, giving a great stimulus to the fishing industry. In 1894 all school fees were finally abolished.

There still remained, however, an acute shortage of land in the island; but the days of the big farms were numbered. In 1901 the Congested Districts Board purchased 3000 acres of the farm of Eoligarry to relieve congestion. Fifty-eight new holdings were created on which crofters from other parts of the island were settled. It was at first intended to establish these as owner-occupiers, but after a short time the occupiers became the tenants of the Board at their own request.

Vatersay was the next big farm to be broken up; the account of its purchase by the Board is given in *Public Administration in the Highlands*,[1] by J. P. Day:

> "The purchase of Vatersay was peculiar. Conditions on the Cathcart estates of Barra and South Uist were almost as difficult as on the Matheson estate in Lewis. In spite of efforts by the estate management to prevent the erection of additional houses, the number of squatters increased. The people, crowded together on a small area, put up their small wooden huts, and appear to have trusted that the proprietrix would not cause them to be evicted or punished. Possibly also they relied on Government intervention or outside agitation. The estate warnings were disregarded, and further proceedings to enforce them were not taken, presumably because they would have entailed considerable suffering to the people. Lady Gordon Cathcart's colonization schemes failed, and the congestion became steadily worse. As a result of what the Government themselves called 'excessive pressure,' the 3000 acres at Barra were bought by the Congested Districts Board, in 1901, and fifty-eight crofters given new holdings. This still left nearly half the landless cottars unprovided for, and congestion was especially severe round Castlebay, where no site had been available for several years. Several of these cottars applied to the Board for ground on the island of Vatersay for planting potatoes in 1902. Vatersay and its adjacent islands constituted the only farm[2] then

1 *Op. cit.*, pp. 215-218.
2 This is not correct; a good deal of Eoligarry still remained intact as a large farm.

left to the Barra estate of Lady Cathcart, and the tenant's terms
proved too high for the Board. The season of 1902 was missed,
but next year the Board was able to buy sixty acres on the island
for £600 and an annual feu duty of 10s. per annum. Fifty-one
cottars obtained potato plots in 1903, and attempted to grow
potatoes. They failed to obtain satisfactory crops, wherefore in
1905 the Board wished to test the soil by a practical experiment,
but the cottars for some reason opposed this,[1] and the Board
could not get any local person to go over to Vatersay to conduct
the experiments. Meantime, the people were becoming irritated
by not knowing whether they were to be allowed to sow oats and
barley on the potato land, whether it was worth their while
starting to collect seaweed for any further land that might be
provided, and by the prospect of another potatoless winter. Early
in 1906 the negotiations for fresh land appeared to be again
breaking down; the tenant asked 10s. an acre for the lease of a
new patch of twenty acres, and the Board were unwilling to
accept that offer or the theory that their own sixty acres were
useless. Thereupon the cottars, in spite of the fact that the
Board's agricultural expert had, in the previous year, impressed
upon them that making a disturbance or threats to do so would
not move the Board but would only bring trouble upon
themselves, threatened to take the land forcibly. Almost
immediately (March 1906) the Board wrote to the cottars saying
that they had rented the twenty acres, and that crops could be
taken from it in 1906 and of corn in 1907.[2] . . .

"To return to Vatersay in 1906; after the Board had notified
the cottars that they might take a potato crop on the twenty
acres, the cottars prepared additional beds on two acres of the
tenant's land, put up some fifteen huts, and brought across their
cattle. Interdicts were obtained by the estate against thirteen
men, served on eleven, and broken by nine. The estate was
preparing complaints for breach of interdict when in July 1907
the Secretary for Scotland (Lord Pentland) sent the Sheriff
(Sheriff Wilson) to try to induce the people to withdraw their
cattle and abandon their illegal conduct. The Sheriff was unsuccessful, but suggested the purchase of the island by the

1 Possibly it was felt that if the experiment was not a success, the land might be lost altogether.
2 A clear proof of the effectiveness of direct action in overcoming official indifference and
procrastination.

Congested Districts Board. Meantime the cottars remained and another application for Government protection for the tenant was refused. In September, however, the Secretary for Scotland wrote suggesting that the proprietrix should co-operate with the Congested Districts Board in forming new holdings in Vatersay. It was pointed out in reply that the proprietrix did not think the island suitable for new holdings because of an insufficient water supply, nor the raiders suitable as tenants, now was she willing to face the contingent liabilities in the way of rates for a new school, or the provision of adequate water. The rest of the year passed in a spirited wrangling between the two sides. Lady Cathcart's position was, that it was unfair and unreasonable to impose upon her a policy which she thought unsuitable, inexpedient, and most likely to result in failure. The Government's position was that they were not responsible for the Vatersay difficulties, but only intervened as offering the assistance of the Congested Districts Board if the proprietrix chose to accept the policy of settling a limited number of tenants upon the island. Eventually the Government abandoned their position, and in February 1909 the Secretary for Scotland informed the Congested Districts Board that he had arranged to purchase Vatersay for £6250, to be paid out of the Board's funds, the Board also having to pay the tenant compensation for renunciation. Fifty-eight holdings were formed and eighty-three applications received. The Board selected fifty-eight tenants, and had to take legal proceedings to remove certain obdurate squatters."

The action of the Board in rejecting as tenants some of the men but for whose initiative Vatersay might never have become available for small tenants not unnaturally aroused intense indignation amongst the squatters, who throughout the summer of 1909 maintained through Duncan Campbell and Neil MacPhee,[1] a most spirited correspondence on behalf of the rejected tenants, addressed to many public men, such as Lord Pentland, Sir Henry Cook (solicitor to the Congested Districts Board) J. G. Swift MacNeill, M.P., Sir John M. Dewar, M.P., and other members of Parliament. The following petition sent to the Secretary for Scotland is an interesting specimen which throws light on the controversy from the squatters' point of view:

1 They also wrote to Lord Balfour and Lord Lovat on behalf of the Small Landholders' Act, which became law in 1911.

Vatersay, Barra, N.B.,
19th June 1909.

To the Right Honourable
Lord Pentland,
Scottish Office,
Whitehall, London.

Right Honourable Sir,
We the undersigned, beg to draw your attention to the fact that
ten of our fellow-cottars, some of whom were imprisoned last
year at Edinburgh, and all of whom were in possession of
holdings here, for over two years, have been rejected as tenants
by the Congested Districts Board, with no apparent reason.

We understand your Lordship is Chairman to the Board, and
we respectfully beg that our fellow-cottars who were rejected, be
immediately restored to their respective holdings, or if they have
no right to their holdings, we beg that we too may share the
same fate, for we cannot be so cowardly as to accept favours, and
see our fellow-men treated in this manner. We crave no favour
this time, my Lord, all we plead is justice.

We beg further to draw your attention to the manner in
which this island was divided by the Board into holdings,
regardless of our protests, and we most earnestly urge the
Government to send a competent neutral judge to compare the
rejected tenants to those selected by the Board from the
mainland of Barra, and to compare our division of the island
with that of the Board.

We beg further to demand an explanation of why the Board
sent some of us by sham ballot, from one end of the island to the
other, while they granted special holdings to others, which were
not balloted.

We beg further to ask whether the Board were advised by
unauthorized parties at Castlebay, and if not, why have such
parties taken part in the proceedings, and why was not each case
considered and judged on its merits?

Lady Gordon Cathcart's policy of rejecting us all was
honourable as compared to the Board's mean methods.

The Board's factor at Castlebay on 16th instant threw the
responsibility of the whole arrangement on your Lordship, when

we asked him to redress our grievance.

We scorn such cowardly excuses, for we believe that had the Board placed the true facts before your Lordship, this trouble would never have happened.

Again, we beg your Lordship to send a competent trustworthy authority on the scene, who will investigate the matter to the root.

Duncan Campbell and 27 others.

In a letter to the Lord Advocate, dated 7th August 1909, the writer very pertinently remarks:

"We have been informed by the Secretary for Scotland that 'the Congested Districts Board purchased Vatersay not for the squatters on the island, but to relieve congestion in Barra.

"My Lord, need we again repeat that it was 'to relieve the congestion in Barra' that we took possession of a few acres each on Vatersay, and are we again to be punished for taking the initiative in a step which the Government itself approves? We may observe that the Secretary for Scotland disputes our right to live here although he acknowledges that the island was bought to relieve the congestion among us when in Barra, but we must leave your Lordships to reconcile these differences."

Despite these and other letters, which reflect no small credit on the ability of the writers (being written in what to them was a foreign language) the Board remained obdurate in rejecting the squatters in question as tenants. Altogether the Board was forced to spend £14,848 in purchasing these areas from the estate, which in this respect certainly got the best of the bargain. It is doubtful if the whole of Barra would fetch such a price at the present time.

The successful raiding of the rest of the farm at Eoligarry, which took place soon after the War, completes the agrarian history of Barra. To-day for the first time for at least 200 years, since the MacNeills left Kismul, there are no large farms on Barra. The wheel has gone full turn. At the census of 1931, the population of Vatersay was returned as 240—Vatersay, of which Lady Gordon Cathcart (who visited Barra once during the fifty-four years that she owned it) had declared that the water-supply was insufficient for small tenants! For this lack of judgement the proprietrix cannot escape a share of the responsibility which in these and similar cases is usually thrust on her agents. Vatersay and Eoligarry are amongst the most successful settlements of the Board of Agriculture, whose standards of management have not been without influence elsewhere.

Subsequent events in Barra are perhaps too near to require recounting in any detail. The first motor car was imported into the island in 1926—a mixed blessing. The steamer services were greatly improved in 1929, but at the same time the lack of a direct service to the mainland is a serious drawback. The present crossing takes twelve hours of which a direct service would save five.

The most regrettable feature of recent years has been the decline to the point of extinction of the magnificent fishery that is described by Rev. Edward MacQueen[1] and MacCulloch.[1] Opinions may differ on the contributory causes of this decline, but no one will disagree that the coming of the steam trawlers has been the chief reason for it. Though the signatories of the North Sea Convention (at which Scotland was not separately represented) agreed in 1882 to prohibit trawling within three miles of the shore, the penalties for violating this limit in Scottish waters have only been made adequate in 1934, and even now the patrol, which has to coal at Greenock, is inadequate in speed to deal with modern trawlers. Moreover, the three-mile limit is an entirely artificial arrangement. It does not correspond with any formation of the sea bed, and some of the best fishing grounds in the Minch are outside it. It has been left to the Sea League, founded in 1933 in Castlebay, to initiate a campaign for the recalling of the North Sea Convention and the complete closing of the Minch to trawlers. Upon the ultimate success of this campaign the future prosperity and economic independence of the Outer Islands may largely depend.

In 1932 Lady Gordon Cathcart died, and her will as published directed

> "her trustees to sell her Long Island Estates of Benbecula, South Uist, and Barra... either in whole or in lots, and to set apart either the estates or the invested proceeds thereof if sold as a separate fund to be known as 'The Emigration Fund' to be applied for the purpose of assisting intending emigrants from the Long Island estates to emigrate to the British Dominions, Colonies, and dependencies, by way of loans to them at a low

1 See pp. 62 and 86.

rate of interest.

"The Trustees are to be the sole judges of how the Emigration Fund shall be applied. If at any time they are of the opinion that the emigration from the Long Island estates has ceased, they shall be at liberty to deal with the Fund as part of the residue of her trust estate and to make over the same to the residuary legatees"[1] (which are charities in Aberdeen and London).

This provision, which was the subject of a considerable amount of criticism when it became known, was, in fact, intended to benefit the islanders; Lady Gordon Cathcart having apparently always thought that emigration has ceased since 1929, there being at present much unemployment in the Dominions, this intention has been rendered ineffective. Far greater good could be done for the inhabitants of these islands by the construction of piers, roads, proper water supplies, and other necessities which have at present to be begged from the County Council or from Parliament, than by the expatriation of individuals. If a plea to this end can have any effect, it is worth while expressing the hope that some means can be found to revise a bequest which, although well intended, is clearly unsuitable under present conditions, since it has for some time been the official policy to improve the conditions of the Hebrideans in their own country rather than to encourage them to seek another.

1 Oban Times, 15 October 1932.

CHAPTER 16

The Literature of Barra

*

J. L. CAMPBELL

The history of the Hebrides during the long period of Norse occupation (800-1266) is still very obscure, and very little if any Old Norse literature of Hebridean origin is now known. But the name at least of one Norse poet who can be presumed to be a Barra man, Ormr Barreyjarskáld, is extant. Two quotations from his works, which are otherwise lost, occur in Snorri's *Edda,* and in the *Sturlunga Saga* a priest is said to have recited his verses, *Ingimundr prestr sagdhi sogu Orms Barreyjarskálds, ok visur margar.*[1] On every account our lack of knowledge about the Norse occupation of the Isles is to be regretted; and at any rate it is worth while to record here the name of the earliest known Barra poet, though his works are no longer in existence.

As Mr Borgström remarks in his chapter on the Norse place-names of Barra, the Gaelic language supplanted Norse completely after the recovery of the Isles by Scotland in 1266. During the succeeding four and a half centuries, Gaelic literature was cultivated in the Islands as on the mainland by the trained poets and historians who were attached to the courts of the chiefs, and also by gifted amateurs of high social rank, such as were represented in Scotland by the Earl and Countess of Argyll, some of whose poems are found in the Dean of Lismore's Book, and in Ireland by Gearóid Iarla and many others. The professional poet historians or *seanchaidhean* were trained in the bardic schools, and received their holdings rent-free, on condition that they and their heirs kept the chronicle of the clan's doings and the chiefs' genealogy. The MacNeills of Barra had *seanchaidhean* of this kind; it is probably one of them, John MacNeill, whom Martin mentions as possessing a manuscript copy of the Life of St Columba in Gaelic; this may be Gaelic MS. XL, now in the possession of the National Library of Scotland. The principal production of these *sean-*

---

1 This information, and the accompanying quotation, is taken from Professor E. V. Gordon's *Introduction to Old Norse* (Oxford University Press, 1827).

chaidhean is, or rather was, the Barra Chronicle, which has now been unfortunately lost for at least fifty years.[1] This probably contained histories and the genealogy of the MacNeill family, with poems in their praise such as are described on page 281. Similar books were kept for all Highland chiefs of any importance, the best known of these being the Black and Red Books of Clanranald, which contain a very readable account of the Montrose Wars. These books were written in the standard literary dialect of Gaelic that was common to Ireland and the Highlands of Scotland before 1700; no one, except a few rebels like the Dean of Lismore and the writer of the Fernaig Manuscript, would have then thought of using any other kind of Gaelic for literary purposes.

No modern[2] Scottish Gaelic poet of any importance is associated with Barra, though the songs of Alexander MacDonald (1700-70) and Neil MacVurich (who died in 1722), both of whom were closely connected with South Uist, are well known in Barra. The only original Barra poetry I have been able to find in print are two poems by Hector MacNeill of Vatersay, *Bu tu marbhtair a' gheòidh* and *Chaidh mi leat do'n Eilean Fhiach* on pages 343 and 345 of Ranald MacDonald's collection of Gaelic poems, published in 1776. These songs are still known by some of the old people on the island. They are in praise of the appearance and prowess in hunting of the then baillie of Barra; deer were apparently not extinct in Muldonich two hundred years ago. But by far the most prominent writer connected with Barra is the late Donald Sinclair, one of the most able and imaginative of modern Gaelic writers, author of *Domhnall na Trioblaid, An Crois-tara, Long nan Og,* and other plays and poems. Calum Ruadh MacKinnon, Bruernish, was also a recent bard of note. His songs have not been printed.

It is, however, the songs, poems, and stories traditionally preserved which have brought Barra its chief literary fame. The three famous collectors of Highland songs and stories—Alexander Carmichael, author of *Carmina Gadelica,* J. F. Campbell, author of *Popular Tales of the West Highlands,* and Mrs Kennedy-Fraser of *Songs of the Hebrides*—have all been very much indebted to Barra singers and reciters for their

1 See *The Clan Macneil,* pp. 25 and 33. The fact that this MS. has been lost for fifty years does not prevent the author from quoting dates in it.
2 Compositions in modern Scottish Gaelic date from the end of the sixteenth century, but the language, as distinct from Irish, had no literary status until the publication of *Gairm an Dé Mhóir,* a translation of *Baxter's Call to the Unconverted,* by the Rev. A. MacFarlane in 1750, and Alexander MacDonald's poems, *Ais-Eiridh na Sean Chánoin Albannaich (The Resurrection of the Ancient Scottish Language)* in 1751.

literary and musical material. In all cases this has not yet been published in full—there is enough of Carmichael's collection to provide two more volumes and of Campbell's for seven—so it is not practical to attempt a catalogue yet, but of the reciters, mention may be made of Alexander MacNeill (Kentangaval), Roderick MacNeill (Mingulay), Alexander MacDonald (Borve), and Hector Boyd (Brevaig), to whom Carmichael and Campbell often refer. There were many others, especially from the islands around Barra. Carmichael collected in 1871 a version of the well-known story of Deirdre from Iain Donn MacNeill, brother of Alexander MacNeill, which was separately published and created much interest; yet Alexander MacNeill himself is supposed to have known the same story in a much better version. These stories have been current in the Highlands and Islands for at least four centuries. Carswell, who translated John Knox's liturgy into Middle Irish in 1567 for the benefit of the Highlanders, denounces his fellow-writers of Gaelic for their absorption in *eachtradha dimhaoineacha buairdheartha bregacha saoghalta*, "vain, hurtful, lying, wordly stories"[1] about Fionn Mac Cumhail and his heroes and other such subjects. It is likely that up till 1700 and even later such tales circulated widely in manuscript in the Highlands as in Ireland. Their history and development has not been worked out, except in a few cases.

The work of Mrs Kennedy-Fraser is of rather a different kind from that of Carmichael and Campbell. Both the latter were collectors in the objective sense of the word, with considerable ability and a first-rate knowledge of colloquial Gaelic. Travelling in the Highlands as Highlanders themselves they collected word for word versions[2] of songs and stories often heard quite informally, which they later published. There is nothing in their work which is not as authentic as it possibly could be.

Mrs Kennedy-Fraser's attitude to her subject was quite a different one. Gaelic she did not know and never came near to mastering. She depended on a collaborator to take down and interpret the words of the songs which she heard, and the methods of her collecting involved formal recitations of a kind that must have been prejudicial to the spontaneity of the singer. It is not too much to say that she regarded the traditional music of the islands as an excellent mine, a source of

1 Rev Thomas MacLauchlan's edition, p. 19. The same opinions about Highland folk-lore can be heard expressed in certain circles at the present time.
2 J. F. Campbell was assisted by various intelligent native collectors.

good musical material to be refined and made presentable for English-speaking audiences. Now the poet and the artist are entitled to take their material where they can find it, and as Mrs Kennedy-Fraser in her autobiography, *A Life of Song*, is quite explicit about the methods which she and the Rev. Kenneth MacLeod used to produce the *Songs of the Hebrides*, it is impossible to complain that they are misrepresented as 'authentic' in the way, for instance, that the *Barzaz Breiz* of de la Villemarqué was presented as a collection of genuine Breton poetry. It is necessary to point out none the less that in *Songs of the Hebrides* the melodies have sometimes been altered in time, sometimes run together; words have been polished up, in some cases suppressed, in others composed for the occasion, while the whole has been set to accompaniments of a kind which have no real origin in Gaelic music at all. The result has been widely acclaimed, and there is no reason to doubt its actual artistic merits. It has also created elsewhere a curiously false impression of the Hebrides based on the author's own romanticized attitude.

The use of folk-songs in this manner has its disadvantages, however. Able as she was, Mrs Kennedy-Fraser was not a de Falla or a Sibelius. The risk is that her arrangements may not stand the test of time, but may go out of fashion in the same way as those of earlier collectors such as Simon Fraser (1816) and Alexander Campbell (1816). Moreover, as long as it is taken for granted that the *Songs of the Hebrides* is a collection of authentic Gaelic airs and words, the danger will remain that the genuinely authentic versions of these songs will perish unrecorded. Meanwhile, the majority of Hebrideans have never been impressed by these arrangements; "it was not that way we sung it to her; she has got it down wrong." This applies, for instance, to the well-known Barra song published under the English name of 'Kishmul's Galley' (of which the proper name is 'Beinn a' Cheathaich'); in Mrs Kennedy-Fraser's version the time of the original is completely altered.

It is to be hoped that future collectors will take a more objective attitude towards their subject; Gaelic music possesses sufficient merits to be studied in its natural form, and deserves better treatment than to be used as a ladder to establish the reputation, however worthy, of any individual singer. In any case, there are still unrecorded songs and stories in Barra which invite investigation, though this will have to be done quickly, as in the majority of cases they are only well known to the older people.

BOOKS

Carmina Gadelica, by Alexander Carmichael; John Grant,
    31 George IV Bridge, Edinburgh.
Popular Tales of the West Highlands, by J. F. Campbell;
    Alexander Gardner, Paisley.
Songs of the Hebrides, by Mrs Kennedy-Fraser and the
    Rev. Kenneth MacLeod; Boosey & Co., Ltd., London.
Gaelic Songs of the Isles of the West; Rev John MacMillan,
    Patrick McGlynn, and F. W. Lewis; Boosey & Co.
The Dialect of Barra in the Outer Hebrides, by Carl Hj. Borgström;
    Norsk Tidsskrift for Sprogvidenskap, Bind VIII. Oslo, 1935.

CHAPTER 17

The Norse Place-names of Barra

*

CARL Hj. BORGSTRÖM

The overwhelming majority of place-names in Barra, as in the Hebrides as a whole, has no connection with the Gaelic language. And those purely Gaelic names which exist, such as *Buaile nam Bodach, Bàgh a Tuath, Loch an Dùin*, etc., are, as a rule, comparatively recent; they are usually made up of current and intelligible words; they belong to modern Gaelic. The 'unintelligible' names, on the other hand, are nearly always Norse. There may, of course, also exist some names of some of the bigger islands; e.g. *Uist* (Gaelic, *Uibhist*) and *Lewis* (Gaelic, *Leodhas*) cannot be reasonably explained either as Norse or as Gaelic; when the Norsemen (in the Sagas) wrote *Ivist* and *Ljódhús*, they only adopted and slightly changed names which existed before them. I believe, therefore, that the name *Barra* (Gaelic, *Barraidh*) is also older than the Norsemen. If the name means 'St Barr's Isle,' we do not understand how the Norse vikings, who were pagans when they first reached the place, could have invented such a name;[1] but they could, of course, adopt it if they heard the original inhabitants use the name. The etymology of this name is, however, not very clear; the first part of it, *Barr-*, can hardly be Norse.

The Norse names were introduced by the Vikings, mostly Norwegians, who settled in the islands from the eighth to the twelfth or thirteenth century A.D. Old Norse must have been almost universally spoken in the Western Isles, and all places got Norse names. But then a complete change of language took place. Perhaps there was an immigration of Gaelic speakers from the mainland; in any case, Norse died out, and Gaelic took its place as the spoken language.[2] But the descendants of the Norsemen continued to inhabit

1 Still less why the uninhabitable island of Suliskeir (off Cape Wrath) should also bear the name Barra. J. L. C.
2 It is probable that the leading Norse families first became Gaelicized, even before the end of Norwegian rule, and their followers abandoned the use of Norse later. See the poem addressed to Angus of Islay, printed by O. Bergin in Vol. IV of *Scottish Gaelic Studies*, p. 57. J. L. C.

their old places and to use the old place-names. These circumstances brought about many changes in the pronunciation of the Old Norse names. The changes have undoubtedly a certain regularity, and obey certain laws, which permits us to recognize and explain the names. Nevertheless, some of their meanings are uncertain, and some names are completely unintelligible to me.

I am indebted to Mr J. L. Campbell, the editor of this work, for a list of early spellings of the place-names of Barra;[1] these often give valuable information about the original pronunciation of many names. But, as a rule, it is the present-day pronunciation of Gaelic speakers which must serve as the foundation of the explanations.

It may be useful to say a few words about the general structure of Old Norse place-names. Many of them are compounds, *i.e.* they are made up of two, sometimes three or more different words. One of these would be a designation of place, such as *ey* (island), *vág(r)* or *vík* (bay), *fjall* (hill, mountain), and so on. The other might be a man's (or a woman's) name, an adjective, or anything describing the place in question. In Old Norse, as in English, the designation of place is put at the end, whereas in Gaelic it is at the beginning; an Old Norse translation of the English *Northbay* (Gaelic, *Bàgh a Tuath*) would thus have been *Nordhr-vágr* or *Nordhr-vík*. If the first word of the compound was a name or a substantive, it would as a rule (though not necessarily) be in the genitive case; the commonest terminations of this case were *-s*, *-ar*, *-a*, and *-u*; each word could of course take only one of these terminations.

I am now going to discuss the more important of the place-names, grouping them together according to the last word of the compound. As a rule I give first the English spelling used in the Ordnance Survey Map, and then the Gaelic spelling, sometimes a little modified, so as to give a clear idea of the pronunciation.

1. OLD NORSE *EY* = ISLAND

Nearly all the islands around Barra contain this word. Proceeding from the south we find the following names: *Berneray,* Gaelic *Bearnaraidh*, comes from Old Norse, *Bjarnarey, i.e.* Björn's Isle. *Björn* was a man's name; *Bjarnar* is the genitive.

Mingulay, Gaelic, *Mi'ulaidh*; by Munro (1549), it is written *Megaly*. There is no doubt that this means 'The Big Isle,' and in Old Norse it

---

1 Taken from the preceding chapters of this book, and from Timothy Pont's map of Barra and Uist. J. L. C.

would be written *Mikiley*. But the written word *mikil* 'big' was certainly, at least in some parts of Norway, pronounced *migil* (with a very weak *g*); and that accounts both for the present pronunciation and for Munro's spelling.

Pabbay, Gaelic, *Pabaidh*, comes from Old Norse, *Papaey* (or *Papey*) 'The Hermit's Isle.' *Papi* was the word for an Irish culdee or hermit; not, as is sometimes said, a priest, which is *prestr* in Old Norse.

Lingay, Gaelic, *Lingeidh*, is from Old Norse, *Lyngey*, 'Heather Isle'; *Flodday*, Gaelic, *Flodaidh*, must have been *Flotaey* or *Flotey*, meaning 'Isle of the Fleet' (or 'Floating Isle'?).

Very difficult are both *Sandray*, Gaelic, *Sanndraidh*, and *Vatersay*, Gaelic, *Bhatarsaidh*. MacBain (*Place-Names, Highlands and Islands of Scotland*) explains them straight away 'from water and sand.' But the Old Norse for 'Sand-Isle' and 'Water-Isle' would be *Sandey* (or *Sandsey*) and *Vatnsey* (without *r*), so this explanation cannot be correct. *Sandray* can perhaps contain a compound of *Sand*, such as *Sand-rif (a)-ey*, 'Isle of the Sand Reefs'; unfortunately I do not know how this suits the nature of the place. As for *Vatersay*, I do not understand it at all.

Next comes *Orosay*, Gaelic, *Oro'osaidh*. There are at least four islands of this name near Barra, and others in Uist. They are small islands, surrounded by a piece of sand which is dry at low tide, so that the *Orosay* then is in connection with a bigger island. MacBain explains it as *Orfirisey*, *i.e.* 'Ebbtide Isle' (Orfiri = ebb). The same name is found in Iceland and in Norway, so the explanation is undoubtedly correct. Munro (1549) spells the name *Orvansay*, and the spelling *Oronsay* is common. The *n* in this form is developed from the second *r* in the Old Norse word in order to make the word more easy to pronounce; in the present pronunciation *n* is regularly dropped before *s*. The 'broken' sound of the second *o* is due to the regular development of *orfi-* to *orofi-* and further to *oro'o-*; cp. Alla'asdal, page 293.

On the north-eastern side of Barra we have the following islands:

Fuiay, which I cannot explain; *Hellisay*, from Old Norse, *Hellisey*, 'Cave Isle.' Difficult is *Gighay*, Gaelic, *Gioghaidh*; perhaps it was *Gýdhuey*, 'Gýdha's Isle'; *Gýdha* was a woman's name in Old Norse. But the explanation is very doubtful. *Fuiday*, Gaelic, *Fúideidh* is an island lying by itself apart from the other islands; its name may come from Old Norse, *Utiey, Utey*, 'Outside Isle' (úti = outside); in Gaelic, *f* is sometimes added to words beginning with a vowel.

Fiaray, Gaelic, *Féaraidh*, may come from Old Norse *Féarey, Fjárey*, meaning 'Cattle Isle'; cp. with a similar meaning *So'olum*, 'Sheep Isle.'

Féar, later *fjár,* is the regular genitive of *fé,* 'cattle.' The name is now felt to mean 'Grass Isle' from Gaelic *féar,* 'grass,' but that can hardly be the original meaning.

Eriskay, Gaelic, *Eirisgeidh,* comes from *Eiriksey,* 'Eric's Isle.' *Eirikr* was common as a man's name.

2. OLD NORSE *NES* = HEADLAND, PENINSULA

This word now has the form *-nish* in the following names: *Bruernish,* from Old Norse, *Brúarnes,* 'Bridge Headland,' from *brú* genitive, *brúar,* 'bridge.' There was probably once a bridge across the 'Bun an t-sruth.' Another possibility, but less likely, I think, is *Brúdharnes,* 'Bride's Headland,' from *brúdhr,* 'a bride'; the *dh,* pronounced like *th* in English *father,* would be dropped.

Leenish, Gaelic *Lè'inis* (open è) must come from *Lœgines,* which means 'Peninsula, where there is an anchoring place' (*lœgi*). The name bears relation to Breivig Bay, which must have been used as an anchoring place by the Vikings who lived near Breivig.

In *Ard Veenish,* Gaelic, *Aird Mh'inis,* only the second part is Norse. It comes from *Midhjunes,* 'Middle Peninsula,' and got its name from the fact that it lies in the middle between Ard Mhór and Bruernish. The initial *m-* is aspirated to *v-* (*mh-*) after the Gaelic word *àird.*

3. OLD NORSE *VÁGR* = BAY

Ending in this we have the names of two bays, *Bay Hulavagh,* Gaelic, *Bàgh Hùileabhagh,* and *Bay Hirivagh,* Gaelic *Bàgh Hiorabhagh.* The first part of both is obscure to me.

4. OLD NORSE *VÍK* = (SMALL) BAY

Ending in this we find the name of the village *Breivig,* Gaelic, *Bréibhig.* The Old Norse form was *Breidhvík,* 'Broad Bay'; this refers, of course, to Breivig Bay, which is very broad and short. *Brevik* (or *Breivik*) occurs as the name of a town in Norway. There are other names in *-vík* on the smaller islands.

5. OLD NORSE *FJALL* - HILL, MOUNTAIN

There are several names of hills ending in *-val* (*fjall*). *Heaval,* Gaelic, *Hèahabhal,* is the highest hill in Barra. One would therefore like to think that the name means something like 'High Hill.' Now the Old Norse for 'High Hill' was *Háfjall,* and that is not a very good starting-point if one wants to explain the pronunciation *Hèahabhal.* I cannot therefore regard the explanation as certain, but I have nothing better to suggest.

Tangaval was Old Norse, *Tangafjall,* 'Headland Hill,' a name suiting its position. *Tangi* meant very much the same as *nes*.

Fjall is also the second part of *Scurrival,* which in Gaelic could be written *Sgaireabhal* or *Sgoireabhal.* It is very uncertain what the first part of the name is. Perhaps we could start from the word *skagi,* 'headland, promontory, cape' (cp. the name *Skagen* of the northern point of Denmark); this word could be used of the northern end of Eoligarry, where Scurrival is. Along the shore there are several rocks, which might be called a reef, Old Norse, *rif;* the name of this reef would naturally be *Skagarif.* Suppose that the reef, a dangerous thing for seagoing people, was better remembered than the promontory; then the hill would be called *Skagariffjall,* 'Hill near the reef of the promontory.' This is perhaps the origin of *Scurrival;* but to understand the modern pronunciation, we must suppose a shortening into *Ska(g)riffjall;* such a shortening could take place in a name of four syllables.

6. OLD NORSE *STÖDHULL* = MILKING PLACE

Two names end in *-sdale, Tangusdale* and *Allasdale.* The last part of these names is the Old Norse, *stödhull,* 'milking place.' The Gaelic, *buaile,* of identical meaning, occurs in the name *Bolnabodach,* Gaelic, *Buaile nam Bodach,* near Bruernish. *Tangusdale,* Gaelic *Tangasdal,* is near Ben Tangaval; it comes from Old Norse, *Tanga-stödhull,* 'the milking-place near the headland.' *Allasdale* is pronounced *Alla'asdal;* the broken *a* shows that there must have been an *f* or *v* after the *l* (cp. what was said under *Oro'osaidh*); the Old Norse name was almost certainly *Alfa-stödhull,* 'the Fairies' Milking-place' (*Alfa* = a fairy). This name, and indeed also *Buaile nam Bodach,* 'The Old Men's (*i.e.* brownies') Milking-place,' were given by people who believed in fairies and in supernatural cattle.

7. MODERN GAELIC, *AIRIGH,* OLD IRISH, *AIRGE,* NORSE, *ERG* = SHEALING

There is a group of names ending in *-ary, -airigh.* This is simply the Gaelic word *airigh,* 'a shealing.' Early Irish, *airge.* The Norsemen borrowed this word, and wrote it *erg.* We have then: *Ersary,* Gaelic, *E'arsairigh,* from Old Norse, *Aefarserg,* 'Aefar's Shealing'; *Skallary,* Gaelic, *Sgallairigh,* from *Skollaerg,* 'Skolli's shealing', and *Gunnery,*

Gaelic, *Gunnairigh*, probably shortened for Old Norse, *Gunnarserg*, 'Gunnar's shealing.' The three names are men's names.

I only mention here the difficult name *Eoligarry*, Gaelic, *Eoiligearraidh*, which I do not understand. Does it contain Old Norse, *gardhr* or *gerdhi*, 'fence, piece of land, farm'? The first part of it cannot be the name *Olafr*, which would require an *s* in composition.

8. OLD NORSE SKER = SKERRY AND *HOLMR* = SMALL ISLAND

Old Norse had the words *sker*, 'skerry' (borrowed in Gaelic as *sgeir*) and *holmr*, 'small island.' The former is found in several names, such as Heisker, from *Hellusker*, 'Flagstone Island.' The latter occurs in *So'olum*, written *Solon More* and *Solon Beg* on the Ordnance Survey Map, from Old Norse, *Saudhaholm(r)*, 'Sheep Isle.' Perhaps it also occurs as -*mul* in *Greanamul*, *Snuasimul*, etc.; but I do not understand the first part of these names.

9. OTHER TERMINATIONS

Vaslin, Gaelic, *Bhàslainn*, is a piece of flat land near the Tràigh Mhór; during winter it is frequently very wet and full of pools. I explain it as Old Norse, *Vátlendi*, 'Wet Land' (vát = wet; lendi = land). The change of *t* to *s* before *l* occurs in many Norse dialects.

A difficult word is *Cuier*, Gaelic, *Cui'eir*. At Cuier in Barra there is a church and a churchyard; the map shows me a Ben Cuier in Vatersay and a burial-ground near it. If both these churchyards are as old as the Norse period, there may be a connection between the name Cuier and the Old Norse word for church; *kyrkja* (*j* = English *y* as in *yes*). I suppose, then, a compound word, *kyrkyugardh(r)*, 'churchyard,' or *kyrkjujordh*, 'ground belonging to the church,' or something like that. But the explanation is not very certain, as we should have to suppose many changes to produce the present *Cui'eir*.

There are also a few names consisting of only one word. The most conspicuous is *Borve*, Gaelic, *Borgh* or *Borogh*, from Old Norse, *Borg*, 'a castle, a town.' This may have been one of the principal settlements of the Norsemen in Barra. The name *Horve*, Gaelic, *Na h-Orgh*, can be explained from Old Norse, *Hogr*, 'a cairn, altar, or place of worship.'

There are not a few Norse loan-words in the Gaelic language; some of them are designations of place. I have already mentioned *sgeir*, from Old Norse *sker*, 'a skerry.' Another is *bodha*, pronounced *bo'o*, 'a rock under the water,' from Old Norse, *bodhi* of the same meaning. The

Gaelic name for the Atlantic Ocean is *Na h-Abh*, pronounced approximately as *na haf;* this comes from Old Norse, *haf,* 'ocean.'

In this very short article I have only collected the most important Norse place-names, and those for which I could find a reasonable explanation. A careful investigation in Barra and the adjacent islands would reveal many more, besides the hundreds or thousands of Norse names which exist in the rest of the Hebrides and on the Mainland.

Appendix

*

ANTIQUITIES

As the antiquities of Barra have been described in the various accounts of the island, it has not been considered necessary to devote a special chapter to them. It is worth mentioning, however, that the only rune-inscribed stone known in the Hebrides was found in the churchyard at Kilbar. It is now in the National Museum of Antiquities. The runic inscription is obscure, and has not been satisfactorily deciphered.

For a detailed description of the antiquities of Barra, readers are recommended to consult the Royal Commission on Ancient Monuments and Constructions of Scotland's volume on the Outer Hebrides, Skye and the Small Isles, and *The Early Christian Monuments of Scotland*, by J. Romilly Allen, Part III., pp. 111-115.

PROPRIETORS

The following are the names and approximate dates of ownership of the proprietors of Barra since the first known charter was granted to Gilleonan MacNeill by the King of the Isles in 1427. The chief source for these is *The Clan Macneil*. See also *Celtic Review*, Vol. III, pp. 216-223.

Gilleonan (Gille Adhamhnáin) MacNeill	1427 – c.1440
Roderick MacNeill	c.1440 – c.1475
Gilleonan MacNeill	c.1475 – c.1510
Gilleonan MacNeill	c.1510 – c.1544
Gilleonan MacNeill	c.1544 – c.1580
Roderick MacNeill	c.1580 – 1598
Roderick MacNeill, "Ruairi an Tartair"	1598 – c.1622
Niall Og (? or Uisteach) MacNeill	c.1622 – c.1655
Gillerane MacNeill	c.1655 – c.1680
Roderick MacNeill	c.1680 – c.1720
Roderick MacNeill	c.1720 – 1763
Roderick MacNeill	1763 – 1822

Roderick MacNeill, last native owner, left Barra in 1827	1822 – 1838
Colonel Gordon of Cluny	1838 – 1858
John Gordon of Cluny	1858 – 1878
Lady Gordon Cathcart	1878 – 1932
Trustees	1932 –

Bernera, Mingulay, and Pabbay now belong to J. H. Russell; the Board of Agriculture owns Vatersay, Sandray, Eoligarry, and the land north of Northbay.

THE PRIESTS OF BARRA[1]

Rev. Dermit Duggan	1652 – 1657
Rev. George Fanning	1671
Rev. Mr Carolan	1687
Rev. Mr Kelly	1725 – 1736
Rev. James Grant	1736 – c.1755
Rev. Aeneas MacDonell	c.1755 – 1762
Rev. Alexander MacDonald	1765 – 1779
Rev. Allan MacDonell	1779 – 1784
Rev. James Allan MacDonell	1784 – 1805
Rev. Angus MacDonald	1805 – 1825
Rev. Neil MacDonald	1825 – 1835
Rev. William Mackintosh	1835 – 1839
Rev. Donald MacDonald	1839 – 1851
Rev. Colin MacPherson	1851 – 1855
Rev. William MacDonell	1856 – 1867
Rev. John MacDonald	1867 – 1883
Canon Chisholm	1883 – 1889

Canon Chisholm completed the church at Castlebay in 1889, and the priests there have been:

Canon Chisholm	1889 – 1903
Rev. (later Canon) William MacMaster	1903 – 1905
Rev. (later Bishop) Donald Martin	1905 – 1908
Monsignor Hugh Cameron[2]	1908 – 1921
Dean (now Canon) Alexander MacDougall	1921 – 1925

1 Taken partly from *The Clan Macneil.*

2 In 1915 Fr Cameron left to join the Forces as Chaplain to the Lovat Scouts, and in his absence Fr Patrick MacDonald acted as parish priest. When the Vatersay Mission Church was opened, Fr Donald MacIntyre, now in Canada, assisted Fr Cameron as curate.

Rev. Donald Campbell, D.D.	1925 – 1935
Rev. John MacQueen	1935 –

At Craigston since 1889:

Rev. Angus MacDonald	1889 – 1893
Rev. William MacKenzie	1893 – 1913
Rev. William MacLellan	1913 – 1919
Rev. Donald MacIntyre	1919 – 1925
Rev. Samuel MacIsaac	1925 – 1929
Rev. James Webb	1929 – 1931
Rev. Dominic MacKellaig	1931 –

The church at Northbay was built in 1906, but until 1919 was served from Craigston. Since 1919 the priests at Northbay have been:

Rev. Joseph Gillies	1919 – 1923
Rev. James MacDonald	1923 – 1929
Rev. John MacMillan	1929 –

CHURCH OF SCOTLAND[1]

Rev. John MacPherson	1734 – 1742
Rev. William MacLeod	1742 – 1750
Rev. Lachlan MacLean	1750 – 1763
Rev. John MacAulay	1763 – 1771
Rev. Angus MacNeill of Vatersay	1771 – 1774
Rev. Edmund MacQueen	1774 – 1813
Rev. Alexander Nicholson	1813 – 1847
Rev. Henry Beatson	1847 – 1871
Rev. Archibald MacDonald	1871 – 1932
Rev. Dugald Munro	1932 – 1934
Rev. Iain MacDougall	1934

APPROXIMATE DISTANCES FROM CASTLEBAY

Oban	95 miles	Ardnamurchan	
Tobermory	70 miles	Point	55 miles
Coll	45 miles	Skye (Cuillins)	55 miles
Tyree	40 miles	Mallaig	65 miles
Lochboisdale	20 miles	Loch Maddy[2]	50 miles

1 Taken from *The Clan Macneil.* Until 1734 the parish of Barra was united with that of South Uist; there was only one Protestant in Barra when Martin visited it in 1695.
2 Police Court for Inverness-shire Outer Isles.

Canna	40 miles	Stornoway	105 miles
Rum	45 miles	Inverness[1]	
Eigg .	55 miles	(via Oban)	205 miles
Muck .	50 miles	(via Mallaig)	185 miles

POPULATION OF BARRA SINCE 1801[2]

1801	1925	1871	1997
1811	2114	1881	2161
1821	2303	1891	2365
1831	2097	1901	2545
1841	2363	1911	2620 (maximum)
1851	1873[3]	1921	2456
1861	1853[3]	1931	2250

Gaelic

Percentage of population speaking Gaelic and English in 1931	69.6
Percentage of population speaking Gaelic only in 1931	17.8
Total percentage of Gaelic speakers in 1931	87.4

The percentage of Gaelic speakers in Barra has never fallen to less than 87.2 per cent. The present percentage of monoglot Gaelic speakers is second only to South Uist in the whole of the Highlands and Islands, a fact upon which Barra may well take pride. The language, however, has no official status under the present régime.

---

1 County Town.
2 Taken from the Census Report of 1931.
3 These low figures were due to the potato famine and Colonel Gordon's evictions.

Bibliography

*

A Description of the Western Islands of Scotland, by MARTIN MARTIN: Glasgow, 1884 (reprint of first edition).

A Description of the Western Islands of Scotland, including the Isle of Man, comprising an account of their geological structure; by JOHN MACCULLOCH, M.D. In three volumes: London, 1819.

A Journey to the Western Islands of Scotland, by Dr SAMUEL JOHNSON: London, 1925 edition.

Gloomy Memories, by DONALD MACLEOD: Glasgow, 1892.

Minutes of Evidence and Report of the Crofters' Commission: Edinburgh, 1884.

New Statistical Account of Scotland: Edinburgh 1845.

(Old) Statistical Account of Scotland, edited by Sir JOHN SINCLAIR, Bart.: Edinburgh, 1794.

Outer Isles, by A. GOODRICH FREER: Westminster, 1902.

Public Administration in the Highlands and Islands of Scotland, by J. P. DAY: London, 1918.

Reliquiae Celticae, Rev. ALEXANDER CAMERON, LL.D.; edited by ALEXANDER MACBAIN and the Rev. JOHN KENNEDY: Inverness, 1882.

Reports of the Society for the Support of Gaelic Schools: Edinburgh, 1811-1845.

Scotland before 1700, edited by P. HUME BROWN: Edinburgh, 1893.

Scottish History Society, Vols. XX-XXIII and LI-LIII.

The Clan Macneil, by the MACNEIL OF BARRA: New York, 1923.

The Highlands and Western Isles of Scotland; containing Descriptions of their Scenery and Antiquities, with an Account of the Political History and Ancient Manners, and of the Origin, Language, Agriculture, Economy, Music, Present Conditions of the People, etc., etc., etc. Founded on a series of annual journies between the years 1811 and 1821, and forming a Universal Guide to that Country, in letters to Sir Walter Scott, Bart. By JOHN MACCULLOCH, M.D., F.R.S., L.S., G.S., etc., etc., etc. In four volumes: London, 1824.

The History of the Highland Clearances, by ALEXANDER MACKENZIE, F.S.A.(Scot.): Inverness, 1883.

The MacNeills of Barra, by the Rev. A. MACLEAN SINCLAIR: Celtic Review, Vol. III, pp. 216-223.

The Fauna and
Flora of Barra

*

THE BIRDS OF THE ISLAND OF BARRA

The following list, compiled by members of the Edinburgh University Biological Society Expedition, comprises the records of John McRury, Wm. L. McGillivray, Harvie-Brown, and the Duchess of Bedford, whose notes and papers are published in the *Annals of Scottish Natural History* 1894-onwards, and in the *Scottish Naturalist* until 1912. The more recent records of the Expedition are also included, while some indication of the status of each species is given.

(H-B) = Harvie-Brown. (B.)= Duchess of Bedford. (McR.)= John McRury. (McG)= Wm. L. McGillivray. (E.U.B.S.)= Edinburgh University Biological Society Expedition.

Status.—O.= Occasional. P.M.= Passage Migrant. R.= Resident. S.M.= Summer Migrant. S.R.= Summer Resident. V.O.= Very Occasional. W.M.= Winter Migrant.

* An asterisk denotes a Hebridean race.

Raven. *Corvus corax corax.* (McR.) (E.U.B.S.) R.
Hooded Crow. *Corvus cornix cornix.* (McR.) (E.U.B.S.) R.
Rook. *Corvus frugilegus frugilegus.* (McR.) O.
Jackdaw. *Corvus monedula spermologus.* (McR.) V.O.
Chough. *Pyrrhocorax pyrrhocorax.* (McR.) Last seen by McGillivray in 1830, now extinct.
Starling. *Sturnus vulgaris vulgaris.* (McR.) (E.U.B.S.) R.
Greenfinch. *Chloris chloris chloris.* (McR.) S.R.
Siskin. *Spinus spinus* (McR.) V.O.
House-Sparrow. *Passer domesticus domesticus.* (McR.) (E.U.B.S.) R.
First appeared in 1893, breeding Castlebay 1895 onwards.
Tree-Sparrow. *Passer montanus montanus.* (McR.) R.
Chaffinch. *Fringilla coelebs coelebs.* (McR.) W.M.
Brambling. *Fringilla montifringilla.* (McR.) V.O.
Linnet. *Acanthis cannabina cannabina.* (McR.) S.M.
Mealy Redpoll. *Acanthis linaria linaria.* (McR.) W.M.
Lesser Redpoll. *Acanthis linaria cabaret.* (H-B.) O.
Greenland Redpoll. *Acanthis linaria rostrata.* (H-B.) V.O.
*Twite. *Acanthis flavirostris bensorum.* (McR.) (E.U.B.S.) R.
Bullfinch. *Pyrrhula pyrrhula.* (McR.) V.O. and W.M.
Crossbill. *Loxia curvirostra curvirostra.* (H-B.) (McR.) O. and S.M.
Corn-Bunting. *Emberiza calandra calandra.* (McR.) (E.U.B.S.) S.R. Breeds
Yellow Bunting. *Emberiza citrinella citrinella.* (McR.) W.M.

Reed-Bunting. *Emberiza schoeniclus schoeniclus.* (McR.) (E.U.B.S.) S.R. Breeds.
Snow-Bunting. *Plectrophenax nivalis.* (McR.) W.M.
Sky-Lark. *Alauda arvensis arvensis.* (McR.) (E.U.B.S.) R.
White Wagtail. *Motacilla alba alba.* (McR.) V.O.
Pied Wagtail. *Motacilla alba yarellii.* (H-B.) O.
Grey Wagtail. *Motacilla cinerea cinerea.* (McR.) V.O.
Meadow-Pipit. *Anthus pratensis.* (McR.) (E.U.B.S.) R.
Rock-Pipit. *Anthus spinoletta petrosus.* (McR.) (E.U.B.S.) R.
British Goldcrest. *Regulus regulus anglorum.* (McR.) S.M.
Great Grey Shrike. *Lanius excubitor excubitor.* (H-B.) V.O.
Whitethroat. *Sylvia communis communis.* (McR.) S.M.
Lesser Whitethroat. *Sylvia curruca curruca.* (H-B.) V.O.
Garden-Warbler. *Sylvia borin.* (H-B.) S.M.
Blackcap. *Sylvia atricapilla atricapilla.* (McR.) P.M.
Barred Warbler. *Sylvia nisoria nisoria.* (H-B.) V.O.
Sedge-Warbler. *Acrocephalus schoenobaenus.* (McR.) (E.U.B.S.) S.R.
Willow-Warbler. *Phylloscopus trochilus trochilus.* (McR.) S.R. Has bred.
Chiffchaff. *Phylloscopus collybita collybita.* (H-B.) V.O.
Mistle-Thrush. *Turdus viscivorus viscivorus.* (B.) V.O.
*Song-Thrush. *Turdus philomelos hebridensis.* (McR.) (E.U.B.S.) R.
Redwing. *Turdus musicus.* (McR.) W.M.
Fieldfare. *Turdus pilaris.* (McR.) W.M.
Blackbird. *Turdus merula merula.* (McR.) (E.U.B.S.) R.
Ring-Ouzel. *Turdus torquatus torquatus.* (McR.) S.M.
Redbreast. *Erithacus rubecula melophilus.* (McR.) (E.U.B.S.) R.
*Stonechat. *Saxicola torquata theresae.* (McR.) (E.U.B.S.) R. Breeds.
Whinchat. *Saxicola rubetra rubetra.* (McR.) S.R. Has bred.
Wheatear. *Oenanthe oenanthe.* (McR.) (E.U.B.S.) S.V. Breeds.
*Hedge-Sparrow. *Prunella modularis hebridensis.* (McR.) (E.U.B.S.) R.
Dipper. *Cinclus cinclus gularis.* (McR.) V.O.
*Wren. *Troglodytes troglodytes hebridensis.* (McR.) (E.U.B.S.) R.
Swallow. *Hirundo rustica rustica.* (McR.) (E.U.B.S.) S.R.
House-Martin. *Delichon urbica urbica.* (McR.) S.M.
Sand-Martin. *Riparia riparia riparia.* (McR.) S.M.
Cuckoo. *Cuculus canoris canoris.* (McR.) S.R.
Swift. *Micropus apus apus.* (McR.) (E.U.B.S.) S.R.
Kingfisher. *Alcedo atthis ispida.* (McR.) V.O.
Long-eared Owl. *Asio otus otus.* (H-B.) V.O.
Short-eared Owl. *Asio flammeus flammeus.* (McR.) S.R. and W.M. Has bred.
Snowy Owl. *Nyctea nyctea.* (McR.) V.O.
Hen-Harrier. *Circus cyaneus cyaneus.* (McR.) ? R.
Buzzard. *Buteo buteo buteo.* (E.U.B.S.) R.
Golden Eagle. *Aquila chrysaëtus chrysaëtus.* (McR.) O. Breeds on adjacent islands.
Sparrow-Hawk. *Accipiter nisus nisus.* (? McR.) (B.) V.O.
White-tailed Eagle. *Haliaetus albicilla* (McR.) V.O. Probably now extinct.
Iceland Falcon. *Falco rusticolus islandus.* (McG.) V.O.
Greenland Falcon. *Falco rusticolus candicans.* (McR.) V.O.
Peregrine Falcon. *Falco peregrinus peregrinus.* (McR.) O. Breeding
    on adjacent islands.
Merlin. *Falco columbarius aesalon.* (McR.) (E.U.B.S.) R.
Kestrel. *Falco tinnunculus tinnunculus.* (McR.) ? R.
Cormorant. *Phalacrocorax carbo carbo.* (McR.) R.

Shag. *Phalacrocorax aristotelis aristotelis.* (McR.) (E.U.B.S.) R.
Gannet. *Sula bassana.* (McR.) (E.U.B.S.) S.R.
Grey Lag-Goose. *Anser anser.* (McR.) W.M.
White-fronted Goose. *Anser albifrons.* (McR.) W.M.
Brent Goose. *Branta bernicla bernicla.* (McR.) W.M.
Barnacle-Goose. *Branta leucopsis.* (McR.) W.M.
Whooper Swan. *Cygnus cygnus.* (McR.) W.M.
Mute Swan. *Cygnus olor.* (McR.) O. Introduced in 1894, has since died out.
Common Sheld-Duck. *Tadorna tadorna.* (McR.) R.
Mallard. *Anas platyrhyncha platyrhyncha.* (McR.) (E.U.B.S.) R.
Gadwall. *Anas strepera.* (McR.) V.O.
Teal. *Querquedula crecca crecca.* (McR.) ? S.R. Has bred.
Wigeon. *Mareca penelope.* (McR.) W.M.
Pintail. *Dafila acuta acuta.* (McR.) W.M.
Pochard. *Nyroca ferina ferina.* (McR.) W.M.
Scaup. *Nyroca marila marila.* (McR.) V.O.
Goldeneye. *Glaucionetta clangula clangula.* (McR.) W.M.
Long-tailed Duck. *Clangula hyemalis.* (McR.) W.M.
Eider. *Somateria mollissima mollissima.* (McR.) (E.U.B.S.) S.R. Breeds.
Red-breasted Merganser. *Mergus serrator.* (McR.) R. and W.M.
Heron. *Ardea cinerea cinerea.* (McR.) (E.U.B.S.) S.R.
Night-Heron. *Nycticorax nycticorax nycticorax.* (McR.) V.O.
Spoonbill. *Platalea leucorodia leucorodia.* (McR.) V.O.
Siberian Crane. *Grus leucoguanus.* (McR.) An escape.
Grey Phalerope. *Phalopus fulicarius.* (McR.) V.O.
Woodcock. *Scolopax rusticola rusticola.* (McR.) W.M.
Common Snipe. *Capella gallinago gallinago.* (McR.) (E.U.B.S.) R.
Jack Snipe. *Lymnocryptes minimus.* (McR.) W.M.
Knot. *Calidris canutus canutus.* (McR.) W.M.
Purple Sandpiper. *Erolia maritima maritima.* (McR.) W.M.
Dunlin. *Erolia alpina alpina.* (McR.) W.M. and S.R. ? Breeds.
Sanderling. *Crocethia alba.* (McR.) W.M.
Redshank. *Tringa totanus totanus.* (McR.) (E.U.B.S.) S.R. and W.M.
Greenshank. *Tringa nebularia.* (McR.) V.O.
Common Sandpiper. *Tringa hypoleucos.* (McR.) (E.U.B.S.) S.R. Breeds.
Bar-tailed Godwit. *Limosa lapponica lapponica.* (McR.) W.M.
Curlew. *Numenius arquata arquata.* (McR.) (E.U.B.S.) S.M.
Whimbrel. *Numenius phaeopus phaeopus.* (McR.) S.M.
Golden Plover. *Pluvialis apricarius apricarius.* (McR.) (E.U.B.S.) S.M. and W.M.
Grey Plover. *Squaterola squaterola squaterola,* (McR.) V.O.
Ringed Plover. *Charadrius hiaticula hiaticula.* (McR.) (E.U.B.S.) R.
Lapwing. *Vanellus vanellus.* (McR.) (E.U.B.S.) R.
Oyster-catcher. *Haematopus ostralegus ostralegus.* (McR.) (E.U.B.S.) R. and W.M.
Turnstone. *Arenaria interpres interpres.* (McR.) W.M. and S.R.
Common Gull. *Larus canus canus.* (McR.) (E.U.B.S.) R.
Herring-Gull. *Larus argentatus argentatus.* (McR.) (E.U.B.S.) R.
Great Black-backed Gull. *Larus marinus.* (McR.) (E.U.B.S.) R.
Lesser Black-backed Gull. *Larus fuscus affinis.* (McR.) (E.U.B.S.) R.
Glaucous Gull. *Larus hyperboreus.* (McR.) V.O.
Iceland Gull. *Larus glaucoides.* (McR.) V.O.
Black-headed Gull. *Larus ridibundus ridibundus.* (McR.) (E.U.B.S.) S.R. and W.M.
Kittiwake. *Rissa tridactyla tridactyla.* (McR.) R.

Common Tern. *Sterna hirundo hirundo.* (E.U.B.S.) S.R.
Arctic Tern. *Sterna macrura.* (McR.) (E.U.B.S.) S.R. Breeds.
Little Tern. *Sterna albifrons albifrons.* (H-B.) S.R. Has bred.Sandwich Tern. *Sterna sandvicensis sandvicensis* (E.U.B.S.) S.R.
Great Skua. *Catharacta skua skua.* (McR.) (H-B.) V.O.
Richardson's Skua. *Stercorarius parasiticus.* (McR.) S.M. and W.M.
Buffon's Skua. *Stercorarius longicaudus.* (McR.) V.O.
Pomatorhine Skua. *Stercorarius pomarinus.* (McR.) O.
Razorbill. *Alca torda.* (McR.) (E.U.B.S.) R.
Guillemot. *Uria aalge aalge.* (McR.) (E.U.B.S.) R.
Black Guillemot. *Uria grylle grylle.* (McR.) (E.U.B.S.) O.
Little Auk. *Alle alle.* (McR.) V.O.
Puffin. *Fratercula arctica grabae.* (McR.) (E.U.B.S.) R.
Storm-Petrel. *Thalassidroma pelagica.* (McR.) O.
Manx Shearwater. *Puffinus puffinus puffinus.* (McR.) O.
Leach's Fork-tailed Petrel. *Oceanodroma leucorrhoea leucorrhoea.* (McR.) O.
Fulmar Petrel. *Fulmarus glacialis glacialis.* (McR.) (E.U.B.S.) R.
Black-throated Diver. *Colymbus arcticus arcticus.* (McR.) W.M.
Great Northern Diver. *Colymbus immer.* (McR.) W.M.
Red-throated Diver. *Colymbus stellatus stellatus.* (McR.) W.M.
Slavonian Grebe. *Podiceps auritus.* (McR.) W.M.
Little Grebe. *Podiceps ruficollis ruficollis.* (McR.) (E.U.B.S.) R. and W.M.
Water-Rail. *Rallus aquaticus aquaticus.* (McR.) V.O.
Corn-Crake. *Crex crex crex.* (McR.) (E.U.B.S.) S.R. Breeds.
Moor-hen. *Gallinula chloropus chloropus.* (McR.) R.
Coot. *Fulica atra atra.* (McR.) (E.U.B.S.) R.
Ring-Dove. *Columba palumbus palumbus.* (McR.) O. and W.M.
Rock-Dove. *Columba livia livia.* (McR.) (E.U.B.S.) R.
Turtle-Dove. *Streptopelia turtur turtur.* (McR.) V.O.
Quail. *Coturnix coturnix coturnix.* (McR.) V.O.
Scottish Red Grouse. *Lagopus scoticus scoticus.* (McR.) (E.U.B.S.) R.

*

List of Flowering-plants, Ferns, Horse-tails and Club-mosses observed by the Edinburgh University Biological Society Expedition to Barra, July 1935.

† A dagger indicates a new record for the Outer Hebrides lacking confirmation.

DICOTYLEDONS
Lesser Meadow Rue. *Thalictrum dunense.*
Creeping Buttercup. *Ranunculus repens.*
Meadow Buttercup. *Ranunculus acris.*
Bulbous Buttercup. *Ranunculus bulbosus.*
Lesser Spearwort. *Ranunculus Flammula.*
Lesser Celandine. *Ranunculus Ficaria.*
Water Crowfoot. *Ranunculus trichophyllus.*
Ivy-leaved Crowfoot. *Ranunculus hederaceus.*
Marsh Marigold. *Caltha palustris.*
White Water-lily. *Castalia alba.*
Long-headed Poppy. *Papaver dubium.*
Fumitory. *Fumaria officinalis.*
Water Cress. *Radicula Nasturtium.*

Cuckoo-flower. *Cardamine pratensis.*
Hairy Bitter Cress. *Cardamine flexuosa.*
Scurvy Grass. *Cochlearia officinalis.*
Shepherd's Purse. *Capsella Bursa-pastoris.*
Hedge Mustard. *Sisymbrium officinale.*
Swine-cress. *Coronopus procumbens.*
Sea Rocket. *Cakile maritima.*
Wild Radish. *Raphanus Raphanistrum.*
Dog Violet. *Viola Riviniana.*
Thyme-leaved Milkwort. *Polygala serpyllacea.*
Common Milkwort. *Polygala vulgaris.*
Sea Campion. *Silene maritima.*
Ragged Robin. *Lychnis Flos-cuculi.*
Red Campion. *Lychnis dioica.*
Mouse-eared Chickweed. *Cerastium vulgatum.*
Viscid Mouse-ear Chickweed. *Cerastium viscosum.*
† Small Mouse-ear Chickweed. *Cerastium semidecandrum.*
Small Mouse-ear Chickweed. *Cerastium tetrandrum.*
Chickweed. *Stellaria media.*
Bog Stitchwort. *Stellaria uliginosa.*
Thyme-leaved Sandwort. *Arenaria serpyllifolia.*
Sea Purslane. *Arenaria peploides.*
Heath Pearlwort. *Sagina subulata.*
Pearlwort. *Sagina apetala.*
Procumbent Pearlwort. *Sagina procumbens.*
Corn Spurrey. *Spergula arvensis.*
Spurrey. *Spergula sativa.*
Water Blinks. *Montia lamprosperma.*
Six-stamened Waterwort. *Elatine hexandra.*
Slender St John's-wort. *Hypericum pulchrum.*
Bog St John's-wort. *Hypericum elodes.*
Cathartic Flax. *Linum catharticum.*
Dove's-foot Crane's-Bill. *Geranium molle.*
Common Stork's-Bill. *Erodium cicutarium.*
Wood-sorrel. *Oxalis Acetosella.*
Sycamore. *Acer Pseudo-platanus.*
Norway Maple. *Acer Platanoides.*
Furze, Gorse or Whin. *Ulex europeus.*
Zig-zag or Meadow Clover. *Trifolium medium.*
Red or Purple Clover. *Trifolium pratense.*
White Clover. *Trifolium repens.*
† Hop Trefoil. *Trifolium procumbens.*
Kidney Vetch. *Anthyllis Vulneraria.*
Bird's-foot Trefoil. *Lotus corniculatus.*
Tufted Vetch. *Vicia Cracca.*
Bush Vetch. *Vicia sepium.*
Meadow Pea. *Lathyrus pratensis.*
Meadow-sweet. *Spirea Ulmaria.*
Bramble. *Rubus fruticosus.*
Silver-weed. *Potentilla Anserina.*
Tormentil. *Potentilla erecta.*
Marsh Cinque-foil. *Potentilla palustris.*
Burnet Rose. *Rosa spinosissima.*

Dog Rose. *Rosa mollis.*
Rowan. *Pyrus Aucuparia.*
Biting Stonecrop. *Sedum acre.*
English Stonecrop. *Sedum anglicum.*
Roseroot. *Sedum Rhodiola.*
English Sundew. *Drosera anglica.*
Common Sundew. *Drosera rotundifolia.*
Spiked Water-Milfoil. *Myriophyllum spicatum.*
Water Starwort. *Callitrice intermedia.*
† Great Willow-herb. *Epilobium hirsutum.*
Hoary Willow-herb. *Epilobium parviflorum.*
Square-stemmed Willow-herb. *Epilobium tetragonum.*
Marsh Willow-herb. *Epilobium palustre.*
Marsh Penny-wort. *Hydrocotyle vulgaris.*
Hemlock. *Conium maculatum.*
Procumbent Celery. *Apium nodiflorum.*
Lesser Water Celery. *Apium inundatum.*
Lesser Water-Parsnip. *Sium erectum.*
† Hemlock Water Dropwort. *Oenanthe crocata.*
Lovage. *Ligustrum scoticum.*
Wild Angelica. *Angelica sylvestris.*
Cow Parsnip. *Heracleum Sphondylium.*
Carrot. *Daucus Carota.*
Hedge Parsley. *Caucalis Anthriscus.*
Common Elder. *Sambucus nigra.*
Common Honeysuckle. *Lonicera Periclymenum.*
Heath Bedstraw. *Galium hercynicum.*
Water Bedstraw. *Galium palustre.*
Lady's Bedstraw. *Galium verum.*
Sticky Willie. *Galium Aparine.*
Common Valerian. *Valeriana officinalis.*
Lamb's Lettuce. *Valerianella olitoria.*
Devil's-bit. Scabiosa Succisa.
Goldenrod. *Solidago Virgaurea.*
Daisy. *Bellis perennis.*
Mountain Everlasting. *Antennaria dioica.*
Elecampane. *Inula Helenium.*
Yarrow. *Achillea Millefolium.*
Sneezewort. *Achillea Ptarmica.*
† Stinking Mayweed. *Anthemis Cotula.*
Corn Marigold. *Chrysanthemum segetum.*
Scentless Mayweed. *Matricaria inodora.*
Rayless Mayweed. *Matricaria suaveolens.*
Tansy. *Tanacetum vulgare.*
Mugwort. *Artemisia vulgaris.*
Colts Tussfoot. *ilago Farfara.*
Butterburr. *Petasites ovatus.*
Marsh Ragwort. *Senecio aquaticus.*
Ragwort. *Senecio jacobaea.*
Groundsel. *Senecio vulgaris.*
Burdock. *Arctium Lappa.*
Spear Thistle. *Cnicus lanceolatus.*
Creeping Thistle. *Cnicus arvensis.*

Marsh Thistle. *Cnicus palustris.*
Knapweed. *Centaurea nigra.*
Smooth Hawk's-beard. *Crepis capillaris.*
Mouse-ear Hawkweed. *Hieracium Pilosella.*
† Alpine Hawkweed. *Hieracium alpinum.*
Cat's-ear. *Hypochoeris radicata.*
Autumnal Hawkbit. *Leontodon autumnalis.*
Dandelion. *Taraxacum vulgare.*
Corn Sowthistle. *Sonchus arvensis.*
Common Sowthistle. *Sonchus asper.*
Common Sowthistle. *Sonchus oleraceus.*
Water Lobelia. *Lobelia Dortmanna.*
Harebell. *Campanula rotundifolia.*
Blaeberry. *Vaccinium Myrtillus.*
Cowberry. *Vaccinium Vitis-idaea.*
Ling. *Calluna vulgaris.*
Bell Heather. *Erica cinerea.*
Cross-leaved Heather. *Erica tetralix.*
Primrose. *Primula vulgaris.*
Cowslip. *Primula veris.*
Yellow Pimpernel. *Lysimachia nemorum.*
Sea Milkwort. *Glaux maritima.*
Pimpernel. *Anagallis arvensis.*
Bog Pimpernel. *Anagallis tenella.*
Ash. *Fraxinus excelsior.*
Common Centaury. *Centaurium unbellatum.*
Field Gentian. *Gentiana campestris.*
Buckbean. *Menyanthes trifoliata.*
Bugloss. *Lycopsis arvensis.*
Water Forget-me-not. *Myosotis palustris.*
Water Forget-me-not. *Myosotis caespitosa.*
Water Forget-me-not. *Myosotis scorpioides.*
† Early Forget-me-not. *Myosotis collina.*
Yellow and Blue Forget-me-not. *Myosotis versicolor.*
† Larger Bindweed. *Calystegia sepium.*
Foxglove. *Digitalis purpurea.*
Common Speedwell. *Veronica officinalis.*
Marsh Speedwell. *Veronica scutellata.*
Water Speedwell. *Veronica Anagallis-aquatica.*
Thyme-leaved Speedwell. *Veronica serpyllifolia.*
Wall Speedwell. *Veronica arvensis.*
Ivy-leaved Speedwell. *Veronica hederaefolia.*
Eyebright. *Euphrasia officinalis.*
Red Bartsia. *Bartsia Odontites.*
Red Rattle. *Pedicularis palustris.*
Lousewort. *Pedicularis sylvatica.*
Yellow Rattle. *Rhinanthus Crista-galli.*
Lesser Bladderwort. *Utricularia minor.*
Common Butterwort. *Pinguicula vulgaris.*
Pale Butterwort. *Pinguicula lusitanica.*
Spear Mint. *Mentha spicata.*
Water Mint. *Mentha aquatica.*
Gypsywort. *Lycopus europeus.*

Wild Thyme. *Thymus neglectus.*
Common Skullcap. *Scutellaria galericulata.*
Self-heal. *Prunella vulgaris.*
Marsh Woundwort. *Stachys palustris.*
Common Hemp-nettle. *Galeopsis Tetrahit.*
Red Dead-nettle. *Lamium purpureum.*
Thrift or Sea Pink. *Armeria maritima.*
Bucks-horn Plantain. *Plantago Coronopus.*
Sea Plantain. *Plantago maritima.*
Ribwort. *Plantago lanceolata.*
Greater Plantain. *Plantago major.*
Shore-weed. *Littorella uniflora.*
Common Orache. *Atriplex hastata.*
Amphibious Bistort. *Polygonum amphibium.*
Persicaria. *Polygonum Persicaria.*
Knotgrass. *Polygonum aviculare.*
Curled Dock. *Rumex crispus.*
Broad Dock. *Rumes obtusifolius.*
Sorrel. *Rumax Acetosa.*
Sheep's-sorrel. *Rumex Acetosella.*
Sun Spurge. *Euphorbia Helioscopia.*
Common Nettle. *Urtica dioica.*
Small Nettle. *Urtica urens.*
Bog Myrtle. *Myrica Gale.*
Common Birch. *Betula alba.*
Alder. *Alnus glutinosa.*
British Oak. *Quercus Robur.*
Bay Willow. *Salix pentandra.*
Common Willow. *Salix alba.*
Round-eared Willow. *Salix aurita.*
Creeping Willow. *Salix repens.*
Aspen. *Populus tremula.*
Black Poplar. *Populus nigra.*
Crowberry. *Empetrum nigrum.*

*

CONIFERS
Juniper. *Juniperus communis.*
Scots Pine. *Pinus sylvestris.*
Larch. *Larix decidua.*

*

MONOCOTYLEDONS
Branched Bur-reed. *Sparganium ramosum.*
Simple Bur-reed. *Sparganium simplex.*
Small Bur-reed. *Sparganium natans.*
Lesser Duckweed. *Lemna minor.*
Grass-wrack. *Zostera marina.*
Broad Pondweed. *Potamogeton natans.*
Broad Pondweed. *Potamogeton polygonifolius.*
Shining Pondweed. *Potamogeton lucens.*

Long Pondweed. *Potamogeton praelongus.*
Fennel Pondweed. *Potamogeton pectinatus.*
Sea Arrow-grass. *Triglochin maritimum.*
Marsh Arrow-grass. *Triglochin palustre.*
Lesser Water Plantain. *Echinodorus ranunculoides.*
Common Twayblade. *Listera ovata.*
Marsh Orchid. *Orchis latifolia.*
Marsh Orchid. *Orchis incarnata.*
Marsh Orchid. *Orchis purpurella.*
Spotted Orchid. *Orchis ericetorum.*
Spotted Orchid. *Orchis Fuchsii.*
Early Purple Orchid. *Orchis mascula.*
Frog Orchid. *Orchis viridis.*
Yellow Flag. *Iris Pseudacorus.*
Spring Squill. *Scilla verna.*
Wild Hyacinth or Bluebell. *Scilla nonscripta.*
Bog Asphodel. *Narthecium ossifragum.*
Common Rush. *Juncus conglomeratus.*
Open-flowered Rush. *Juncus effusus.*
Wood Rush. *Juncus sylvaticus.*
Jointed Rush. *Juncus articulatus.*
Bulbous Rush. *Juncus bulbosus.*
Heath Rush. *Juncus squarrosus.*
Gerard's Rush. *Juncus Gerardi.*
Toad Rush. *Juncus bufonius.*
Great Woodrush. *Luzula sylvatica.*
Hairy Woodrush. *Luzula pilosa.*
Field Woodrush. *Luzula campestris.*
Bog-rush. *Schoenus nigricans.*
White Beak-Sedge. *Rhynchospora alba.*
Creeping Sedge. *Eleocharis palustris.*
Many-stalked Sedge. *Eleocharis multicaulis.*
Sea Sedge. *Scirpus maritimus.*
Sea Sedge. *Scirpus Tabernaemontani.*
Deer's Grass. *Scirpus caespitosus.*
Bristle Sedge. *Scirpus setaceus*
Floating Sedge. *Scirpus fluitans.*
Narrow Beak-Sedge. *Blysmus rufus.*
Common Cotton-grass. *Eriophorum angustifolium.*
Sheathing Cotton-grass. *Eriophorum vaginatum.*
Flea Sedge. *Carex pulicaris.*
Dioecious Sedge. *Carex dioica.*
Star-headed Sedge. *Carex echinata.*
Oval Sedge. *Carex leporina.*
Sand Sedge. *Carex arenaria.*
Common Sedge. *Carex Goodenowii.*
Bottle Sedge. *Carex rostrata.*
Green-ribbed Sedge. *Carex binervis.*
Tawny Sedge. *Carex fulva.*
Yellow Sedge. *Carex flava.*
Glaucous Sedge. *Carex glauca.*
Carnation Sedge. *Carex panicea.*
Pill-headed Sedge. *Carex pilulifera.*

Vernal Grass. *Anthoxanthum odoratum.*
Marsh Foxtail. *Alopecurus geniculatus.*
Timothy Grass. *Phleum pratense.*
Fiorin-grass. *Agrostis alba.*
Fine Bent-grass. *Agrostis tenuis.*
Bent-grass. *Agrostis canina.*
Marram. *Ammophila arenaria.*
Early Hair-grass. *Aira praecox.*
Tufted Hair-grass. *Deschampsia caespitosa.*
Wavy Hair-grass. *Deschampsia flexuosa.*
Yorkshire Fog. *Holcus lanatus.*
Wild Oat. *Avena pubescens.*
False Oat. *Arrhenatherum avenaceum.*
Heath Grass. *Triodia decumbens.*
Common Reed. *Phragmites vulgaris.*
Crested Dog's-tail. *Cynosurus cristatus.*
Crested Koeleria. *Koeleria cristata.*
Purple Moor-grass. *Molinia caerulea.*
Cock's-foot Grass. *Dactylus glomeratus.*
Flote-grass. *Glyceria fluitans.*
Meadow-grass. *Poa pratensis.*
Roughish Meadow-grass. *Poa trivialis.*
Annual Meadow-grass. *Poa annua.*
† Hard Fescue. *Festuca rigida.*
Meadow Fescue. *Festuca rubra.*
Sheep's Fescue. *Festuca ovina.*
Soft Brome-grass. *Bromus hordaceus.*
Couch-grass. *Agropyron junceum.*
Couch-grass. *Agropyron repens.*
Perennial Rye-grass. *Lolium perenne.*
Mat-grass. *Nardus stricta.*

FERNS, HORSE-TAILS AND CLUB-MOSSES
Filmy Fern. *Hymenophyllum Wilsoni.*
Bracken. *Pteris aquilina.*
Hard Fern. *Blechnum Spicant.*
Black Spleenwort. *Asplenium Adiantum-nigrum.*
Sea Spleenwort. *Asplenium marinum.*
Common Spleenwort. *Asplenium Trichomanes.*
Wall-Rue. *Asplenium Ruta-muraria.*
Lady Fern. *Athyrium Filix-foemina.*
Brittle Bladder-fern. *Cystopteris fragilis.*
Male Fern. *Lastraea Filix-mas.*
Broad Shield-fern. *Dryopteris spinulosa.*
Prickly Shield-fern. *Dryopteris aristata.*
Fragrant Fern. *Dryopteris aemula.*
Oak Fern. *Dryopteris montana.*
Common Polypody. *Polypodium vulgare.*
Beech Fern. *Phegopteris polypodioides.*
Royal Fern. *Osmunda regalis.*
Adder's-tongue. *Ophioglossum vulgatum.*
Moonwort. *Botrychium Lunaria.*
Field Horse-tail. *Equisetum arvense.*

Meadow Horse-tail. *Equisetum pratense.*
Wood Horse-tail. *Equisetum sylvaticum.*
Marsh Horse-tail. *Equisetum palustre.*
Smooth Horse-tail. *Equisetum limosum.*
Fir Club-moss. *Lycopodium Selago.*
Lesser Club-moss. *Selaginella selaginoides.*
Quillwort. *Isoetes echinospora.*

*

LEPIDOPTERA OF BARRA[1]
The list appended below is in no way meant to be complete. All we have done is to record the commoner and more noticeable species.
All the Butterflies with the exception of the Large White and the Small Tortoise-shell are Northern varieties.

Large White. *Pieris brassicae.* Not common.
Small Tortoise-shell. *Aglais urticae.* Common.
Dark Green Fritillary. *Argynnis aglaia.* Common.
The Grayling. *Hipparchia (Satyrus) semele.* Common.
The Meadow Brown. *Epinephele jurtina.* Common
Common Blue. *Polyommatus (Lycaena) icarus.* Common
Puss Moth. *Dicranura vinula.* Common on willows.
Oak Eggar. *Lasiocampus quercae* var. *callunae.*
Fox Moth. *Macrothylacia rubi.*
Emperor. *Saturnia pavonia.*
Wood Tiger. *Parasemia plantaginis.*
Garden Tiger. *Arctia caia.*
Silver Y. *Plusia gamma.* A notorious migrant.
Magpie. *Abraxas grossulariata.* Breeds on the heather moor.
Belted Beauty. *Nyssia zonaria.* Adults not seen, but larvae about in thousands on the "Machair."

*

THE FISHES OF BARRA
(H-B.) = J.A. Harvie-Brown. *A Vertebrate Fauna of the Outer Hebrides.* Edinburgh, 1888.
(E.U.B.S.) = Edinburgh University Biological Society. *Expedition to Barra.* July 1935.

Pristiurus melanostomus. Black-mouthed dog-fish.
    Not uncommon on W. coast of Scotland (H-B.)
Scyllium canicula. Small-spotted dog-fish. Barra. (H-B.)
Scyllium catulus. Large-spotted dog-fish. Not so common on the W.
    of Scotland as *S. canicula.* (H-B.)
Selache maxima. Basking Shark. Formerly appeared in large shoals
    off Barra, where it was speared. (H-B.)
Acanthias vulgaris. Common or picked dog-fish.
    Plentiful on W. coast of Scotland. (H-B.)
Raia clavata. Thornback ray. Very plentiful over W. coast of Scotland. (H-B.)
Raia maculata. Spotted ray. Plentiful in shallow water at Barra. (H-B.)
Raia batis. Skate. Abundant on W. coast of Scotland. (H-B.)

1 See also p. 23.

Clupea harengus. Herring. Fine herring at Barra. (H-B.)

Salmo salar. Salmon. Plentiful in the Hebrides. (H-B.)

Salmo trutta. Sea Trout. Plentiful in Hebrides. (H-B.)

Salmo trutta. Common Trout. Everywhere in streams, a fine variety in Loch St Clair,
Barra. (H-B.) In several lochs of Barra, L. an Duin, L. na Cartach, L. nic
Ruaidhe. (E.U.B.S.)

Anguilla vulgaris. Eel. Plentiful in Hebridean lochs. (H-B.)
Several lochs and streams. (E.U.B.S.)

Conger vulgaris. Conger. Plentiful throughout the West. (H-B.)

Gasterosteus aculeatus. Three-spined stickleback.
Common in salt, fresh and brackish water all round the coast from Lewis to
Barra. (H-B.) Common in L. St Clair and L. na Doirlinn, and the streams
below them. (E.U.B.S.)

Spinachia vulgaris. Fifteen-spined stickleback. Common from Lewis to Barra. (H-B.)

Orthagoriscus mola. Sun-fish. Off Barra. (H-B.)

Gadus aeglefinus. Haddock. A local fish in the W. of Scotland. (H-B.)

Gadus morrhua. Cod. A plentiful western fish. Finest banks, Barra. (H-B.)

Gadus luscus. Bib or Pout. Loch Obe, Barra. (E.U.B.S.)

Gadus pollachius. Pollack or Lythe.
Equally numerous with the Coal fish on W. of Scotland. (H-B.)
Loch Obe, Barra. (E.U.B.S.)

Gadus virens. Coal fish. Numberless all over the W. Taken form Lewis to the Clyde.
(H-B.)

Molva vulgaris. Ling. General. (H-B.)

Onos tricirratus. Three-bearded rockling. Taken over most of W. of Scotland. (H-B.)

Brosmius brosme. Tusk. Off Barra, numbers sent to the curers at Castlebay. (H-B.)

Blennius pholis. Shanny. Numerous in rock pools in Barra. (H-B.)

Lepadogaster bimaculatus. Doubly-spotted sucker. Plentiful in Barra. (H-B.)

Lophius piscatorius. Angler fish. Plentiful all over W. coast of Scotland. (H-B.)

Gobius flavescens. Two-spotted goby. Barra. (H-B.)

Hippoglossus vulgaris. Halibut. Off Barra. (H-B.)

Pleuronectes platessa. Plaice. Abundant. Barra. (H-B.)

Trigla gurnardus. Grey gurnard. Common around W. coast of Scotland. (H-B.)

Cottus scorpius. Short-spined Cottus. Barra. (H-B.)

Cottus quadricornis. Four-horned Cottus. Barra. (H-B.)

Cottus bubalis. Father-lasher. Barra. (H-B.)

Cyclopterus lumpus. Lumpsucker.
Common all along W. coast of Scotland. (H-B.)

Ctenolabrus rupestris. Goldsinny. Loch Obe. (E.U.B.S.)

Centrolabrus exoletus. Rock cook. Loch Obe. (E.U.B.S.)

Caranx trachurus. Horse mackerel.
Generally diffused on W. coast of Scotland. (H-B.)

Scomber scombrus. Mackerel. Common throughout W. coast waters. (H-B.)

Zeus faber. John Dory. One caught from shore, December 1935.

General Index

*

Index of Persons

*

Index of Places

*

[The Index of Persons and the Index of Places record for the most part only persons and places directly connected with the Island of Barra.]